Derek Sumeray

Discovering
London
Plaques

British Library Cataloguing in Publication Data: Sumeray, Derek. Discovering London Plaques 1. Historical markers – England – London – Guidebooks 2. London (England) – Guidebooks I. Title 914.2'1'04859. ISBN 0 7478 0395 1

Front cover: *A selection of London commemorative plaques, and the house at 96 Cheyne Walk, SW10, where James Whistler, the American painter, lived after 1859. A plaque records his residence there.*

Back cover: *A plaque on Christie Cottage, Cresswell Place, SW10, records that Agatha Christie, the celebrated writer of detective stories, once lived there.*

ACKNOWLEDGEMENTS
Thanks are due to: the Corporation of the City of London, London Borough of Barking and Dagenham, London Borough of Barnet, London Borough of Bexley, London Borough of Brent, London Borough of Bromley and Orpington, London Borough of Camden, London Borough of Croydon, London Borough of Enfield, London Borough of Hackney, London Borough of Hammersmith and Fulham, London Borough of Harrow, London Borough of Hounslow, London Borough of Islington, London Borough of Kensington and Chelsea, London Borough of Kingston-upon-Thames, London Borough of Lambeth, London Borough of Lewisham, London Borough of Merton, London Borough of Richmond-upon-Thames, London Borough of Southwark, London Borough of Sutton, London Borough of Tower Hamlets, London Borough of Waltham Forest, London Borough of Wandsworth, London Borough of Westminster, Loughton Town Council, English Heritage, Comic Heritage, the Heath and Old Hampstead Society, Eric Tucker (for his assistance in finding and locating private plaques), and Ralph Temple (for his assistance on my many photographic journeys). Special thanks are due to Pam Whiffen of English Heritage, Gillian Dawson of Westminster City Council and, last but not least, my wife Loretta for her patience whilst I have been researching this book.

Published in 1999 by Shire Publications Ltd, Cromwell House, Church Street, Princes Risborough, Buckinghamshire HP27 9AA, UK. (Website: www.shirebooks.co.uk)
Copyright © 1999 by Derek Sumeray. First published 1999. Number 291 in the Discovering series. ISBN 0 7478 0395 1.
Derek Sumeray is hereby identified as the author of this work in accordance with Section 77 of the Copyright, Designs and Patents Act, 1988.

Printed in Great Britain by CIT Printing Services Ltd, Press Buildings, Merlins Bridge, Haverfordwest, Pembrokeshire SA61 1XF.

Contents

Author's preface

Interest in commemorative plaques has never been greater than it is today, and not only English Heritage and its predecessors but several of the London boroughs as well as local historical societies have responded to public curiosity about the homes of famous and historical figures and the sites and landmarks of London. This is a guide to most of the significant commemorative plaques on the exteriors of London buildings, not only in the city centre, but in the surrounding boroughs and the countryside within the circle of the M25 motorway. It is written for those who live in London, for those who work in London and for those who visit London.

The first official London plaques were erected in 1867 by the Royal Society of Arts at the instigation of William Ewart MP. By 1901 they had erected thirty-six plaques, the oldest of which now surviving are those commemorating Napoleon III and the poet John Dryden, both erected in 1875. The responsibility for erecting the plaques passed on to the London County Council in 1901, who had extended the total to 298 by the time the Greater London Council took over in 1965. The official plaque scheme was extended further until the GLC was disbanded in 1985. The first plaque set up by English Heritage was erected in 1986, and more than twelve a year have been put up by them since that date. In total there are about 700 official plaques and most of them are blue with white lettering.

Since the early 1900s local authorities and private individuals have erected their own plaques. In the City of London the rectangular blue glazed plaques of the Corporation mark many historical sites. The green plaques set up by Westminster City Council are now a familiar sight, and further afield there is a variety of different types, sizes and colours, to be found in most areas of London.

The unveiling of a new plaque is often marked by a small ceremony, where a celebrity pulls a cord to draw the curtains for a first viewing of the plaque. The occasion is usually marked by speeches about the person or event commemorated and is followed by a small reception. These ceremonies are frequently attended by relatives, descendants or associates of the named person and press photographers to record the occasion.

The plaques listed are all on the exterior of buildings and can be seen easily by the public. Local plaques not of general interest or significant importance have mainly been omitted, as have heritage trails. This has still resulted in a compilation of over fourteen hundred plaques.

The descriptive detail has been kept brief, as this is intended only to highlight the relevant facets of the lives of the persons commemorated or the historical detail of a building or event. Some persons have been commemorated in more than one place, in different parts of London, by different organisations (examples are William Blake, Noel Coward, Charles Dickens, Benjamin Waugh and Mary Wollstonecraft). In such cases all plaques are listed under the name concerned, together with the appropriate addresses.

The authority or organisation responsible for erecting the plaque is given in italics either at the end of the entry or, in the case of multiple plaques, after the address. The borough councils mentioned are as stated on the plaques and are not necessarily as the current borough boundaries.

New plaques are continually being erected, and, regrettably, some do occasionally disappear through redevelopment or theft. Those listed are the ones of which I am aware at the time of going to print.

D. S.

Gazetteer of London commemorative plaques

ABBAS, Ali Mohammed (1922-79). **33 Tavistock Square, WC1**
Barrister and one of the founders of Pakistan; lived here 1945-79. *Camden Borough Council*

ACRES, Birt (1854-1918). **19 Park Road, Barnet**
American-born inventor and pioneer cameraman. He came to Barnet in 1892 and worked as a manager for a local firm producing photographic plates, before setting up his own business. At this address he produced the first British movie film in February 1895. *Cinema 100*

ADAM, Robert (1728-92). **1-3 Robert Street, Adelphi, WC2**

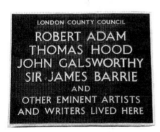

British architect, lived at No. 3 1778-85; Thomas Hood (1799-1845), poet (q.v.), lived at No. 2 1828-30; Sir James Barrie (1860-1937), dramatist (q.v.), lived in a flat here from 1909 until his death in 1937; the engraver Henry Ryall lived at No. 1 1841-50; John Galsworthy (1867-1933), writer (q.v.), and other eminent artists and writers also resided here. See also Royal Society of Arts. *London County Council*

ADAMS, Henry Brooks (1838-1918). **98 Portland Place, W1**
American historian; lived here. Grandson of John Quincy Adams, sixth US president, and great-grandson of John Adams, second US president, he taught American history at Harvard and wrote many important works, one of which was awarded the Pulitzer prize in 1919. This building was also used as the US Embassy in 1863-6, when his father was ambassador. *Greater London Council*

ADAMS, John (1735-1826). **9 Grosvenor Square, W1**
American statesman and president; lived here. He was first American minister to Great Britain May 1785 to March 1788, afterwards second president of the United States. The plaque states: 'From here his daughter Abigail was married

to Colonel William Stephen Smith, first secretary of the legation and an officer in the revolutionary army, on Washington's staff. John Adams and Abigail his wife through character and personality did much to create understanding between the two English-speaking countries. In their memory this tablet is placed by the Colonial Dames of America 1933.' *Colonial Dames of America*

ADAMS-ACTON, John (1830-1910). 14 Langford Place, NW8
English sculptor; lived here 1882-1906. He was born 1830, not as stated on the plaque. He adopted the name Acton, after his birthplace, in 1869 to avoid confusion with other artists of the same name. He executed the Wesley memorials at Westminster Abbey and the City Road Chapel, the Cruikshank memorial in St Paul's Cathedral and that of Cardinal Manning (q.v.) in Westminster Cathedral. He also created statues of Queen Victoria and Gladstone. King Edward VII sat for him on several occasions. *Westminster City Council*

ADELPHI TERRACE. The Adelphi, WC2

This building stands on the site of Adelphi Terrace, built by the brothers Adam in 1768-74. Among the occupants of the terrace were Topham (1739-80), friend of Dr Johnson (q.v.), and Lady Diana Beauclerk (1734-1808) (q.v.), amateur artist; David Garrick (1717-79) (q.v.), actor; Richard D'Oyly Carte (1844-1901), Savoy Opera promoter; Thomas Hardy (1840-1928) (q.v.), poet and novelist; and George Bernard Shaw (1856-1950) (q.v.) author and playwright. The London School of Economics and Political Science and the Savage Club also had their premises here. The original four-storey terrace was demolished in 1936 and rebuilt as the present building. *London County Council*

AIR-RAID PRECAUTION CENTRE. 24 Rossendale Street, E5
Civil Defence Centre for North Hackney. It was built 1938 and used in the Second World War. *Borough of Hackney*

AIR RAIDS, first night. Hotel Bedford, Southampton Row, WC1
The plaque records that on 24th September 1917 thirteen people were killed and twenty-two injured near this spot, on the steps of the old Bedford Hotel, by a 112 pound bomb dropped by an enemy plane, in one of London's first night air raids. *Private*

ALDERSGATE. 1 Aldersgate Street, EC1
Aldersgate, or Ealdred Gate, as it was originally known, was one of the oldest London gates and the most important exit from the old City to the north of England. Rebuilt in 1617 and repaired in 1670 after being damaged in the Great

Fire of London (1665), it was finally demolished in 1761. *Corporation of the City of London*

ALDGATE. 88 Aldgate Street, EC3
This was one of the six gates to the City built by the Romans. It was rebuilt in the early twelfth century, and in 1215 the Barons came through it at the time of Magna Carta. Between 1374 and 1385 the room above it was leased to the writer Geoffrey Chaucer. The gate was again rebuilt 1606-9 but was demolished in 1761. *Corporation of the City of London*

ALEXANDER, Sir George (1858-1918). **57 Pont Street, SW1**
Actor-manager, born in Reading; lived here. He managed the St James's Theatre from 1891 until his death. He appeared in *Lady Windermere's Fan*, *The Importance of Being Earnest*, *The Second Mrs Tanqueray*, etc. *London County Council*

ALLENBY, Edmund Henry Hyman, First Viscount (1861-1936). **24 Wetherby Gardens, SW5**
Field marshal during the First World War; lived here from 1928 until his death. He served in South Africa 1884-5 and in the second Boer War. In the First World War he served in France, becoming Commander of British Forces. He later commanded the Egyptian Expeditionary Force against the Turks in Palestine and, as field marshal, routed the Egyptians at Megiddo in 1918. He was High Commissioner in Egypt 1919-25. *London County Council*

ALMA-TADEMA, Sir Lawrence (1836-1912). **4 Grove End Road, NW8**
Dutch-born painter; lived here 1886-1912. He is famous for his classic idyllic scenes. He was knighted in 1899 and awarded the Order of Merit in 1905. *Greater London Council*

AMBEDKAR, Dr Bhimrao Ramji (1893-1956). **10 King Henry's Road, NW3**
Indian politician and champion of the depressed castes; lived here 1921-2. Born near Bombay and educated in New York and the London School of Economics, Ambedkar was a member of the Bombay Legislative Assembly and the leader of sixty million 'untouchables'. Appointed law minister in 1947, he was the principal author of the Indian constitution. He published *Annihilation of Caste* 1937. *Private*

ANAESTHETIC. 52 Gower Street, NW1
The first anaesthetic given in England was administered in a house on this site on 19th December 1846. See also Clover, Dr Joseph T., and Snow, Dr John. *The Association of Anaesthetists of Great Britain and Ireland*

ANCHOR BREWERY, site of. Park Street, SE1
The plaque lists seven different brewers who occu-

7

Above: *The site of the old Anchor Brewery in Park Street, SE1.*

pied the former premises from 1616 until the demolition of the brewery in 1986. *Private*

ANDERSON, Elizabeth Garrett (1836-1917). London Guildhall University, Commercial Road, E1 *Borough of Tower Hamlets;* **20 Upper Berkeley Street, W1** *London County Council*

The first woman registered as a doctor and surgeon in Great Britain (1865) was born in a house formerly on the site in Commercial Road; she lived in Upper Berkeley Street 1860-74. She established a hospital for women in London (1866), later named Elizabeth Garrett Anderson Hospital. She was elected the first woman mayor in England (Aldeburgh) in 1908.

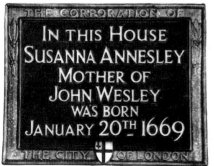

ANNESLEY, Susanna (1669-1742). 7 Spitalyard, Bishopsgate, E1

Mother of John Wesley (q.v.); born in this house 20th January 1669. She married Samuel Wesley in 1690 and gave birth to seventeen children, outliving her husband. *Corporation of the City of London*

ANSDELL, Richard, RA (1815-85). **1 St Albans Grove, W8**
English artist and painter of animals; lived in Lytham House, on this site 1862-84. He exhibited at the Royal Academy from 1840 and gained the Heywood Medal three times at Manchester exhibitions. *Private*

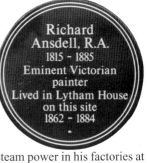

ARKWRIGHT, Sir Richard (1732-92). **8 Adam Street, WC2**
Inventor and manufacturing pioneer; lived here for a short time. He developed the spinning frame in 1768 for the cotton trade and used steam power in his factories at the beginning of the industrial revolution. *Greater London Council*

ARNE, Thomas Augustine (1710-78). **31 King Street, Covent Garden, WC2**
English composer; lived here. He wrote the opera *Rosamond* (1733), the operetta *Tom Thumb* and *Comus* (1738). He is best known as the composer of 'Rule Britannia'. His son Michael (1740-86), also a musician, composed 'Lass with a Delicate Air'. *English Heritage*

ARNOLD, Benedict (1741-1801). **62 Gloucester Place, W1**
US revolutionary soldier and traitor to the American cause; moved to this house in 1796, where he died in poverty. A merchant in New Haven, Connecticut, he joined the colonial forces. Having distinguished himself in battle and been promoted to major-general, he became commander of West Point but plotted to betray it to the British. He fled to the British lines and was given a command, coming to England in 1781. *Private*

Left: *Sir Richard Arkwright from an engraving by J. Jenkins.*

ARNOLD, Sir Edwin (1832-1904). **31 Bolton Gardens, SW5**
English poet and journalist; lived and died here. He taught in Birmingham and in 1856 went to India, where he remained for five years. On his return he joined the *Daily Telegraph* and became editor in 1863. He wrote *Light of India* (1879) and *Light of the World* (1891). *London County Council*

ARNOLD, Matthew (1822-88). **2 Chester Square, SW1**
English poet and critic; lived here. The son of Thomas Arnold, renowned headmaster of Rugby School, he was educated at public schools and at Oxford. He was Inspector of Schools 1851-86 and Professor of Poetry at Oxford 1857-67. His poems include 'Thyrsis' and 'Dover Beach' (1867). He also wrote several works of criticism. *London County Council*

ARTISTS RIFLES. 8 St George Street, W1
The Artists Rifles was formed here in 1860 at the studio of Henry Wyndham Phillips (1820-68), a portrait painter who exhibited at the Royal Academy from 1838. Among those present at the first meeting were the artists Millais (q.v.), Lord Leighton (q.v.) and George Caley. The regiment became known as the 38th Middlesex (Artists) Rifle Volunteers, and Phillips was the first commanding officer. A Royal Academy memorial can be found at Burlington House commemorating the 2003 members of the Artists Rifles killed in the First World War. In 1921 the regiment became the 1st 28th Battalion (London) regiment. *Private*

ARUP, Sir Ove Nyquist (1895-1988). **28 Willifield Way, NW11**
British civil engineer of Danish parents; lived here 1932-9. He was responsible for the structural design of Coventry Cathedral designed by Sir Basil Spence, the Sydney Opera House, designed by Jørn Utzon, and other well-known buildings. *Borough of Barnet*

ASHBEE, Charles Robert (1863-1942). **Onyx House, 401 Mile End Road, E3**
English designer, architect, writer and founder of the Guild and School of

Handicraft (1888), where he remained a director for twenty years and which once stood on this site. He was much influenced by William Morris (q.v.) and John Ruskin (q.v.). Although his speciality was church restoration, he was also a capable silversmith. *Borough of Tower Hamlets*

ASHFIELD, Lord Albert Henry Stanley (1874-1948). **43 South Street, W1**
First Chairman of London Transport; lived here. *Greater London Council*

ASHLEY, Laura (née Mountney) (1925-85). **83 Cambridge Street, SW1**
British designer; began printing fabrics here with her husband, Bernard, 1954-6. She was the founder of an international chain of shops, which marketed her range of Victorian-style furnishings, fabrics, clothing and wallpapers. *Westminster City Council*

ASQUITH, Herbert Henry, First Earl of Oxford and Asquith (1852-1928). **20 Cavendish Square, W1** *London County Council;* **27 Maresfield Gardens, NW3** *Hampstead Plaque Fund*
Liberal prime minister, 1908; lived at both addresses, the latter from 1887 to 1892. He formed a coalition government in May 1915 but was ousted by Lloyd George in December 1916. Asquith received his earldom in 1925.

ASTAFIEVA, Princess Seraphine (1876-1934). **152 King's Road, SW3**
Ballet dancer; lived and taught here. She came to England with Diaghilev in 1910 and established a teaching school here from 1916 until her death. Her pupils included Margot Fonteyn, Anton Dolin and Alicia Markova. *Greater London Council*

ASTOR, Viscountess Nancy Witcher Langhorne (1879-1964). **4 St James's Square, SW1**
American-born British politician; lived here. The wife of William Waldorf Astor (1879-1952), she succeeded her husband as Conservative MP for Plymouth in 1919, becoming the first woman to sit in the House of Commons. *English Heritage*

The plaque to Princess Seraphine Astafieva can be seen by the upstairs window, to the left of the entrance of this building in King's Road, SW3.

ATTLEE, Clement Richard, First Earl Attlee (1883-1967). **17 Monkham's Avenue, Woodford Green** *Greater London Council;* **Heywood Court, London Road, Stanmore** *Harrow Heritage Trust*
Socialist politician; lived at Monkham's Avenue and on the site of Heywood Court. First elected to Parliament 1922, he became leader of the Labour Party in 1935. He was deputy prime minister in Churchill's wartime coalition government 1940-5, prime minister 1945-51 and opposition leader 1951-5.

AUSTEN, Jane (1775-1817). **23 Hans Place, SW1** *Private;* **10 Henrietta Street, Covent Garden, WC2** *Westminster City Council*
English novelist; stayed with her brother Henry in a house on the first site, 1814-15; stayed with her brother John at Henrietta Street and wrote many letters from there. Born in Hampshire, she was the daughter of a rector. Her novels, *Sense and Sensibility* (1811), *Pride and Prejudice* (1813), *Mansfield Park* (1814), *Emma* (1816), *Persuasion* (1818) and *Northanger Abbey* (1818) have enjoyed enduring popularity. She is buried in Winchester Cathedral.

The plaque to Jane Austen at 23 Hans Place, SW1.

AUTOMOBILE ASSOCIATION. 18 Fleet Street, EC4
The AA opened its first office in this building in 1905. The plaque marks its diamond jubilee. *Private*

AVEBURY, John Lubbock, First Baron (1834-1913). **29 Eaton Place, SW1**
English banker and politician; born here. He was a Liberal and Liberal Unionist MP 1870-1900 and was responsible for the Bank Holidays Act (1871) and many other bills. He was chairman of LCC 1890-2. He is also noted for his researches on primitive man and the habits of bees and ants. *London County Council*

AYER, Professor Sir Alfred Jules (1910-89). **51 York Street, W1**
English philosopher; lived here. He was professor of logic at Oxford University 1959-78. His published works include *Language, Truth and Logic* (1936), *Probability and Evidence* (1972) and *Philosophy in the Twentieth Century* (1982). *Westminster City Council*

BABBAGE, Charles (1791-1871). **Corner of Larcom Street and Walworth Road, SE17** *Southwark Council;* **Dorset Street, W1** *Westminster City Council*
English mathematician and astronomer; born near the first site; lived in a house on the second. He devised a calculating machine, the 'Difference Engine', and another, the 'Analytical Engine' (never built in his lifetime), which were forerunners of the modern computer. He wrote one hundred books, mainly about the economics of machinery.

BACON, Francis (1909-92). **7 Cromwell Place, SW7**
Irish-born British artist; lived here. He settled in England in 1923 and is regarded as one of Britain's most important post-war artists. His abstract style developed into mainly tortured figures, many with religious associations. The plaque is shared with the artists Millais (q.v.) and Hoppe (q.v.). *National Art Collections Fund*

BADEN-POWELL, Robert Stephenson Smythe, First Baron (1857-1941). **9 Hyde Park Gate, SW7**
British general and founder of the Scout Association; lived here 1861-76. He fought in the defence of Mafeking (1899-1900), founded the Boy Scout movement (1908) and was the author of *Scouting for Boys* (1908). He was knighted in 1929. *Greater London Council*

The Chief Scout, Sir Robert Baden-Powell.

13

BAGEHOT, Walter (1826-77). **12 Upper Belgrave Street, SW1**
British banker, writer and economist; lived here. He was editor of *The Economist* magazine 1860-77. His works include *The English Constitution* (1867) and *Lombard Street* (1873). *Greater London Council*

BAGNOLD, Enid (1889-1981). **29 Hyde Park Gate, SW7**
English novelist and playwright; lived here. She was an associate of Katherine Mansfield (q.v.) and of Henri Gaudier-Brzeska (q.v.), who sculpted her head. Among her novels are *National Velvet* (1935; later filmed) and *The Loved and the Envied* (1950). She also had several poems published. *English Heritage*

BAILLIE, Joanna (1762-1851). **Bolton House, Windmill Hill, Hampstead, NW3**
Scottish poet and dramatist; lived here *c.*1791-1851. She published three volumes of *Plays on the Passions* (1798, 1802 and 1812). Her most successful play was *The Family Legend* (1810). She also published several poems and ballads. Baillie lived in this house for nearly sixty years and was visited by many eminent writers and scientists of the time. *Royal Society of Arts*

BAIRD, John Logie (1888-1946). **3 Crescent Wood Road, Sydenham, SE26** *Greater London Council;* **22 Frith Street, W1** *London County Council;* **132-5 Long Acre, WC2** *The Royal Television Society.* Scottish engineer who first developed television (1926); lived at the first address; first demonstrated television at the second; and broadcast the first television programme in Britain (30th September 1929) from the third. His system was adopted by the BBC in 1929, and improvements led to the first regular public transmissions in 1936. His further research succeeded in producing colour and three-dimensional images (1944), as well as screen projection and stereophonic sound. See also Television.

The plaque at 22 Frith Street, W1.

BAIRNSFATHER, Bruce (1888-1959). **1 Sterling Street, SW7**
British cartoonist; lived here. He became famous for his First World War 'Old Bill' cartoons and was an official war cartoonist attached to the US Army during the Second World War. *Greater London Council*

BAKER, Hylda (1905-86). **Brinsworth House, Staines Road, Twickenham**
Lancashire-born comedy actress. She first went on stage at the age of ten and had a leading part by the time she was fourteen. Her best-known comedy routine was with a tall silent man in woman's clothing, whom she ridiculed, saying to the audience 'She knows you know'. Her popular television show with Jimmy Jewel was entitled *Nearest and Dearest,* and her film work included roles in *Saturday Night and Sunday Morning* (1960), *Up the Junction* (1967) and *Oliver* (1968). This plaque is located on the rear of a retirement home for show business people. *Comic Heritage*

BALCON, Sir Michael (1896-1977). **57a Tufton Street, SW1**
British film producer; lived here. His productions include the comedies *Kind Hearts and Coronets* (1949), *Whisky Galore* (1949) and *The Lavender Hill Mob* (1951). *Westminster City Council*

BALDWIN, Stanley, First Earl Baldwin of Bewdley (1867-1947). **93 Eaton Square, SW1**
Conservative politician; lived here. He entered Parliament in 1908 and was Chancellor of the Exchequer (1922-3) and thrice prime minister (1923-4, 1924-9, 1935-7). He was in office during the General Strike (1926) and the abdication crisis (1936) and was made a peer in 1937. *Greater London Council*

BALFE, Michael William (1808-70). **12 Seymour Street, W1**
Irish-born composer; lived here 1861-5. Born in Dublin, he was a child prodigy violinist and singer. Balfe visited London in 1823 and studied under Rossini in Italy in 1825-6, returning to England in 1833. In 1846 he was appointed conductor of the London Italian Opera at Her Majesty's Theatre. His many compositions include *The Bohemian Girl* (1843). *London County Council*

BALLANTYNE, R. M. (Robert Michael) (1825-94). **Duneaves, Mount Park Road, Harrow**
Scottish author of boys' books; lived here. His experiences in Canada in 1841-8 inspired him to write his early novels, which included *The Young Fur Traders* (1856), *Coral Island* (1857) and *Martin Rattler* (1858). *Greater London Council*

BANKS, Sir Joseph (1743-1820). **32 Soho Square, W1**
English botanist; lived in a house on this site from 1777. He visited Newfoundland in 1766, collecting plants, and travelled round the world 1768-71 with James Cook on the *Endeavour*. He was president of the Royal Society 1778-1819 and was also a founder of Kew botanical gardens. The botanists Robert Brown (q.v.) and David Don (1800-41) also lived here. The Linnaean Society met here 1821-57. *London County Council*

BARBAULD, Anna Laetitia (1743-1825). **113 Stoke Newington Church Street, N16**
English poet and author; lived in this house from 1802 until her death. Her works include *Poems* (1773), *Early Lessons for Children* and *Hymns in Prose for Children*. With her brother John Aikin she began the series *Evenings at Home* in 1792. *Borough of Hackney*

BARBIROLLI, Sir John (1899-1970). **Bloomsbury Park Hotel, Southampton Row, WC1**
British conductor and cellist; born here. He played in leading string quartets before becoming conductor of the New York Philharmonic Orchestra (1937-42). Barbirolli returned to England as conductor of the Hallé Orchestra in 1943, in which position he excelled until his death in 1970. *Private*

BARBON, Nicholas (died 1698). **Essex Hall, Essex Street, WC2**
Architect, who laid out the grounds of Essex Street (q.v.) in 1675. He graduated as MD at Utrecht in 1661, wrote two treatises on money and was the originator of fire insurance in England. He was MP for Bramber in 1690 and 1695. After the Fire of London he was one of the most prolific builders of the new City of London. Barbon is included as one of the names in the Essex Street plaque. *London County Council*

BARBOSA, Ruy (1849-1923). **17 Holland Park Gardens, W14**
Brazilian statesman and lawyer; lived here 1895. He was Minister of the Treasury in the new republic of Brazil (1889). Five years later he fled after the establishment of a military dictatorship. Barbosa spent a year in exile in this house, during which time he started a law practice. *Anglo-Brazilian Society*

BARING, Sir Evelyn, First Earl of Cromer (1841-1917). **36 Wimpole Street, W1**
British statesman, diplomat and colonial administrator; lived and died here. He spent much of his overseas posting in Egypt and the Sudan, during which time he greatly improved the infrastructure and Britain's standing in the area. Baring was created a viscount in 1899 and an earl in 1901. *English Heritage*

BARING, Sir Francis (1740-1810). **Manor House Library, Old Road, Lee, SE13**
Merchant and banker, founder of Baring's Bank; lived here 1797-1810. Baring was created a baronet in 1793 by William Pitt (q.v.). *Baring Bros & Company Limited; Borough of Lewisham*

BARKER, Cicely Mary (1895-1973). **23 The Waldrons, Croydon**
Author and illustrator of the 'Flower Fairy' children's books; lived and worked here 1924-61. *Borough of Croydon*

BARLOW, William Henry (1812-1902). **'Highcombe', 145 Charlton Road, SE7**
Engineer; lived and died here. He worked extensively in the design of the Midland Railway, and the 'saddleback' form of rail bears his name. Barlow worked with Sir John Hawkshaw on the completion of Brunel's (q.v.) Clifton Suspension Bridge. He was a member of the court of enquiry into the Tay Bridge disaster and active in the design of its replacement. He received many international awards for his work, and his portrait hangs at the Institute of Civil Engineers. *English Heritage*

BARNARDO, 'Dr' Thomas John (1845-1905). **58 Solent House, Ben Johnson Road, E1** *London County Council;* **30 Coborn Street, EC3** *Bow Heritage.*
Irish-born philanthropist; began his work for destitute children in a building on the first site, 1866, lodging in Coborn Street on coming to London. Though not medically qualified, he was known as 'Dr', and his philanthropic work was the basis of the

16

Right: *The plaque to Cicely Mary Barker in Croydon.*

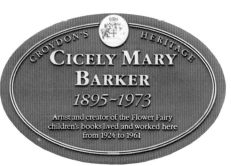

Left: *The plaque to Sir Cecil Beaton in Langland Gardens, NW3.*

present-day charity 'Dr Barnardo's', which maintains over one hundred children's homes in Britain and abroad.

BARNES WALLIS. See **WALLIS, Barnes**

BARNETT, Dame Henrietta (1851-1936) and **Canon Samuel** (1844-1913).
Heath End House, Spaniards Road, NW3
Founders of Hampstead Garden Suburb and Toynbee Hall, respectively; lived here. Henrietta was a founder of the Whitechapel Art Gallery and an ardent supporter of Toynbee Hall. She raised a considerable sum for the preservation of Hampstead Heath. In 1903 she and Samuel, her husband, who was a notable social reformer, formed the Hampstead Garden Suburb Trust, which raised money for the development of a new residential area (begun 1907). Dame Henrietta took up painting at the age of seventy-two and had a picture hung at the Royal Academy. She was appointed CBE in 1917 and DBE in 1924.

Greater London Council

BARRATT, Thomas J. (1841-1914). **East Heath Road, NW3**
Historian of Hampstead; lived in a house, 'Bell Moor', on this site 1877-1914. He was a deputy-lieutenant of the City of London and the chairman of A. & F. Pears, the soap manufacturers. He published the three-volume work *Annals of Hampstead* in 1912. *Hampstead Borough Council*

17

BARRETT, Elizabeth. See **BROWNING, Elizabeth Barrett**

BARRIE, J. M. (Sir James) (1860-1937). **100 Bayswater Road, W2** *London County Council;* **1-3 Robert Street, Adelphi, WC2** *London County Council*
Novelist and dramatist; lived in Bayswater Road from 1902 to 1909, when he moved to Robert Street (see Adam, Robert). His famous *Peter Pan* was written at the first address after inspiration received during walks in nearby Kensington Gardens.

BARRY, Sir Charles (1795-1860). **The Elms, Clapham Common North Side, SW4**
English architect; lived and died here. He had studied in Italy, and his work showed the influence of the Italian Renaissance. Among his designs are the Manchester Athenaeum (1836), the Reform Club (1837) and the Houses of Parliament (1840-60). *London County Council*

BARTÓK, Béla (1881-1945). **7 Sydney Place, SW7**
Hungarian composer; stayed at this address when performing in London. A child prodigy, he toured as an eminent pianist and developed his own style of recreated folk music. He left his homeland in 1940 and settled in the USA. His work includes the opera *Duke Bluebeard's Castle*, ballets, two violin and three piano concertos and six string quartets. *English Heritage*

BASEVI, George (1794-1845). **17 Savile Row, W1**
Architect; lived here 1829-45. Born in London, he designed the Fitzwilliam Museum, Cambridge, and many country mansions and Gothic churches and was responsible for the layout of part of Belgravia. Basevi fell to his death whilst surveying Ely Cathedral. *London County Council*

BASTIAN, Dr Henry Charlton (1837-1915). **8 Manchester Square, W1**
English biologist; lived and worked here. He was professor of pathological anatomy at University College London (1867), hospital physician there (1871) and professor of clinical medicine (1887-95). Bastian's work made him one of the founders of British neurology. *Westminster County Council*

BATEMAN, H. M. (Henry Mayo) (1887-1970). **40 Nightingale Lane, SW12**
Australian-born cartoonist; lived here 1910-14. He worked for *Punch* and other periodicals. *English Heritage*

BAX, Sir Arnold Edward Trevor (1883-1953). **13 Pendennis Road, Streatham, SE16**
English composer; born here. His works were often based on Celtic legends and include seven symphonies, tone poems, chamber music, piano solos and concertos. He was appointed Master of the King's Musick in 1942. *English Heritage*

BAXTER, George (1804-67). **City University, Northampton Square, EC1** *Private;* **Entrance, Baxter Field, Sydenham, SE26** *Sydenham Society*
English engraver, printer and illustrator who invented a process of high-quality colour printing; he conducted his business in numbers 11 and 12 Northampton Square (since demolished) between 1844 and 1860, retiring to Sydenham, where Baxter Field is named after him.

The plaque to George Baxter at the entrance to Baxter Field in Sydenham, SE26.

BAYLIS, Lilian Mary (1874-1937). **27 Stockwell Park Road, SW9**
Theatre manager; lived and died here. Born in London, a daughter of musicians, she became a music teacher before helping in the management of the Royal Victoria Hall (afterwards the Old Vic). Becoming manager in 1912, she developed it into a home for Shakespearian plays and opera. She also acquired the Sadler's Wells Theatre in 1931, for the presentation of opera and ballet. *Greater London Council*

BAZALGETTE, Sir Joseph William (1819-91). **17 Hamilton Terrace, NW8**
British civil engineer; lived here. A notable pioneer of public health engineering, he designed London's sewerage system (completed 1865) and the Victoria Thames Embankment. *Greater London Council*

BEACONSFIELD, Earl of. See **DISRAELI, Benjamin**

BEARD, John (*c*.1716-91). **Hampton Branch Library, Rose Hill, Hampton**
Actor and vocalist; lived here. He was one of the finest singers of his time, appearing at Drury Lane and Covent Garden, of which he become a shareholder and manager. Beard retired to Hampton and is buried at Hampton church. The plaque is shared with William Ewart (q.v.). *English Heritage*

BEARDSLEY, Aubrey Vincent (1872-98). **114 Cambridge Street, SW1**
English illustrator; lived here. He is famous for his black-and-white Art Nouveau drawings. He illustrated Oscar Wilde's *Salome* (1894), also the *Yellow Book Magazine* (1894-6) and his own *Book of Fifty Drawings*. Beardsley died of tuberculosis in the south of France. *London County Council*

BEATON, Sir Cecil (1904-80). **21 Langland Gardens, NW3**
English photographer and designer; was born and lived here until 1911. He was

noted for his portraits of royalty and celebrities but also designed scenery and costumes for stage and film productions. His publications include *The Glass of Fashion* (1959), *The Magic Image* (1975) and several volumes of autobiography (1961-78). (Photograph, page 17) *Heath and Old Hampstead Society*

BEATTY, David, First Earl Beatty (1871-1936). **Hanover Lodge, Outer Circle, NW1**
English naval commander; lived here 1910-25. Beatty served in the Sudan 1896-8 and the China War 1900, and in the First World War he commanded the British fleet at the Battle of Jutland. He became First Sea Lord in 1919. The plaque is shared with Thomas Cochrane (q.v.). *Greater London Council*

Earl Beatty, when a Vice Admiral.

BEAUCLERK, Lady Diana (1734-1808). Included in the **ADELPHI TERRACE** plaque.
Artist and illustrator. The daughter of the second Duke of Marlborough, she married Topham Beauclerk, a descendant of Charles II and Nell Gwynne (q.v.).

IN MEMORY OF
HARRY BECK
THE ORIGINATOR OF THE
DISTINCTIVE LONDON UNDERGROUND MAP
WHO LIVED NEAR HERE AND USED
THE STATION REGULARLY
THE MAP IS USED BY MILLIONS DAILY
AND HAS BECOME RECOGNISED
AS A CLASSIC
WORLD-WIDE

BEAUFORT, Sir Francis (1774-1857). **51 Manchester Street, W1**
British naval officer and hydrographer; lived here. He developed the 'Beaufort Scale' of wind force, and the Beaufort Sea in the Arctic was named after him. Beaufort was wounded twice during active service. *London County Council*

BECK, Harry (1903-74). **Finchley Central station, N3**
Originator of the London Underground railway map; lived near here and used the station regularly. Modifications of his famous design are gazed upon each day by thousands of commuters and visitors. The plaque is sited on the southbound platform, from which he travelled to work each day, alongside copies of his original map and its updated version. *London Transport*

BECKET, Thomas à (1118-70). **90 Cheapside, EC2**
Saint and martyr; born in a house formerly near this spot. He became Chancellor of England in 1155 and Archbishop of Canterbury in 1162. After a disagreement with King Henry II's policy, he was murdered in Canterbury Cathedral by four knights wishing to gain favour with the monarch. *Corporation of the City of London*

BEECHAM, Sir Thomas (1879-1961). **31 Grove End Road, NW8**
British conductor and impresario; lived here. The son of the 'Beecham Pills' founder, Beecham began his career with the New Symphony Orchestra in 1906, becoming principal conductor at Covent Garden in 1932 and, in 1943, conductor of the New York Metropolitan Opera. In 1947 he founded the Royal Philharmonic Orchestra, promoting the works of Delius, Sibelius and Richard Strauss. He was also noted as an after-dinner speaker. *Greater London Council*

BEERBOHM, Sir Max (1872-1956). **57 Palace Gardens Terrace, W8**
English caricaturist and writer; born here. The half-brother of Sir Herbert Beerbohm Tree (q.v.), he published his first volume, *The Works of Max Beerbohm,* in 1896. He succeeded George Bernard Shaw (q.v.) as drama critic of *The Sunday Review* and published various essays and a full-length novel, *Zuleika Dobson* (1912). From 1935 he made several broadcast talks. *Greater London Council*

BEETON, Mrs Isabella Mary (1836-65). **513 Uxbridge Road, Hatch End**
English writer of the *Book of Household Management;* lived in a house on this site 1856-62. Her famous cookery book was first published in parts for her husband's magazine in 1859. *Harrow Heritage Trust*

THE SITE OF 2 CHANDOS VILLAS,
HOME OF COOKERY WRITER
ISABELLA BEETON
AND HER PUBLISHER HUSBAND
SAMUEL
1856-62
HARROW
HERITAGE TRUST

BELL. Bell Yard, Carter Lane, EC4
The plaque reads: 'Upon

this site formerly stood The Bell, Carter Lane, from whence Richard Quiney wrote the letter to William Shakespeare dated 28th October 1598. This is the only letter extant addressed to Shakespeare, and the original is preserved in the museum at his birthplace, Stratford-upon-Avon. This tablet was placed upon the present building by leave of the Postmaster General, 1899.' *Private*

BELLO, Andres (1781-1865). **58 Grafton Way, W1**
Venezuelan patriot, poet, jurist and philologist lived here in 1810. A second blue plaque at this address commemorates Francisco de Miranda (q.v.). *English Heritage*

BELLOC, Hilaire Pierre (1870-1953). **104 Cheyne Walk, SW10**
French-born English author; lived here 1900-5. A friend of G. K. Chesterton (q.v.), Belloc is best known for his children's books of verse, though he also wrote travel, religious and historical books. He was also a Liberal MP 1906-10. A second plaque here commemorates Walter Greaves (q.v.). *Greater London Council*

BENEDICT, Sir Julius (1804-85). **2 Manchester Square, W1**
German musician and composer; lived and died here. Benedict settled in London in 1836. His best-known composition was 'Lily of Killarney' (1862). *London County Council*

BENES, Dr Edward (1884-1948). **26 Gwendolen Avenue, Putney, SW15**
Czechoslovak politician; lived here. He worked with Masaryk (q.v.) during the First World War and became premier of newly formed Czechoslovakia (1921-2), succeeding Masaryk as president in 1935. Due to Nazi interference he left the country in 1938. During the Second World War he led a government in exile in Britain. Though re-elected president in 1946, he resigned after the Communist coup of 1948. *Greater London Council*

BEN-GURION, David (1886-1973). **75 Warrington Crescent, W9**
Polish-born Israeli politician; lived here. He settled in Palestine in 1906 and became a leader of the Zionist movement. He was first prime minister of Israel in 1948-53 and held the office again in 1955-63. *Greater London Council*

BENNETT, Arnold (1867-1931). **75 Cadogan Square, SW1**
English novelist; lived here 1921-30. He became a journalist and in 1896 the editor of *Woman* magazine. His first novel, *The Man from the North,* was published in 1898. His noted works were *Anna of the Five Towns* (1902), *The Old Wives' Tale* (1908) and the *Clayhanger* series of books (1910-16), which were set in the Potteries district of Staffordshire, where he was born. *London County Council*

Right: *The plaque at Chagford Street, W1.*

Left: *The plaque at Cadogan Square, SW1.*

BENNETT, Sir William Sterndale (1816-75). **38 Queensborough Terrace, W2**
English composer and pianist; lived here. He was the founder of the Bach
Society (1849) and professor of music at Cambridge (1856). In 1868 he became
principal of the Royal College of Music. *English Heritage*

BENSON, E. F. (Edward Frederic) (1867-1940). **25 Brompton Square, SW3**
English novelist; lived here. The son of an Archbishop of Canterbury, he
published several novels, including *Dodo* (1893), *Queen Lucia* (1920) and *Miss
Mapp* (1922). *English Heritage*

BENTHAM, George (1800-84). **25 Wilton Place, SW1**
English botanist; lived here. The nephew of the reformer Jeremy Bentham, he
was secretary of the Horticultural Society of London in 1828-40 and compiled
many important botanical works. *Greater London Council*

BENTLEY, John Francis (1839-1902). **43 Old Town, Clapham, SW4**
British architect; lived here. He was the designer of Westminster Cathedral
(built 1895-1903). *London County Council*

BENTLEY MOTOR CAR. 49 Chagford Street, W1
The first Bentley motor car was produced in the workshops at this address in
1919. (Photograph, page 21) *Private*

BERG, Jack (Kid) (1909-91). **Noble Court, Cable Street, E1**

English boxer; born in a house near here. Nick-
named the 'Whitechapel Whirlwind', not 'Windmill' as the plaque states, he was light-welter-
weight world champion in 1930. He defended
his title nine times in fifteen months in the USA
and was also British lightweight champion in
1934. *Stepney Historical Trust*

BERLIOZ, Hector (1803-69). **58 Queen Anne Street, W1**
French composer; stayed here in 1851. He was awarded the Prix de Rome in
1830. His compositions include *Symphonie Fantastique* (1830), *Romeo and
Juliet* (1838), *The Damnation of Faust* (1846), sacred music and three operas.
Greater London Council

BESANT, Annie (1847-1933). **39 Colby Road, SE19**
English theosophist, social reformer and promoter of birth control; lived here in
1874. She was an associate of Charles Bradlaugh and
the Fabian Society (q.v.) and the sister-in-law of Sir
Walter Besant (q.v.). She lived for many years in India
and became president of the Indian National Congress
(1917). *London County Council*

BESANT, Sir Walter (1836-1901). **18 Frognal Gardens, NW3**
English writer and social reformer; lived here from
1893 until his death. He wrote several novels in
collaboration with James Rice (1844-82). His own
novels described conditions in the London slums,
and he also wrote on the history of London. A

Sir Walter Besant.

22

second plaque at this address commemorates Hugh Gaitskell (q.v.). *London County Council*

BETHLEHEM HOSPITAL. Liverpool Street, EC2 *Corporation of the City of London;* **9 London Wall, EC2** *Corporation of the City of London*
The first Bethlehem hospital (1247-1676) was built on the first site by Simon FitzMary and remained for over four hundred years until it was moved to London Wall. The second hospital (1676-1815), designed by Robert Hooke, could accommodate 150 patients. It was removed to Lambeth in 1815. (Photograph, page 24)

BEWDLEY, Earl Baldwin of. See **BALDWIN, Stanley**

BIBLE, first printed. Post Office, Borough High Street, SE1
The first English edition of the Bible to be printed in Great Britain was produced here in 1537. *Borough of Southwark*

BIGGIN HILL AIRFIELD. Main Road, Biggin Hill
Site of the RAF fighter station which was one of the most important fighter airfields in the 'Battle of Britain' during the Second World War. Two plaques, one of which bears the RAF station motto, 'the strongest link'. *Borough of Bromley*

Biggin Hill Airfield with the two plaques, one either side of the entrance.

BILLIG, Dr Hannah (1901-87). **198 Cable Street, E1**
Physician; lived and had her surgery here from 1935 to 1964. She tended the sick and injured throughout the Blitz of the Second World War and was known locally as 'the Angel of Cable Street'. Billig was awarded the George Medal, for her bravery, and the MBE. She also served in the army with the rank of captain and did famine relief work in India. Her final years were spent in Israel. *Borough of Tower Hamlets*

BINNEY, Captain Ralph Douglas (1888-1944). **Birchin Lane, EC3**
Captain in the Royal Navy. The plaque reads: 'This plaque was given by the Royal Navy in memory of Captain Ralph Douglas Binney, CBE, Royal Navy, who, on 8th December 1944, died from injuries received, when, bravely and alone, he confronted violent men raiding a jeweller's shop in this lane and struggled to prevent their escape. To honour this courageous act, Captain Binney's fellow officers and other friends founded the Binney Memorial Awards for civilians of the City and metropolitan areas of London who, in face of great danger and personal risk, have followed Captain Binney's example and

The plaque in Liverpool Street, EC2, where the first Bethlehem Hospital was situated.

steadfastly upheld law and order. Unveiled by HRH the Duke of Edinburgh, KG KT, on Thursday 4th December 1986.' *Royal Navy*

BIRKENHEAD, Earl of. See **SMITH, F. E.**

BLACKFRIARS PRIORY, site of. 7 Ludgate Broadway, EC4
A group of Dominicans formed a community here in 1221, and in 1278 Robert Fitzwalter gave them property for a larger monastery. The monks prospered, and many important people were buried at the priory. In the fourteenth century Parliament met here and the monastery was used as a depository for state records. Although it was dissolved in 1538 it continued to be used in part for various purposes, for example the Blackfriars playhouse. The remaining parts of the building were destroyed in 1666 by the Great Fire. *Corporation of the City of London*

BLACKHEATH FOOTBALL CLUB. The 'Princess of Wales' public house, Montpelier Row, SE3
The oldest Rugby Union club in the world, founded 1858, was based here and played on the heath for many years. A second plaque records that the England team for the first RU International in 1871 was organised here. The game, held in Edinburgh on 25th March, was between England and Scotland and was won by Scotland. *Private*

BLACKHEATH HALL. Bennett Park, Blackheath, SE3
Film studios of the General Post Office and Crown Film Units 1933-42. *Private*

BLACKWELL, Dr Elizabeth (1821-1910). **Royal Free Hospital, Pond Street, Hampstead, NW3**
English-born physician who became the first woman doctor in America; lived

and died here. She emigrated with her father to the USA in 1832 but returned to England in 1868, after having had a successful practice in New York. The plaque was unveiled in 1914 by the women's suffragist and social reformer Millicent Fawcett (q.v.). *Private*

BLAKE, William (1757-1827). **8 Marshall Street, W1** *Private;* **17 South Molton Street, W1** *Corporation of the City of London;* **'Old Wyldes', North End, Hampstead,**

The plaque at 23 Hercules Road, SE1, the site of one of Blake's homes.

NW3 *Private;* **23 Hercules Road, SE1** *Corporation of the City of London;* **37 Woolstone Road, SE23** *Greater London Council*
English poet, artist, engraver and visionary; the five plaques mark, respectively, the site of his birthplace, one of his homes, the home of John Linnell (where he stayed), the site of another of his homes, and another house where he stayed with Linnell. Apprenticed to an engraver (1771-8), he went on to produce many prints and paintings of a unique mystical and visionary nature, including *Songs of Innocence* (1789), *Songs of Experience* (1794), illustrations to the *Book of Job* (1825) and illustrations to Dante's *Divine Comedy* (1824-7). His followers and friends included Samuel Palmer (q.v.) and 'The Ancients', Henry Fuseli (q.v.). and John Flaxman (q.v.). In later years he was financially supported by his friend John Linnell (q.v.).

BLAND, Dorothea. See **JORDAN, Dorothy**

BLIGH, Captain William (1754-1817). **100 Lambeth Road, SE1** *London County Council;* **Reardon Street, E1** *History of Wapping Trust*
Captain of the famous *Bounty*; lived at the first address 1794-1813 and on the site of the second. Cast adrift by mutineers, he sailed 4000 miles to safety. He served under James Cook (q.v.), Sir Joseph Banks (q.v.) and Lord Nelson (q.v.) and was promoted admiral before his retirement in 1811. The second plaque records that he transplanted breadfruit from Tahiti to the West Indies.

BLISS, Sir Arthur (1891-1975). **East Heath Lodge, 1 East Heath Road, NW3**
British composer; lived here 1929-39. Born in London, he was music director of the BBC in 1942-4 and became Master of the Queen's Musick in 1953. He wrote orchestral and film music, the opera *The Olympians* (1949), chamber music and piano and violin works. *English Heritage*

BLOOMFIELD, Robert (1766-1823). **Kent House, Telegraph Street, EC2**
English poet; lived in a house on this site. He was the author of *The Farmer's Boy* (1800), *Rural Tales* (1802) and *Wild Flowers* (1806). He died in poverty. *Corporation of the City of London*

BLOOMSBURY GROUP. 50 Gordon Square, WC1
Literary group formed around the time of the First World War; several members lived here and in neighbouring houses. The group took its name from Bloomsbury Square and consisted of Leonard and Virginia Woolf (q.v.), Clive and Vanessa Bell, Lytton Strachey (q.v.), Roger Fry, John Maynard Keynes (q.v.), E. M. Forster (q.v.) and Duncan Grant. They had a great influence on the English modernist movement. *Camden Borough Council*

BLUMLEIN, Alan Dower (1903-42). **37 The Ridings, Ealing, W5**
English electronics engineer and inventor; lived here. He designed the 'in

flight' radar system used by Bomber Command during the Second World War. *Greater London Council*

BLUNT, Wilfred Scawen. See **SCAWEN-BLUNT, Wilfred**

BLYTON, Enid Mary (1897-1968). **83 Shortlands Road, Bromley** *Borough of Bromley;* **207 Hook Road, Chessington** *English Heritage*
English children's author; lived at both addresses (Hook Road 1920-4). She published over six hundred books. Her most famous character was 'Noddy'.

BOARD OF GUARDIANS, Jewish. Middlesex Street, E1.
The plaque reads: '1896-1956. This plaque was unveiled on 26th June 1989 by the Right Honourable the Lord Mayor Sir Christopher Collett, GBE, MA, DSc, to mark the 130th anniversary of the Board of Guardians and trustees for the relief of the Jewish poor registered (known as the Jewish Board of Guardians) who occupied these premises for sixty years.' *Private*

BOLAN, Marc (1947-77). **25 Stoke Newington Common, N16**
Stage name of Mark Feld, musician; lived here. Lead singer of the group 'T Rex', he died tragically in a car crash. *Borough of Hackney*

BOLÍVAR, Simon (1783-1830). **4 Duke Street, W1**
South American revolutionary leader; stayed here 1810. Known as 'The Liberator', he led the revolution against Spanish colonial forces, freeing Venezuela in 1821, Colombia and Ecuador in 1822, Peru in 1824 and Upper Peru (renamed Bolivia in his honour) in 1825. *Private*

BOMB, first (First World War). 31 Nevill Road, N16
The first bomb of the First World War to fall from a Zeppelin on London dropped in the garden of the Nevill Arms public house on 30th May 1915. *Borough of Hackney*

BOMB, first (Second World War). Fore Street, EC2
The first bomb to fall on the City of London in the Second World War fell on this site at 12.15 am on 25th August 1940. *Private*

BOMBERG, David (1890-1957). **10 Fordwych Road, NW2**
English artist; lived and worked here 1928-34. He studied under Sickert (q.v.) at the Slade school (1911-13) and was a founder member of the London Group (1913). Bomberg travelled widely and in his younger days associated with Modigliani and Picasso. *English Heritage*

BONHAM-CARTER, Lady Violet, Baroness Asquith of Yarnbury (1887-1969). **43 Gloucester Square, W2**
English Liberal politician and writer; lived here.

The daughter of H. H. Asquith (q.v.), she was president of the Liberal Party 1944-5 and governor of the BBC 1941-6. She was created a peeress in 1964. *English Heritage*

BONHOEFFER, Dietrich (1906-45). **2 Manor Mount, Forest Hill, SE23**
German Lutheran theologian; lived here 1933-5. He came to England in 1933 and was pastor of the church in Forest Hill until 1935, when he returned to Germany. His anti-Nazi views resulted in his imprisonment in 1943 and subsequent execution, one month before VE Day. His best-known and most interpreted work was *Ethics,* published posthumously in 1949. A statue of him can be found above the west door of Westminster Abbey (1998). *Lewisham Council*

BONN, Leo (1850-1929). **22 Upper Brook Street, W1**
He founded what is now the Royal National Institute for deaf people in this building on 9th June 1911. The plaque was unveiled by HRH the Duke of Edinburgh. *Westminster City Council*

BOOTH, Charles (1840-1916). **6 Grenville Place, SW7**
Liverpool-born shipowner and social reformer; lived here. He settled in London in 1875 and was a pioneer of old age pensions. *London County Council*

BOOTH, William (1829-1912). **33 Lancaster Avenue, Hadley Wood**
Founder and first general of the Salvation Army (q.v.); lived here from 1903 until his death. He became a Methodist minister in 1844 and held his first Christian Mission meeting in New Road, E1, in 1865. This eventually developed into the worldwide Salvation Army. *Borough of Enfield.*

BOOTHBY, Lord Robert John Graham, First Baron Boothby of Buchan and Rattray Head (1900-86). **1 Eaton Square, SW1**
Unionist MP; lived here 1946-86. He was parliamentary private secretary to Winston Churchill (q.v.) 1926-9. A supporter of the EEC (now EU), he was a well-known popular radio and television broadcaster and panellist. *Private*

BOROUGH, Stephen. See **WILLOUGHBY, Sir Hugh**

BOROUGH, William. See **WILLOUGHBY, Sir Hugh**

BORROW, George Henry (1803-81). **22 Hereford Square, SW7**
English writer and traveller; lived here. His journeys in Europe and Russia were mainly on foot, exploiting his linguistic abilities. Borrow published *The Zincali* (1840), *The Bible in Spain* (1843), *Lavengro* (1851), *Wild Roses* (1862) and several other books, some about gypsy life. *London County Council*

BOSWELL, James (1740-95). **122 Great Portland Street, W1** *London County Council;* **8 Russell Street, Covent Garden, WC2** (shared plaque) *Greater London Council*
Scottish author and biographer; lived and died in a house in Great Portland Street. He studied law in his younger days and travelled extensively in Europe, where he met Voltaire (q.v.) and Jean-Jacques Rousseau. He met Dr Johnson (q.v.) at Russell Street on his second visit to London. Their friendship developed,

The unveiling of the English Heritage plaque commemorating Sir Adrian Boult on 31st July 1998 by Andrew Davis, Principal Conductor of the BBC Symphony Orchestra. Over one hundred people were present to watch the ceremony.

and in 1773 he joined Johnson's literary club. His biography of the great man was published in two volumes in 1791.

BOULT, Sir Adrian Cedric (1889-1983). **78 Marlborough Mansions, Cannon Hill, NW6**
British conductor; lived at this address 1966-77. He was the conductor of the BBC Symphony Orchestra 1930-50 and the London Philharmonic 1950-7. He continued to conduct until 1981 and published his autobiography in 1973. He was knighted in 1937. *English Heritage*

BOW STREET. 19-20 Bow Street, WC2
Formed in 1637 and so named because it was in the shape of a bent bow. It has been the residence of many notable men, among whom were: Henry Fielding

The plaque in Bow Street, WC2.

(1707-54) (q.v.), novelist; Sir John Fielding (1721-80), magistrate; Grinling Gibbons (1648-1721), wood carver; Charles Macklin (*c*.1697-1797), actor; John Radcliffe (1650-1714), physician; Charles Sackville, Earl of Dorset (1638-1706), poet; and William Wycherley (*c*.1640-1716), dramatist. *London County Council*

BRAIDWOOD, James (1800-61). **33 Tooley Street, SE1**
Superintendent of the London Fire Brigade who was killed near this spot 'in the execution of his duty at the great fire on 27th June 1861'. This is one of the oldest commemorative tablets in London. *Private*

BRAILSFORD, Henry Noel (1873-1958). **27 Belsize Park Gardens, NW3**
English socialist author and political journalist; lived here. He was editor of *The New Leader* (1922-6) and wrote for several newspapers, including the *Daily Herald* and the *Manchester Guardian*. His first published work in 1898 described his experiences of the Greek-Turkish war (1897). The plaque refers to him as a 'champion of equal and free humanity'. *Greater London Council*

BRAIN, Dennis (1921-57). **37 Frognal Gardens, Hampstead, NW3**
London-born horn player and organist; lived here. He was the chief horn player of the Royal Philharmonic and Philharmonia orchestras. *English Heritage*

BRANDON, Thomas. See **SUFFOLK, Duke of**

BRANGWYN, Sir Frank (1867-1956). **51 Queen Caroline Street, W6**
Artist; lived here. Born in Belgium to Welsh parents, he was apprenticed to William Morris (q.v.). He produced furniture, pottery and interior designs, in addition to etchings, lithographs and murals. *English Heritage*

BRAY, John. 13 Little Britain, EC1
The plaque reads: 'Adjoining this site stood the house of John Bray, scene of Charles Wesley's evangelical conversion, May 21st 1738.' *Corporation of the City of London*

BRIDEWELL PALACE. 14 Farringdon Street, EC4
The plaque reads: 'Here stood the palace of Bridewell, built by Henry VIII in 1523 and granted by Edward VI in 1553 to the City of London to house Bridewell Royal Hospital, founded by royal charter in the same year. The present building was erected in 1802, and in 1862 the court room of Bridewell Royal Hospital was incorporated therein.' *Private*

BRIDGE, Frank (1879-1941). **4 Bedford Gardens, W8**
English composer and conductor; lived here. He was the tutor of Benjamin Britten (q.v.) and conducted frequently at the Promenade Concerts. Among his works are *Sea* (1912) and *Ovation* (1930). *English Heritage*

BRIDGEMAN, Charles (died 1738). **54 Broadwick Street, W1**
Landscape gardener to George II and Queen Caroline; lived here 1723-38. He was responsible for the landscaping of the gardens at Kensington Palace and the layout of those at Marble Hill (1723), a stately home near Richmond, Surrey. *Greater London Council*

BRIDGEMAN, Sir Orlando (1608-74). Included in the **ESSEX STREET** plaque.
English judge. He practised as a conveyancer during the Civil War but at the Restoration held various offices, becoming Lord Keeper of the Great Seal (1667-72). *London County Council*

BRIGHT, John (1811-89). **69 Fleet Street, EC4**
British Liberal politician; closely associated with the Anti-Corn Law League, whose offices were on this site 1844-60. He was also a campaigner against the Crimean War. The plaque is shared with Richard Cobden (q.v.), with whom he led the struggle for free trade. An eloquent speaker, he sat in Gladstone's cabinet. He was Chancellor of the Duchy of Lancaster 1873-4 and 1880-2. *Private*

BRIGHT, Richard (1789-1858). **11 Saville Row, W1**
British physician; lived here 1830-58. From 1820 he spent many years at Guy's Hospital, where he made numerous important observations. 'Bright's Disease' is named after him. *Greater London Council*

BRITTAIN, Vera Mary (1893-1970). **58 Doughty Street, WC1** *English Heritage;* **11 Wymering Mansions, Wymering Road, W9** *Westminster City Council*
English socialist writer; lived at both addresses. Her *Testament of Youth* (1933) described her experiences as a nurse during the First World War. She was the mother of

John Bright.

the Labour and SDP MP Shirley Williams. The Doughty Street plaque is shared by Winifred Holtby (q.v.).

BRITTEN, Sir Benjamin (1913-76). **8 Halliford Street, N1** *Islington Borough Council;* **45a St John's Wood High Street, NW8** *Westminster City Council*
English composer; lived at both addresses (Halliford Street from 1970). He studied under Frank Bridge (q.v.) and at the Royal College of Music. Britten composed in many forms but is best known for his operas and choral music. He was a founder of the Aldeburgh Festival (1948) and lived at the St John's Wood address with Peter Pears (q.v.), who shares the plaque.

BRITTON, Thomas (1644-1714). **Jerusalem Passage, EC1**
English coal merchant and musician; lived in a house on this site. He founded a musical club over his shop. His weekly concerts were attended by composers of his day including Handel (q.v.) and Pepusch. He also studied chemistry and the occult and was one of the founders of the Harleian Collection in the British Library. *Islington Borough Council*

BROCKWAY, Lord Archibald Fenner (1888-1988). **60 Myddleton Square, EC1**
English socialist politician and pacifist; lived here 1908-10. He sat approximately forty years in parliament and was a founder of CND. He was created a life peer in 1964. This plaque was, contrary to usual practice, erected during his lifetime. *Islington Borough Council*

BRODERERS' HALL, site of (1515-1940). **32 Gutter Lane, EC2**
English embroidery was famous throughout Europe, and the hall of the embroiderers' (broderers') livery company stood in Gutter Lane from 1515 until destroyed by enemy action in 1940. It had been rebuilt after the 1666 fire but, being little used, by the nineteenth century served as a warehouse. *Corporation of the City of London*

BROOKE, Sir Charles Vyner (1874-1963). **13 Albion Street, W2**
Last rajah of Sarawak; lived here. He was rajah of Sarawak (Borneo) from 1917 until he arranged for its transfer to the British Crown in 1946. *Greater London Council*

BROOKS, James (1825-1901). **42 Clissold Crescent, N16**
British architect; lived and died in this house, which he designed and built, *c.*1862. He designed and restored a number of buildings, including churches, rectories, schools and private houses. His London churches include St Michael, Shoreditch; St Columba and St Chad, both Hoxton; Holy Innocents, Hammersmith; and St John the Baptist, Kensington. *Borough of Hackney*

BROUGHAM, Lord Henry Peter (1778-1868). **5 Grafton Street, W1**
Scottish-born Whig politician and lawyer; lived here for the last thirty years of his life. He was advisor to Queen Caroline of Brunswick, a founder of London University and Lord Chancellor 1830-4. The brougham horse-drawn carriage was named after him. (Photograph, page 32) *City Lands Committee*

The plaque to Lord Henry Peter Brougham, the Whig politician and lawyer, at 5 Grafton Street, W1.

HENRY PETER, LORD BROUGHAM.
RESIDED IN THIS HOUSE FOR
THE LAST 30 YEARS OF HIS LIFE
BORN 1778 — DIED 1868

ON 29 JULY 1871
THE AUSTRIAN COMPOSER
ANTON BRUCKNER
1824—1896
STAYED IN THE HOUSE
WHICH USED TO OCCUPY THIS SITE
BRUCKNER STARTED WORK ON HIS
SECOND SYMPHONY DURING HIS
PERIOD IN LONDON

BRUNEL UNIVERSITY

Above: *The plaque on City Gate House, Finsbury Square, EC2, is to the Austrian composer Anton Bruckner.*

Artist

Sir Edward Coley
Burne-Jones
1833-1898
Lived at The Grange
on this site
1867-1898

Left: *One of three plaques to the artist Sir Edward Burne-Jones, this one is on Samuel Richardson House, North End Crescent, W14.*

BROWN, Ford Madox (1821-93). **56 Fortress Road, Kentish Town, NW5**
British Pre-Raphaelite painter; lived here. Born in France, he was an associate of Dante Gabriel Rossetti (q.v.) and William Morris (q.v.), for whose company he produced some designs of furniture and stained glass. Among his best-known works are *The Last of England* (1855) and the murals at Manchester Town Hall. *Greater London Council*

BROWN, Robert (1773-1858). Listed on the plaque of **BANKS, Sir Joseph**
Scottish botanist and pioneer of plant classification.

BROWNING, Elizabeth Barrett (1806-61). **50 Wimpole Street, W1** *Royal Society of Arts;* **99 Gloucester Place,W1** *London County Council*
English poet, wife of Robert Browning (q.v.); lived in a house on the Wimpole Street site 1838-46 and in Gloucester Place. She moved with her family to Wimpole Street from Durham, and her first poems were published at the age of nineteen. She first met Browning in 1845. After their marriage in 1846 he took her to Italy, where she continued writing. She suffered ill health for many years.

ROBERT
BROWNING
LIVED IN THIS HOUSE
1887-1889
FROM HERE
HIS BODY WAS TAKEN
FOR INTERMENT
IN
POETS' CORNER
WESTMINSTER ABBEY

BROWNING, Robert (1812-89). **179 South-ampton Way, SE5** *Private;* **Warwick Crescent, W2** *Westminster City Council;* **29 De Vere Gardens, W8** *Private*
English poet, husband of Elizabeth Barrett Browning (q.v.); lived at all three addresses and died in De Vere Gardens. Born in Camberwell, he had his first poem published in 1833. After their marriage, he and Elizabeth lived in Pisa and Florence. On her death he settled in London, living in Warwick Crescent for fifteen years (1862-87) and moving finally to De Vere Gardens (1887-9).

BRUCKNER, Anton (1824-96). **City Gate House, 39-45 Finsbury Square, EC2**
Austrian composer; stayed in a house on this site. He was organist at Linz Cathedral (1856-68) and a professor at the Vienna Conservatoire. His work, which was influenced by Wagner, included nine symphonies (the second of which was written in London) and many choral pieces. *Brunel University*

BEAU
BRUMMELL
1778-1840
Leader of Fashion
lived here

BRUMMELL, George Bryan ('Beau') (1778-1840). **4 Chesterfield Street, W1**
British dandy and fashion leader; lived here. He was a friend of the Prince Regent, with whom he quarrelled in 1813. Gambling debts forced him to flee to France in 1816, where he eventually died penniless in an asylum. *Greater London Council*

BRUNEL, Isambard Kingdom (1806-59). **98 Cheyne Walk, SW10**
English engineer and inventor; lived here 1808-25. Son of Marc Isambard Brunel (q.v.), with whom he shares the plaque. He was engineer for the Great Western Railway (1833) and designed the Clifton suspension bridge (1864) and

Isambard Kingdom Brunel (second from the right) and others at the launching of the 'Great Eastern'.

the Saltash bridge. His shipbuilding designs included the *Great Western* (1838), the *Great Britain* (1845) and the *Great Eastern* (q.v.) (1858), which laid the first transatlantic telegraph cable. *London County Council*

BRUNEL, Sir Marc Isambard (1769-1849). **98 Cheyne Walk, SW10**
French-born engineer and inventor; lived here. He was the father of Isambard Kingdom Brunel (q.v.), with whom he shares this plaque. He settled in England in 1799 after six years in America. His most outstanding work was the construction of the Thames tunnel from Rotherhithe to Wapping (1825-43). *London County Council*

BUCHANAN, Jack (1890-1957). **44 Mount Street, W1**
Scottish-born actor, dancer, manager, film producer and director; lived here. He appeared on the London and American stages in many light comedy roles, in pantomime and in a number of both British and Hollywood films. Buchanan controlled the Garrick Theatre, London, and was one of the most popular entertainers in the 1930s and 1940s. *Private*

BUCKINGHAM, Second Duke of (1628-87). **Newcastle Court, College Hill, EC4**
English politician and courtier; lived in a house on this site. Brought up with Charles I's children, he escaped during the Civil War and returned with Charles II, afterwards spending many years in Parliament. He was also the author of several comedies. *Corporation of the City of London*

BULL AND MOUTH INN, site of. 1 St Martin-le-Grand, EC1
The inn was a regular meeting place of the Quakers and, before the coming of the railway, a coach office but was demolished in 1888 to make way for the Post Office. *Corporation of the City of London*

BURGOYNE, General John (1722-92). **10 Hertford Street, W1**
British soldier and playwright; lived and died here. He fought in the American

War of Independence but after some successes surrendered at Saratoga (1777). He served in Parliament as both a Tory and a Whig. His comedies included *The Maid of Oaks* (1775) and *The Heiress* (1786). A second plaque at this address commemorates Richard Brinsley Sheridan (q.v.). *London County Council*

General John Burgoyne

BURKE, Edmund (1729-97). **37 Gerrard Street, W1**
Irish-born British politician; lived here 1787-90. He served the Whig party in Parliament from 1765 until 1794. A highly skilled orator, he denounced the French Revolution but defended the American colonists and is regarded as one of the greatest Conservative theorists. This plaque was erected in 1876 and is one of the oldest official plaques still surviving. *Royal Society of Arts*

BURNE-JONES, Sir Edward Coley (1833-98). **Samuel Richardson House, North End Crescent, W14** *Borough of Hammersmith and Fulham;* **17 Red Lion Square, WC1** *London County Council;* **41 Kensington Square, W8** *English Heritage*
British artist; lived at The Grange on the North End Crescent site; also lived at the other two addresses. He was influenced by Dante Gabriel Rossetti (q.v.) and William Morris (q.v.), of whom he was a close associate. His works were often inspired by Arthurian legends and Greek myths. (Photograph, page 32)

BURNETT, Frances Hodgson (1849-1924). **63 Portland Place, W1**
English-born writer; lived here 1893-8. She emigrated to the USA in 1865 with her family but returned to London after her marriage. Her most famous books are the children's stories *Little Lord Fauntleroy* (1886) and *The Secret Garden* (1909). *Greater London Council*

BURNEY, Fanny (Madame D'Arblay) (1752-1840). **11 Bolton Street, W1**
English novelist and diarist; lived here briefly in 1818. Her successful *Evelina* was published in 1778. A friend of Dr Johnson (q.v.), she belonged to the court of Queen Charlotte in 1786. Other novels include *Cecilia* (1782), *Camilla* (1796) and *The Wanderer* (1814), which could be considered forerunners of the modern 'soaps'. *Royal Society of Arts*

BURNS, John (1858-1943). **110 North Side, Clapham Common, SW4**
British socialist politician; lived here. He was elected to Parliament in 1892 and became Britain's first working-class cabinet minister. *London County Council*

BURTT, John (1855-1925) and **Lewis 'Daddy' BURTT** (1860-1935). **Hoxton Market, N1**
The founders (respectively, superintendent and honorary secretary) of Hoxton Market Christian Mission. Founded in 1886, the mission operated in these premises from 1915, 'For the benefit of local people', states the plaque. *Borough of Hackney*

BUSHEY POLICE STATION. 26 High Street, Bushey
The plaque reads: 'This building was the first Metropolitan Police station in Bushey 1840-84'. *Private*

BUTT, Dame Clara (1873-1936). **7 Harley Road, NW3**
English contralto; lived here 1901-29. She was one of the most popular singers of her day. *Greater London Council*

BUTTERFIELD, William (1814-1900). **42 Bedford Square, W1**
English architect; lived here. An important exponent of the Gothic revival, he designed Keble College, Oxford; St Augustine's College, Canterbury; All Saints' Church, Margaret Street, London; and several imposing buildings in other parts of Britain. *Greater London Council*

BYRON, Lady Anne (1792-1860). **Thames Valley University, St Mary's Road, W5**
Wife of the poet, whom she left after twelve months of marriage. She founded the co-operative school nearby (1834-59). *Private*

CAGE (or Old Watch House). Vestry House, Vestry Road, Walthamstow, E17
It was erected here in 1765 and removed in 1912. *Walthamstow Borough Council*

CALDECOTT, Randolph (1846-86). **46 Great Russell Street, WC1**
English illustrator of children's books; lived here. His work included *The House That Jack Built* (1878) and *Aesop's Fables* (1883). He was also a contributor to *Punch* magazine. *Greater London Council*

CALMAN, Mel (1931-94). **64 Linthorpe Road, N16**
Cartoonist and writer; lived here 1931-57. He worked as a cartoonist first for the *Daily Express* and then, from 1979, for *The Times.* Other work included book illustration and a series of short plays for Radio Three. He also exhibited regularly at the Royal Academy Summer Exhibition. *Borough of Hackney*

CAMPBELL, Colen (1676-1729). **76 Brook Street, W1**
Scottish architect; lived and died here. An exponent of the Palladian style, he designed Burlington House (1718-19). *Greater London Council*

CAMPBELL, Mrs Patrick (1865-1940). **33 Kensington Square, W8**
English actress; lived here. Married at nineteen, she went on the stage in 1888. Mrs Campbell appeared in *The Second Mrs Tanqueray* (1893), Shakespearian plays and *Pygmalion* (specially written for her by George Bernard Shaw). *Private*

CAMPBELL, Thomas (1777-1844). **8 Victoria Square, SW1**
Scottish poet; lived here 1840-4. He settled in London after his marriage in 1803 and also travelled extensively in Europe. Campbell's best-known poems are 'Ye Mariners of England' and 'Hohenlinden'. He is buried in Westminster Abbey. *Duke of Westminster (1908)*

CAMPBELL-BANNERMAN, Sir Henry (1836-1908). **6 Grosvenor Place, SW1**
Liberal prime minister 1905-8; lived here 1877-1904. Born in Glasgow, he entered Parliament in 1868 and became Liberal Party leader in 1899. *London County Council*

CANALETTO (Giovanni Antonio Canal) (1697-1768). **41 Beak Street, W1**
Venetian painter; lived here. He is famous for his detailed views of Venice and London (1746-56). *London County Council*

CANNING, George (1770-1827). **50 Berkeley Square, W1**
English Tory politician; lived here 1806-7. Canning entered Parliament in 1794, serving as Foreign Secretary in 1807-10 and 1822-7 and as prime minister in the last year of his life. He is buried in Westminster Abbey. *Greater London Council*

CARLILE, Wilson (1847-1942). **34 Sheffield Terrace, W8**
Anglican clergyman; lived here 1881-91. He founded the Church Army in 1882. *Greater London Council*

CARLYLE, Thomas (1795-1881). **33 Ampton Street, WC1** *London County Council;* **24 Cheyne Row, SW3** *Carlyle Society*
Scottish historian and essayist; lived in Ampton Street and later in Cheyne Row from 1834 until his death. His works include *Sartor Resartus* (1833), *The French Revolution* (1837), *Chartism* (1839), *Oliver Cromwell's Letters and Speeches* (1845), *History of Frederick the Great* (1858-65) and various essays, translations and pamphlets. He was acquainted with Coleridge (q.v.), Hazlitt (q.v.), Thomas Campbell (q.v.), J. S. Mill (q.v.) and Ralph Waldo Emerson.

CARTE, Richard D'Oyly (1844-1901). Listed under **ADELPHI TERRACE**.
English theatrical impresario and producer of the Gilbert and Sullivan operettas.

Left: *Thomas Carlyle.*

Below: *The plaque to Thomas Carlyle in Ampton Street, WC1.*

He built the Savoy Theatre (q.v.) in 1881.

CARTER, Howard (1874-1939). **19 Collingham Gardens, SW5**
Egyptologist; lived here. He joined Flinders Petrie's (q.v.) expedition in Egypt (1891), returning from 1907 under the patronage of Lord Carnarvon. Among his many discoveries were the tombs of Hatshepsut, Tuthmosis IV and, most notably, Tutankhamun (1922). *English Heritage*

CASLON, William (1692-1766). **21-3 Chiswell Street, N1**
English typefounder; his foundry stood on this site 1737-1909. 'Caslon' type was popular with printers in the eighteenth and nineteenth centuries and, after a revival, is used in the present day. *London County Council*

CASTLEREAGH, Viscount Robert Stewart (1769-1822). **Loring Hall, Water Lane, North Cray**
British statesman; lived and died here. He was Chief Secretary for Ireland in Pitt's government (1797-1801) and Foreign Secretary (1812-22). In 1809 Castlereagh duelled with George Canning (q.v.). He committed suicide in this house and is buried in Westminster Abbey. *English Heritage*

CATHERINE OF ARAGON (1485-1536). **49 Bankside, SE1**
First wife of Henry VIII and mother of Mary Tudor; the plaque states that she took shelter here on her first landing in London in 1502. Her marriage to the king was annulled because she was unable to give him an heir. The plaque is shared with Sir Christopher Wren (q.v.). *Private*

CATO STREET CONSPIRACY. 1a Cato Street, W1
Conspirators met in a stable loft here in 1820 and planned to murder the Cabinet at a meeting to be held in Grosvenor Square. However, their plot was uncovered and they were arrested by the Bow Street Runners. Five of the conspirators were hanged outside Newgate Prison and the remainder were transported to Australia. *Greater London Council*

CATTLE POUND OF HENDON. The Quadrant, Hendon, NW4
The pound stood here in medieval times and was still shown in a painting of 1850. Its purpose was to prevent cattle straying on to the lord of the manor's land. *Hendon Corporation*

CATTLEY, William (1788-1835). **Cattley Close, Wood Street, Barnet**
English botanist; lived and worked here. Famous as one of the first successful growers of epiphytic orchids in England, he was also a patron of John Lindley (1799-1865), to whom he paid a regular salary for drawing and describing new plants. *Borough of Barnet*

CAVAFY, Constantine (1863-1933). **14-15 Queensborough Terrace, W2**
Greek poet (pen name of Constantinos Petrou Kavafis); lived here 1873-6. He published one book only, in 1904, and was not generally well

known until English translations of his work appeared in the 1950s. *The London Hellenic Society (1974)*

CAVELL, Edith Louisa (1865-1915). **London Hospital, Whitechapel, E1** *English Heritage;* **St Leonard's Hospital, Kingsland Road, N1** *Borough of Hackney*
British nurse; trained and worked at the first address, 1896-1901; the second plaque records her time as assistant matron at the Shoreditch Infirmary, 1903-6. She assisted British soldiers to escape the Germans in Belgium during the First World War and was tried and executed by the enemy.

The plaque at the London Hospital in Whitechapel, E1.

CAVENDISH, The Honourable Henry (1731-1810). **11 Bedford Square, WC1**
English physicist; lived here. Grandson of the Duke of Devonshire, he discovered hydrogen and invented a device for estimating the density of the earth. *Erected by the Duke of Bedford c.1903 and adopted by the GLC in 1983*

CAYLEY, Sir George (1773-1857). **20 Hertford Street, W1**
English engineer and inventor; lived here 1840-8. He constructed and piloted the first glider in 1853. He also invented the caterpillar tractor and worked in railway engineering. With Quintin Hogg (q.v.), he was a founder of the Regent Street Polytechnic. *London County Council*

CAYLEY ROBINSON. See **ROBINSON, E. Cayley**

CECIL, Robert Gascoyne. See **SALISBURY, Third Marquess of**

CECIL, Robert, First Viscount Cecil of Chelwood (1864-1958). **16 South Eaton Place, SW1**
English Tory statesman; lived here 1923-58. He first entered Parliament in 1903. As Under-secretary for Foreign Affairs in 1918 he helped to draft the League of Nations covenant. He was president of the League of Nations 1923-45 and winner of the Nobel peace prize in 1937. A second plaque at this address commemorates Philip Noel-Baker (q.v.). *Greater London Council*

CEDAR LAWN. Cattley Close, Wood Street, Barnet
This building was the former Victoria Maternity Hospital 1924-87. A second plaque at this same address commemorates William Cattley (q.v.). *Borough of Barnet*

CHADWICK, Sir Edwin (1801-90). **5 Montague Road, Richmond**
English social reformer; lived here. He was a prominent campaigner for public health reforms and commissioner of the first Board of Health 1848-54. *English Heritage*

CHALLONER, Bishop Richard (1691-1781). **44 Old Gloucester Street, WC1**
English Roman Catholic prelate and writer; died here. He converted to Roman Catholicism during

childhood. Having spent twenty-six years at the English College in Douai (1704-30), he became a missionary priest in London. In 1758 he became vicar apostolic of the London District. Challoner wrote thirty-four books, many of which are still used by Roman Catholics today. *English Heritage*

CHAMBERLAIN, (Arthur) Neville (1869-1940). **37 Eaton Square, SW1**
English Tory statesman and prime minister; lived here 1923-35. His policy of appeasement did not prevent the outbreak of the Second World War. He was lord mayor of Birmingham 1915-6, Minister of Health 1924-9, Chancellor of the Exchequer 1923-4 and 1931-7 and prime minister 1937-40. *London County Council*

CHAMBERLAIN, Joseph (1836-1914). **188 Camberwell Grove, SE5** *London County Council;* **25 Highbury Place, N5** *London County Council*
English politician; lived at both addresses. By 1874 he had made a fortune with a screw-manufacturing business. Three times mayor of Birmingham, he became a left-wing Liberal MP in 1876. He was President of the Board of Trade in 1880 and Colonial Secretary in Salisbury's Conservative government in 1895. He was the father of Neville Chamberlain (q.v.).

CHAMPAGNE CHARLIE. See **LEYBOURNE, George**

CHAPLIN, Charlie (Charles Spencer) (1889-1977). **277 Walworth Road, SE17** *Southwark Council;* **287 Kennington Road, SE11** *Vauxhall Society;* **39 Methley Street, SE11** *The Dead Comics Society*
Actor, comedian, film star and director; born in East Lane, Walworth (first address) and lived at the other two addresses. He started his career as a child in the music halls. He went to Hollywood in 1914 and appeared in silent movies as the famous tramp. As the film industry progressed he turned to directing as well as acting. His left-wing sympathies caused him to emigrate to Switzerland during the McCarthy anti-communist period in 1952. He was knighted in 1975.

This plaque to Charlie Chaplin is at Kennington Road, SE11.

CHARLES, Elizabeth Rundle (1828-96). **Coombe Edge, Branch Hill, NW3**
Author of *The Chronicles of the Schönberg-Cotta Family*; lived here 1874-96. In all, she wrote some fifty novels. *Rundle Charles Memorial Fund (1897)*

CHARLOTTE, Queen (1744-1818). Mentioned on the plaque to **WHITBREAD, Samuel.**
Wife of George III, to whom she bore fifteen children.

CHATEAUBRIAND, François René, Vicomte de (1768-1848). **Paddington Street Gardens, Paddington Street, W1**
French statesman and writer; 'lived as an émigré in a garret close to this site and began his literary career', states the plaque. As a supporter of the royalists, he lived in exile during the French Revolution. He visited the USA in 1791 and from 1793 to 1800 lived in London. Returning to England as ambassador in 1822-4, he lived in Portland Place. His major literary work, *Mémoires d'outre-tombe,* filled six volumes and was not published in full until 1902. *Private*

CHATHAM, Earl of. See **PITT, William**

CHATTERTON, Thomas (1752-70). **39 Brooke Street, EC1**
English poet; died in a house on this site. He wrote poems in a medieval style, purporting to have been written by a fifteenth-century monk. In 1769 he sent an essay to Horace Walpole, which he claimed was the work of this same monk, but Walpole was not deceived. Living in poverty, he committed suicide the following year. *Corporation of the City of London*

CHEESMAN, Wallace Bligh (1865-1947). **8 Highbury Grange, N5**
English trade union leader; lived here 1926-7. A delegate to the TUC and executive of the Labour Representation Committee, he founded the Fawcett Association and the Civil Service Federation. He was also a delegate to the founding conference of the Labour Party (1900). *Islington Borough Council*

CHELSEA CHINA. 16 Lawrence Street, SW3
Chelsea china was manufactured in a house at the north end of Lawrence Street, 1745-84. The plaque is shared with Tobias Smollett (q.v.). *London County Council*

CHESTERFIELD, Philip Stanhope, Second Earl of (1633-1713), **CHESTERFIELD, Philip Stanhope, Third Earl of** (1672-1726); **CHESTERFIELD, Philip Dormer Stanhope, Fourth Earl of** (1694-1773). **45 Bloomsbury Square, WC1** *Duke of Bedford (1907);* **Ranger's House, Chesterfield Walk, SE10** *London County Council*
English aristocrats; all three earls lived at the first address; the fourth earl, a statesman and author, also lived at Ranger's House. The second earl was educated mainly in Holland. Three times married, he was a gambler and drunkard, committed to the Tower of London for duelling and his involvement in Royalist plots. The third earl was borne by his father's third wife. The fourth earl was ambassador to Holland 1728-32 and 1744, Lord Lieutenant of Ireland 1745-6 and Secretary of State 1746-8. He was also a member of the literary circle of Swift, Pope (q.v.) and Bolingbroke and was the infamous 'patron' of Dr Johnson (q.v.). He purchased Ranger's House in 1748 and made extensive alterations.

CHESTERTON, G. K. (Gilbert Keith) (1874-1936). **11 Warwick Gardens, W14** *London County Council;* **32 Sheffield Terrace, W8** *Private*
London-born novelist, biographer and poet; lived at both addresses. Chesterton's first writings were mainly essays in periodicals, and his first published books

The plaque to three of the Earls of Chesterfield at 45 Bloomsbury Square, WC1

were collections of poems. Author of the *Father Brown* stories, he also contributed illustrations to novels by Hilaire Belloc (q.v.). Chesterton wrote biographies of Browning (q.v.), Dickens (q.v.), R. L. Stevenson (q.v.) and St Francis of Assisi.

CHEVALIER, Albert (1861-1923). **17 St Ann's Villas, W11**
Music-hall entertainer; born here. His memorable songs were 'My Old Dutch' and 'Knocked 'em in the Old Kent Road'. *London County Council*

CHICHESTER, Sir Francis (Charles) (1901-72). **9 St James's Place, SW1**
English yachtsman and navigator; lived here 1944-72. He won the first trans-atlantic yacht race in 1957 and was knighted in 1967, having made a solo circumnavigation of the world. *Westminster City Council*

CHIPPENDALE, Thomas (1718-79). **61 St Martin's Lane, WC2**
English furniture designer and craftsman; established his workshop in St Martin's Lane in 1753, where the business was afterwards continued by his son until 1813. He worked mainly in mahogany and styled Rococo, Chinese, Gothic and Neo-Classical designs. *London County Council*

CHISHOLM, Caroline (1808-77). **32 Charlton Place, N1**
English-born social worker and philanthropist who settled in Australia in 1838; lived here. Known as 'the emigrants' friend', she set up a shelter for new arrivals in the 1840s and helped them to find work. She also established the Family Colonisation Loan Society. Chisholm came to England in 1846, returned again to Australia in 1854 and finally retired to England in 1866, receiving a civil pension. *Greater London Council*

43

The plaque at 4 St James's Place, SW1.

CHOPIN, Frédéric (1810-49). **4 St James's Place, SW1** *Greater London Council;* **99 Eaton Place, SW1** *Private*
Polish composer and pianist; gave his first London concert at Eaton Place and was residing at St James's Place on the day he gave his last performance; both in 1848. Chopin made his debut at the age of eight. He went to Paris in 1831 and was introduced to Madame Dudevant (George Sand) by Liszt (q.v.) in 1836; they had a close relationship and she nursed him through tuberculosis in Majorca (1838-9). He visited England in 1837 and 1848. His compositions include fifty mazurkas, twenty-five preludes, two piano concertos and a funeral march.

CHRISTIE, Dame Agatha Mary Clarissa (1890-1976). **Christie Cottage, Cresswell Place, SW10**
English novelist; lived here. She was the writer of more than seventy detective stories, mainly featuring the characters 'Hercule Poirot' or 'Miss Marple'. Several of her books have been filmed or adapted for television. She also had successes with plays, including the record-breaking *The Mousetrap. Private*

CHRIST'S HOSPITAL, site of. Newgate Street, EC1
Situated here 1552-1902, it was founded by Edward VI as a hospital for orphans. It was severely damaged in the Great Fire (1666) but rebuilt, under the supervision of Sir Christopher Wren (q.v.). *Corporation of the City of London*

CHURCH COMMON. Former postal sorting office, Vestry Road, E1
The playground opposite the plaque was part of Church Common, one of the three in the borough before the Enclosure Act (1850), and will remain an open space. *Borough of Walthamstow*

CHURCH HOUSE, site of. The Greyhound, Church End, NW4
Founded in 1321, former location of parish meetings. The Greyhound Inn is the last of a series of buildings on this site. Vestry meetings were held here regularly, and the name 'Greyhound' first appears in records of 1655. *Hendon Corporation*

CHURCHILL, Lord Randolph Henry Spencer (1849-95). **2 Connaught Place, W2**
British statesman and father of Sir Winston Churchill (q.v); lived here 1883-92. Son of the seventh Duke of Marlborough, he became a Conservative politician, entering Parliament in 1874. He became Secretary of State for India (1885-6) and Chancellor of the Exchequer in 1886. *London County Council*

CHURCHILL, Sir Winston (Leonard) Spencer (1874-1965). **Caxton Hall, Caxton Street, SW1** *Westminster City Council;* **34 Eccleston Square, SW1** *Private;* **3 Sussex Square, W2** *Private;* **28 Hyde Park Gate, SW7** *Greater London Council*
English statesman and prime minister during the Second World War; spoke at

The plaque commemorating Lord Randolph Churchill at 2 Connaught Place, W2.

the former Caxton Hall (1937-42); lived in Eccleston Square (1909-13), in a former house in Sussex Square (1921-4) and in Hyde Park Gate, where he died. Son of Lord Randolph Churchill (q.v.), he was often described as the 'greatest living Englishman'. His eventful lifetime saw him through campaigns in India and the Sudan, the Boer Wars, two World Wars and the 'Cold War'. He was President of the Board of Trade 1908-10, Home Secretary 1910-11, First Lord of the Admiralty 1911-15, Minister of Munitions 1918, Secretary of State for War 1919-21, Chancellor of the Exchequer 1924-9 and prime minister 1940-5 and 1951-5. An accomplished amateur artist and skilled bricklayer, he also wrote *The World Crisis* (1923-9), *Marlborough* (1933-8), *The Second World War* (1948-54) and *History of the English Speaking Peoples* (1956-8).

CITY OF LONDON SCHOOL, site of (1835-82). **3 Milk Street, EC2**
The foundation stone was laid by Lord Brougham (q.v.). Because of lack of space the school was moved to the Thames embankment. *Corporation of the City of London*

CITY PEST HOUSE. Bath Street, EC1
The City Pest House was built in 1594 to isolate persons suffering from leprosy and other infectious diseases, notably the great plague (1665). It was demolished 1736. *Islington Borough Council*

CITY ROAD TURNPIKE. 112 City Road, EC1
This turnpike stood near here from 1766 to 1864. *Islington Borough Council*

CLAPHAM SECT. Holy Trinity Church, Clapham Common, SW4
The Clapham Sect was active in the 1780s and 1790s as an Anglican movement for evangelical reform. Prominent members were William Wilberforce (q.v.) and his cousin, the economist Henry Thornton (1760-1815). The vicar of Clapham at the time was John Venn (1759-1813). The plaque is shared with William Wilberforce. *Greater London Council*

CLARENCE, Duke of (1765-1837). **22 Charles Street, W1** *Private;* **Ashberry Cottage, Honor Oak Road, SE23** *Private*

Later William IV (1830-7); lived in Charles Street 1826 and in Ashberry Cottage from 1790 to 1811 with Mrs Jordan (q.v.), who bore him ten children. He married Adelaide of Saxe-Meiningen in 1818 and was known as the 'Sailor King'.

CLARK, William Tierney (1783-1852). **Upper Mall, Hammersmith, W6**
Civil engineer; lived on this site *c.*1839. He was the designer of the first Hammersmith bridge. *Borough of Hammersmith and Fulham*

CLARKSON, Willy (1861-1934). **41-3 Wardour Street, W1**
Theatrical wig maker; lived and died here. The building was designed for him in 1905, and brass plaques commemorate the fact that Sarah Bernhardt and Sir Henry Irving (q.v.) laid the foundation stone. *Greater London Council*

CLAYTON, The Reverend Philip Thomas Byard ('Tubby') (1885-1972). **43 Trinity Square, EC3**
Founder of the 'TOC H' Christian fellowship; lived here. TOC H was founded in 1922 to teach the younger generation racial reconciliation and unselfish service. Clayton toured the world promoting these values and served as chaplain in the Indian Ocean and Mediterranean during the Second World War. He was awarded a special Salvation Army diploma in 1971. *English Heritage*

CLEARY, Frederick, CBE (1905-84). **Cleary Gardens, Huggin Hill, EC4**
A chartered surveyor by profession, he founded and became chairman of a large property company, renowned for its restoration of old buildings and responsible for some of the largest office developments in the City of London. Cleary, who was a councillor, seized every opportunity to add beauty in every available space in the City and this garden was given his name. The plaque states he was 'tireless in his wish to create open space in the City'. *Corporation of the City of London.*

CLEGHORN, Elizabeth. See **GASKELL, Mrs**

CLEMENS, Samuel Langhorne. See **TWAIN, Mark**

CLEMENTI, Muzio (1752-1832). **128 Kensington Church Street, W8**
Italian pianist and composer; lived here 1820-3. He settled in London in 1782 after earlier visits and opened a piano and music business. His collection of piano studies (in fact exercises), *Gradus ad Parnassum* (1817), is still used today. *London County Council*

CLERKS' WELL. 14-16 Farringdon Lane, EC1
Clerks' Well was mentioned as early as 1174 and gave its name to the district of Clerkenwell. It was here that parish clerks performed miracle plays in medieval times. A pump was placed over the well in 1800 for public use but was lost during rebuilding in the nineteenth century. During further reconstruction the well was rediscovered in 1924 and it can be seen by request to the local

authority. *Borough of Finsbury*

CLINK PRISON. Clink Street, SE1
The wall to which the plaque is attached is part
of the original fourteenth-century prison used
for religious and political prisoners. It was first
owned by the Bishops of Winchester and later
buildings survived as a prison (1580-1745) until
it was finally closed in 1840. It is now a museum open to the public. *Private*

CLIVE, Robert, Baron of Plassey (1725-74). **45 Berkeley Square, W1**
English soldier and administrator; lived here from 1761 until his death. He
overthrew the French in India (1751) and the Nawab of Bengal (1757), establishing British supremacy in India. *London County Council*

CLOCK TOWER. Heath Street, NW3
This well-known Hampstead landmark, states the plaque, started its life as the
local fire station. A permanent lookout was kept at the top of the clock tower.
Hampstead Plaque Fund

CLOVER, Dr Joseph T. (1825-82). **3 Cavendish Place, W1**
Pioneer anaesthetist; lived in a house on this site 1853-82. *Westminster City
Council*

COATES, Eric (1886-1957). **7 Willifield Way, NW11**
English composer; lived here 1925-31. Among his best-known works are *The
London Suite* (1933), which includes the 'Knightsbridge March'; 'By the
Sleepy Lagoon' (1939); and 'The Dambusters March' (1942). *Borough of
Barnet*

COBDEN, Richard (1804-65). **23 Suffolk Street, SW1** *London County Council;* **69 Fleet Street, EC4** *Private*
English Liberal politician and economist; co-founded the Anti-Corn-Law
League, whose offices were in Fleet Street 1844-6; died in Suffolk Street. He
and John Bright (q.v.) founded the League in 1839. He entered Parliament in
1841 and was a campaigner for free trade. He opposed trade unionism and the
Crimean War.

COBDEN-SANDERSON, Thomas James (1840-1922). **15 Upper Mall, W6**
English bookbinder and printer; lived and died here. He worked with William
Morris (q.v.) and Burne-Jones (q.v.). He founded the Doves Bindery (1893) and
Press (1900) in this house. The press closed in 1916 after publishing some fifty
books, and Cobden-Sanderson threw the type into the nearby river Thames.
Greater London Council

COBORN, Charles (1852-1945). **Coborn Street, E3**
Stage name of Colin Whitton McCallum, a music-hall entertainer who took his name from this street, where he lived in his youth. He is remembered for his popular songs 'Two Lovely Black Eyes' (1886) and 'The Man Who Broke the Bank at Monte Carlo' (1890). *Bow Heritage*

COCHRANE, Thomas, Tenth Earl of Dundonald (1775-1860). **Hanover Lodge, Outer Circle, NW1**
British admiral; lived here 1830-45. Hanover Lodge was designed by John Nash in the 1820s, and Cochrane lived here in the 1830s and early 1840s. The house was enlarged in 1909 by Lutyens, and Lord Beatty (q.v.) lived here 1910-25. Cochrane entered the Navy in 1793 and had an eventful career, often plundering the French, while rapidly gaining promotion. He spent a year in prison after accusations of fraud, for which he was later pardoned. He served as naval commander for Chile and Peru (1818-22), Brazil (1823-5) and Greece (1827-8). He became a rear admiral of Great Britain in 1854 and is buried in Westminster Abbey. The plaque is shared with Lord Beatty. *Greater London Council*

COCKERELL, Charles Robert (1788-1863). **13 Chester Terrace, NW1**
English architect and antiquary, lived and died here. He was professor of architecture at the Royal Academy of Arts (1840-57) and designed the Taylorian Institute at Oxford and the Fitzwilliam Museum, Cambridge. *English Heritage*

COFFEE HOUSE, first London. St Michael's Alley, EC2
Opened in 1652 by a Turk from Smyrna named Pasqua Rosee. *Private*

COLE, Sir Henry (1808-82). **3 Elm Row, NW3** *Hampstead Plaque Fund;* **33 Thurloe Square, SW7** *English Heritage*
English designer and writer; lived at both addresses. He published the first Christmas card and was responsible for the first adhesive postage stamps,

The first London coffee house was in St Michael's Alley, EC2.

proposed by Sir Rowland Hill (q.v.). He was a founder and director of the Victoria and Albert Museum.

COLE, King (died 1868). **Meath Gardens, E2**
Aborigine cricketer; plaque commemorates the donation of a eucalyptus tree to the Aboriginal Cricket Association in his honour (1988). He died on the first ever Australian cricket tour of Britain, having contracted tuberculosis, and was buried in a pauper's grave in Victoria Park cemetery, now Meath Gardens. *Private*

COLERIDGE, Samuel Taylor (1772-1834). **7 Addison Bridge Road, W14**
London County Council; **71 Berners Street, W1** *London County Council;* **3 The Grove, N6** *St Pancras Borough Council*
English poet and writer; lived at the first address, on the site of the second (1812-13) and also at the third (1823-34). He was a friend of William Wordsworth and Charles Lamb (q.v.). In later life he was addicted to opium. His poems include 'The Rime of the Ancient Mariner' (1798) and 'Kubla Khan' (1816).

COLERIDGE-TAYLOR, Samuel (1875-1912). **30 Dagnall Park, South Norwood, SE25**
English composer; lived here. His most notable work was *Hiawatha's Wedding Feast* (1898), a cantata based on Longfellow's poem. He was the son of a West African doctor and an English mother. *Greater London Council*

COLLINS, José (Josephine) (1887-1958). **St Olave's Hotel, High Road, Loughton**
Actress and singer; lived here. She appeared with Harry Lauder in both music hall and pantomime and worked in New York 1911-16. She was at Daly's Theatre 1916-21 and at the Gaiety 1922-4 and was known as a true soprano with a tempestuous personality. *Loughton Town Council*

COLLINS, Michael (1890-1922). **5 Netherwood Road, W14**
Irish nationalist and Sinn Fein leader;

lived here 1914-15. He fought in the 1916 Easter Rising and was prominent in the establishment of the Irish Free State. He became head of state ten days before being killed in an ambush. *Borough of Kensington and Chelsea*

COLLINS, William Wilkie (1824-89). **65 Gloucester Place, W1**
English novelist; lived here 1868-76. He was one of the earliest to write stories of crime, mystery and suspense. His novels include *The Woman in White* (1860), *No Name* (1862), *Armadale* (1866) and *The Moonstone* (1868). *London County Council*

COLLINS' MUSIC HALL. 10-11 Islington Green, N1
Opened in 1862 by Sam Collins, a performer who died in 1865, the music hall was used until destroyed by fire in 1958. It featured many well-known artists, including Charlie Chaplin (q.v.), Marie Lloyd (q.v.), Harry Lauder (q.v.) and George Robey. *Greater London Council*

COLLINSON, Peter (1694-1768). **Wall of Mill Hill School, The Ridgeway, Mill Hill, NW7**
English author, naturalist and botanist; lived in Mill Hill from 1749, in Ridgeway House on this site. He was noted for his contributions to the Sir Hans Sloane and British Museums. A friend of Benjamin Franklin (q.v.), he corresponded regularly with him and sent him details of electrical experiments being conducted in Germany. From his advice American settlers began growing flax, hemp, sisal and vines. He was elected to the Royal Society in 1728. *Hendon Corporation*

COLYER, Ken (1928-88). **11-12 Great Newport Street, WC2**
English jazz musician; played New Orleans jazz here in the basement, 'Studio 51', 1950-73. *Westminster City Council*

COMPTON-BURNETT, Ivy (1892-1969). **Braemar Mansions, Cornwall Gardens, SW7**
English novelist; lived here 1934-69. She was noted for her skilful use of dialogue, and many of her novels have been adapted for broadcasting. Her first published work, *Dolores* (1911), was followed by others, including *Pastors and Masters* (1925), *Brothers and Sisters* (1929), *Parents and Children* (1941) and *Mother and Son* (1955). The original private plaque was replaced by English Heritage in 1997. *English Heritage*

CONNELL, Jim (1852-1929). **22a Standon Park, SE23**
Irish socialist; lived here 1915-29. He wrote the anthem of the British Labour Party, 'The Red Flag', in 1889 whilst travelling on a train between Charing Cross and New Cross. *Lewisham Council*

CONRAD, Joseph (1857-1924). **17 Gillingham Street, SW1**
Polish-born, naturalised British novelist; lived here. He joined an English merchant ship at the age of twenty and in the following years sailed between Singapore and Borneo until 1896, when he married and settled in Kent. His best-known works include *Lord Jim* (1900), *Nostromo* (1904), *The Secret Agent* (1907) and *Under Western Eyes* (1911). As well as novels he wrote many short stories and is regarded as one of the greatest novelists of the twentieth century. *Greater London Council*

CONS, Emma (1837-1912). **136 Seymour Place, W1**
English philanthropist and founder of the Old Vic Theatre; lived and worked here. *Greater London Council*

CONSTABLE, John (1776-1837). **2 Lower Terrace, NW3** *Hampstead Plaque Fund;* **Mansion Gardens, West Heath Road, NW3** *Hampstead Plaque Fund;* **40 Well Walk, NW3** *London County Council*
English landscape painter; stayed at the first address 1821, 1822; painted a well-known view from the second, described in the plaque; lived at the third 1827-34. His best-known paintings include 'The Haywain' (1821), 'Flatford Mill' (1825) and 'Salisbury Cathedral from the Meadows (1831). Many of his works can be seen in the National and Tate Galleries. The plaque at Mansion Gardens also commemorates Sir Herbert Beerbohm Tree (q.v.).

The plaque at 40 Well Walk, NW3.

COOK, Don. Kennistoun House, Leighton Road, NW5
The plaque commemorates him as the leader of the famous St Pancras rent strike in the late 1950s when tenants rebelled against the government's Act to increase council rent charges. Residents at Kennistoun House lived for several weeks behind barricades and barbed wire until the bailiffs forced entry, and in September 1960 Cook's family, together with two others, were finally evicted, to much media attention. A typical increase at the time for a three-bedroom flat was from £1 15s 0d to £2 14s 3d a week. *Private*

COOK, Captain James (1728-79). **88 Mile End Road, E1** *Greater London Council;* **326 The Highway, E1** *Stepney Historical Trust*
English navigator and explorer; lived in houses on both sites. He surveyed the St Lawrence river (1759) and, from 1768, made three major voyages to New Zealand, Australia and the Pacific Ocean, charting many then undiscovered lands. He was killed by natives on the island of Hawaii.

COOKS' HALL, site of. 10 Aldersgate Street, EC1
The Company of Cooks was established in the reign of Edward IV. The hall was built in 1500 but destroyed by fire in 1771. *Corporation of the City of London*

COOPER, Tommy (1922-84). **Teddington Studios, Broom Road, Teddington**
Welsh-born comedian and magician; worked here. He entertained troops during the Second World War and afterwards performed at the Windmill Theatre. His popularity was secured when he appeared on television, and he had his own series during the 1950s and 1960s. He is remembered for his red fez and the catchphrase 'Just like that'. *Comic Heritage*

COPEMAN, Sydney Monkton (1862-1947). **57 Redcliffe Gardens, SW10**
English physician; lived here. He developed the vaccine used for immunisation against smallpox. *English Heritage*

COPENHAGEN HOUSE AND FIELDS. The Clocktower, Market Road, N7
The 'fields' were said to have been named by a Dane who lived there in the seventeenth century. From the early seventeenth century until 1855 the fields were used as a pleasure ground, with a tavern and tea garden, and later they were used for political meetings. In the nineteenth and early twentieth centuries there was a cattle and pedlars' market here. *Islington Borough Council*

COPPICE ROW TURNPIKE. GPO Sorting Office, Farringdon Road, EC1
The turnpike stood near here *c*.1750 to 1830. It was one of London's many tollgates. *Islington Borough Council*

CORBOULD, Edward Henry (1815-1905). **52 Victoria Road, W8**
Art tutor to the children of Queen Victoria; lived here. *Private*

CORY, William Johnson (1823-92). **8 Pilgrim's Lane, NW3**
English poet and teacher; lived and died in this house. He was an assistant master at Eton College 1845-72, published a book of poems in 1858 and wrote the words for the 'Eton Boating Song'. *Hampstead Plaque Fund*

COUNTY HALL. Main Entrance, County Hall, SE1
The home of London government 1922-86. London County Council was based here until 1965 and the Greater London Council 1965-86. *Greater London Council*

COURT LEET AND COURT BARON, site of the meeting place of. The White Bear, The Burroughs, NW4
The original White Bear inn served as a court house for a very long period under the jurisdiction of the lord of the manor in medieval times. The Court Leet exercised criminal jurisdiction, but its powers declined after the Act of 1267 which exempted members of the clergy and noblemen from attendance. The Court Baron met twice a year, dealing mainly with matters pertaining to the manor estate, and was in use until 1916. The present building on this site was erected in 1932. *Hendon Corporation*

COWARD, Sir Noël Pierce (1899-1973). **17 Gerald Road, SW1** *Private;* **131 Waldegrave Road, Teddington** *English Heritage;* **56 Lenham Road, Sutton** *Borough of Sutton*
English actor, playwright and composer; born at the Teddington address; lived at the Sutton one; lived in Gerald Road 1930-56. Coward's first stage appearance was at Sutton Public Hall, aged eight. His first play, *I'll Leave It to You* (1920), was followed by many successes, including *Bitter Sweet* (1929), *Private Lives* (1930), *Cavalcade* (1931), *Blithe Spirit* (1941) and *This Happy Breed* (1943). He also produced several films, including *In Which We Serve* (1942) and *Brief Encounter* (1945).

COX, David (1783-1859). **34 Foxley Road, SW9**
English landscape painter; lived here. He worked in both oils and watercolours. Many of his works can be seen at the Tate Gallery and the Birmingham Art Gallery. *London County Council*

CRANE, Walter (1845-1915). **13 Holland Street, W8**
English artist and illustrator; lived here. He was an associate of William Morris (q.v.) and is particularly noted for his book illustrations for both adults and children. The illustration of Spenser's *Faerie Queen* (1894-6) was one of his greatest achievements. *London County Council*

CRAPPER, Thomas (1837-1910). **12 Thornsett Road, SE20**
English plumber; lived here. He is attributed with the invention of the syphonic toilet flush. Although he never lodged a patent for this, he was known to be one of the leading contractors for their installation in the 1870s and 1880s. He installed thirty toilets and drains for Queen Victoria at Sandringham House during its refurbishment, and the name 'Thomas Crapper' can still be found on manhole covers in many public buildings. *Borough of Bromley*

CREED, Frederick George (1871-1957). **20 Outram Road, Addiscombe, Croydon**
Canadian inventor of the teleprinter machine (1897); lived and died here. *Greater London Council*

CRIPPLEGATE, site of. Alphage Gardens, Barbican, EC2
First built by the Romans and rebuilt in 1490 for use as a prison and gateway, the gate was destroyed in the reign of Charles II and the building was finally demolished in 1760. *Corporation of the City of London*

CRIPPS, Sir Richard Stafford (1889-1952). **32 Elm Park Gardens, SW10**
British socialist politician; born here. He was ambassador to Moscow 1940-2, Minister of Aircraft Production 1942-5 and Chancellor of the Exchequer 1947-50. He was also a nephew of Beatrice Webb (q.v.). *English Heritage*

CROMPTON, Richmal (R. C. Lamburn) (1890-1969). **The Glebe, Oakley Road, Bromley Common**
English novelist and author of the 'William' stories for children; lived here. Struck down with poliomyelitis in 1923, she took to writing thereafter and published fifty adult books as well as the 'William' stories. *Private*

Richmal Crompton authoress lived here 1928~1954 *Bromley*

CROMPTON, Colonel Rookes Evelyn Bell (1845-1940). **48 Kensington Court, W8**
After a distinguished military career he went on to found an electrical lamp manufacturing company, Crompton & Co. He was twice president of the Institute of Electrical Engineers and a founder member of the Royal Automobile Club. *English Heritage*

CROOKES, Sir William (1832-1919). **7 Kensington Park Gardens, W11**
English physicist and chemist; lived here from 1880 until his death. He discovered the metal thallium (1861), invented the radiometer (1873-6) and improved vacuum tubes and electric lighting. *Greater London Council*

CROSBY, Brass (1725-93). A lord mayor of London. See **ESSEX STREET**

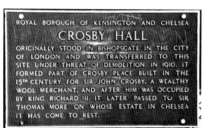

CROSBY HALL, Cheyne Walk, SW3
The plaque states that it 'originally stood in Bishopsgate in the City of London and was transferred to this site under threat of demolition in 1910. It formed part of Crosby Place, built in the fifteenth century for Sir John Crosby, a wealthy wool merchant, and after him was occupied by King Richard III. It later passed to Sir Thomas More on whose estate in Chelsea it has come to rest.' It is now privately owned. *Borough of Kensington and Chelsea*

CROSS, Mary Ann. See **ELIOT, George**

CROSSKEYS INN, Bell Yard, EC3
The crossed keys of St Peter were the arms of the papal see, and the inn was in the shadow of a church dedicated to St Peter. The inn was destroyed in 1666 in the Great Fire. *Corporation of the City of London*

CRUDEN, Alexander (1699-70). **45 Camden Passage, N1**
Scottish bookseller and scholar; lived and died here. He came to London

The unusual plaque to Alexander Cruden in N1.

from Aberdeen in 1719 and by 1732 had set up as a bookseller. His greatest achievement was a biblical concordance, published in 1737. He suffered from mental illness but managed to work as a proofreader, assuming the title 'Alexander the Corrector'. He also toured the country reproving Sabbath-breaking. *Camden Passage Association*

CRUFT, Charles Alfred (1852-1939). **Ashurst Lodge, Highbury Grove, N5** Dog show promoter; lived near here 1913-38. He was the general manager of Spratts dog-food manufacturers, for whom he worked from 1865 until 1895. He held his first show in 1886, and the shows have continued annually ever since. Cruft was largely responsible for the high standards now observed in dog breeding. *Islington Borough Council*

CRUIKSHANK, George (1792-1878). **69-71 Amwell Street, EC1** *Islington Borough Council;* **263 Hampstead Road, NW1** *Royal Society of Arts* London-born cartoonist and illustrator; lived at both addresses, 1824-49 and 1850-78 respectively. He made his name as a political caricaturist but is best known for his illustrations to Dickens's (q.v.) *Sketches by Boz* and *Oliver Twist*, also Daniel Defoe's (q.v.) *Robinson Crusoe*. In later years he was an ardent supporter of the temperance movement.

CUBITT, Thomas (1788-1855). **3 Lyall Street, SW1** English master builder; lived here. He rebuilt most of Belgravia and the east front of Buckingham Palace. *London County Council*

CURTIS, William (1746-99). **51 Gracechurch Street, EC3** English botanist and entomologist; lived in a house on this site. Students visited his botanical gardens at Bermondsey and Lambeth. He was a member of the Linnaean Society (q.v.). *Corporation of the City of London*

CURZON, George Nathaniel, First Marquess Curzon of Kedleston (1859-1925). **1 Carlton House Terrace, SW1** British Conservative politician; lived and died here. An outstanding figure of his time, he served as Viceroy of India 1899-1905, a member of the War Cabinet in 1916 and Foreign Secretary 1919-24. *Greater London Council*

CUTLERS' HALL. Cloak Lane, EC4 The first hall opened in 1285 in Poultry and moved to Cloak Lane in 1416. This second hall was rebuilt 1451 and again in 1660, only to be destroyed in the Great Fire in 1666. The fourth hall was opened 1671 and was compulsorily demolished in 1883 to make way for the railway. The present Cutlers' Hall is in Warwick Lane. *Corporation of the City of London*

DADD, Richard (1817-86). **15 Suffolk Street, SW1**
English painter; lived here. Dadd suffered a mental breakdown in 1843, when he murdered his father. His remaining years were spent in asylums, but he continued painting in an amazingly detailed style, depicting fairy themes. *Greater London Council*

DAILY COURANT. 12 Ludgate Circus, EC4
The first London newspaper. It was published in a house near this site in 1702. *Corporation of the City of London*

DALE, Sir Henry Hallett (1875-1968). **Mount Vernon House, Mount Vernon, NW3**
English physiologist; lived here. He became director of the National Institute for Medical Research (1928) and shared the Nobel prize for physiology and medicine in 1936 for work on the chemical transmission of nervous effects. *Greater London Council*

DANCE, George, the younger (1741-1825). **91 Gower Street, WC1**
English architect and painter; lived and died here. He rebuilt Newgate Prison (1770-83) and was one of the first members of the Royal Academy. *Greater London Council*

DANIELL, Thomas (1749-1840). **14 Earls Terrace, W8**
English landscape painter; lived and died here. Daniell went to India in 1784 and stayed there for ten years. This had a marked impression on his art and he painted many oriental-style pictures. He became a member of the Royal Academy in 1799. *English Heritage*

DARWIN, Charles Robert (1809-82). **Biological Science Building, University College London, Gower Street, WC1,**
English scientist; lived in a house on this site 1838-42. He was the originator of the theory of evolution by natural selection. His house at Downe, Orpington, Kent, is open to the public and is a museum of his work and collections from his travels. *London County Council*

DAVIES, Emily (1830-1921). **17 Cunningham Place, NW8**
Founder of Girton College, Cambridge; lived here 1862-86. *Greater London Council*

DAVIES, Thomas (*c.*1712-85). **8 Russell Street, WC2**
English bookseller, who introduced James Boswell (q.v.) to Johnson (q.v.) at premises on this site in 1763. He also published some of his own work including *Life of Garrick* (1780). *Greater London Council*

DAWSON, Margaret Damer (1875-1920). **10 Cheyne Row, SW3**
Founder (1915) of the Women's Police Service and holder of Danish and Finnish awards for her work in animal protection; lived here. She studied music in her early years and was a holder of a gold medal and diploma from the London Academy of Music. *Private*

DAY-LEWIS, Cecil (1904-72). **6 Crooms Hill, Greenwich, SE10**
Irish-born poet and Poet Laureate (1968-72); lived here. During the 1930s he was associated with left-wing causes, together with Stephen Spender and W. H. Auden. He taught at Cheltenham College 1930-5 and, in addition to his early poems, wrote literary criticism. He was professor of poetry at Oxford 1951-6 and at Harvard 1964-5. His published works include *Poetry for You* (1944), *The Poetic Image* (1947), *The Poetic Impulse* (1965) and a series of detective novels under the pseudonym Nicholas Blake. *English Heritage*

DEFOE, Daniel (*c*.1661-1731). **95 Stoke Newington Church Street, N16**
English writer; lived in a house on this site. Best known for *Robinson Crusoe* (1719) and *Moll Flanders* (1722), he spent two years in prison for his *The Shortest Way with Dissenters* (1702), was bankrupted three times and changed his political persuasions several times. Defoe wrote numerous pamphlets and issued one of the first newspapers. His writing was prolific, and many books have been attributed to him. *London County Council*

DE GAULLE, Charles Andre Joseph Marie (1890-1970). **4 Carlton Gardens, SW1** *Greater London Council;* **99 Frognal, Hampstead, NW3** *Hampstead Plaque Fund*
French general and president; set up the headquarters of the Free French Forces in Carlton Gardens in 1940; lived at Frognal 1940-2. He was president of the

This plaque to Charles de Gaulle can be seen at 99 Frognal, Hampstead, NW3.

French National Committee, leader of the Free French forces 1940-4 and head of the provisional French Government 1944-6. He was later (1959-69) first president of the Fifth Republic.

DE LA MARE, Walter (1873-1956). **195 Mackenzie Road, Beckenham** *Borough of Bromley;* **Southend House, Montpelier Row, Twickenham** *English Heritage*
English poet and writer; lived at both addresses (Southend House 1940-56). He is best known for his verse for children and his short stories. His later works included poems for adults.

DE LA RAMÉE, Maria Louisa. See **OUIDA**

DE LASZLO, Philip A. (1869-1937). **3 Fitzjohn's Avenue, NW3**
Hungarian-born British portrait painter; lived and worked here 1921-37. He painted many famous people including Edward VII and was president of the Royal Society of British Artists from 1930. *Private*

DELFONT, Sir Bernard, Baron Delfont of Stepney (1909-94). **Prince of Wales Theatre, Coventry Street, W1**
Theatrical impresario. He was born Boris Winogradsky in Russia and was brought to England with his older brother Sir Lew Grade in 1912. They both started in show business as dancers and progressed to being theatrical agents. Bernard turned to theatre management and acquired many properties and companies, cinema and television interests. He also owned the London Hippodrome and presented the annual Royal Variety Performance. *Comic Heritage*

DE MORGAN, William Frend (1839-1917) and **Evelyn** (1855-1919). **127 Old Church Street, SW3**
English ceramic artists; lived and died here. William first moved to Chelsea in 1872, where he started to produce pottery. Later associations with Burne-Jones (q.v.) and William Morris (q.v.) led him to produce tiles at Morris's factory, though he was not financially successful. In 1887 he married Evelyn, who became a notable Pre-Raphaelite ceramicist and painter in her own right. In 1910 they moved to Old Church Street, and William began writing, producing several successful novels. *London County Council*

DENMAN, Thomas, First Baron Denman (1779-1854). **50-1 Russell Square, WC1**
English lawyer and Lord Chief Justice; lived in a house on this site 1816-34. With Henry Brougham (q.v.), he defended Queen Caroline (1820). He was a Whig MP from 1818 until 1826, and Attorney-General 1830-2, becoming Lord Chief Justice afterwards. His son, the **Rt Hon George Denman,** who became a high court judge (1872-92), was born here in 1819. *Private*

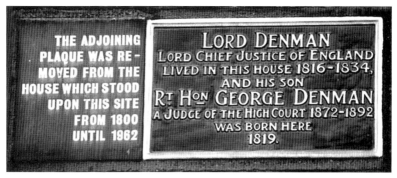

THE ADJOINING PLAQUE WAS REMOVED FROM THE HOUSE WHICH STOOD UPON THIS SITE FROM 1800 UNTIL 1962

LORD DENMAN
LORD CHIEF JUSTICE OF ENGLAND LIVED IN THIS HOUSE 1816-1834, AND HIS SON
RT HON GEORGE DENMAN A JUDGE OF THE HIGH COURT 1872-1892 WAS BORN HERE 1819.

DE QUINCEY, Thomas (1785-1859). **36 Tavistock Street, WC2**
English author; his best-known work, *Confessions of an English Opium Eater*, was written in this house and published in 1822 in serial form. He was a friend of the poets Wordsworth and Coleridge (q.v.), with whom he settled in the Lake District (1809). De Quincey moved in 1828 to Edinburgh, where he died. This plaque spells his name without the 'E'. *Greater London Council*

DERBY, Edward Geoffrey Smith Stanley, Fourteenth Earl of (1799-1869). **10 St James's Square, SW1**
British prime minister three times between 1852 and 1868; lived here 1837-55. He introduced the Bill for the abolition of slavery and led the Tory party for twenty years. The plaque is shared with William Pitt (q.v.) and W. E. Gladstone (q.v.). *London County Council*

DE ROKESLEY, Gregory (died 1291). **72 Lombard Street, EC3**
Eight times lord mayor of London, 1274-81 and 1285; lived in a house on this site. *Corporation of the City of London*

DEVIL TAVERN. 1 Fleet Street, EC4
Its first name was St Dunstan tavern, owing to its proximity to the church of St Dunstan. It was called 'Devil' as the sign illustrated the story about St Dunstan pulling the Devil by the nose with a pair of tongs. It was demolished 1787. *Corporation of the City of London*

DEVINE, George (1910-66). **9 Lower Mall, Hammersmith, W6**
English actor and stage director; lived here. He founded the English Stage Company, which resided at the Royal Court Theatre (1956-65). *English Heritage*

DE WORDE, Wynkyn (died 1535). **Stationers' Hall, Ave Maria Lane, EC4**
Dutch-born English printer; first set up his press near this address. He was a pupil of William Caxton. His press, set up in 1500, produced hundreds of books, and made great improvements in printing and typesetting techniques. *Private*

WYNKYN de WORDE
Father of Fleet Street
first set up his Press
by Shoe Lane
near this Hall
circa 1500

DICKENS, Charles (1812-70). **141 Bayham Street, NW1** *Dickens Fellowship;* **6 Chandos Place, WC2** *Private;* **48 Doughty Street, WC1** *London County Council;* **14 Great Russell Street,**

The plaques to Charles Dickens at 141 Bayham Street, NW1 (right), and at 26 Wellington Street, WC2 (below).

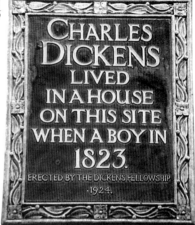

WC1 *Private;* **Prudential Buildings, High Holborn, WC1** *Private;* **92 North Road, Highgate, N6** *Haringey Borough Council;* **BMA House, Tavistock Square, WC1** *Private;* **26 Wellington Street, WC2** *Private;* **15-17 Marylebone Road, NW1** *Private;* **1 Devonshire Terrace, W2** *Private*
English author, noted for his characterisation of figures portraying the social evils of Victorian Britain. There appear to be nine plaques commemorating him in London, the greatest number for any individual person. Respectively they denote that he: lived on this site in 1823 (Bayham Street); worked here 1824-5 (Chandos Place); lived here (Doughty Street); invented a character (Charles Kitterbell in *Sketches by Boz*) who lived here (Great Russell Street); lived and wrote *The Pickwick Papers* near here in 1836 (Prudential Buildings); stayed here in 1832 (North Road); lived near here (BMA House); lived and ran a magazine, *All the Year Round,* from here 1859-70 (Wellington Street); lived and wrote six of his novels here (Marylebone Road); lived on this site 1839-51 (Devonshire Terrace). He started writing as a reporter for a London newspaper, and his *Sketches by Boz* were published individually. They were followed by *Pickwick Papers* (1836), *Oliver Twist* and *Nicholas Nickleby* (1839), *Barnaby Rudge* (1840), *The Old Curiosity Shop* (1841) and *David Copperfield* (1849). Among his later books were *A Tale of Two Cities* (1859) and *Great Expectations* (1861). Dickens had ten children by his wife Catherine but separated from her in 1858. Around this time he began public readings of his works. These proved to be very popular, especially in the USA, where he toured.

DICKINSON, Goldworthy Lowes (1862-1932). **11 Edwardes Square, W8**
Writer and humanist; lived here. He was a Cambridge lecturer 1896-1920. His works include *The Greek View of Life* (1896), *The Meaning of Good* (1901), *Religion and Immortality* (1911), and *War, Its Nature Cause and Cure* (1923). *Private, adopted by London County Council in 1956*

DICK-READ, Dr Grantley (1890-1959). **25 Harley Street, W1**
British gynaecologist who promoted natural childbirth; practised here 1935-41. *Westminster City Council*

DILKE, Sir Charles Wentworth (1843-1911). **76 Sloane Street, SW1**
English statesman and author; lived here.
He was a member of Parliament 1868-86
and 1892-1911. A radical Liberal, he was
largely responsible for the legalisation of
trade unions and supported a minimum wage.
He was also an authority on defence and
foreign affairs. *London County Council*

**DISRAELI, Benjamin, First Earl of
Beaconsfield** (1804-81). **22 Theobalds
Road, WC1** *London County Council;* **6
Frederick's Place, EC2** *Corporation of the
City of London;* **93 Park Lane, W1** *Private;* **19 Curzon Street, W1** *London
County Council*

The plaque at 22 Theobalds Road, WC1.

Prime minister 1868 and 1874-80; responsible for the purchase of the Suez
Canal and creating Queen Victoria 'Empress of India'. Disraeli was born and
spent his childhood at 22 Theobalds Road; from 1821 to 1824 he was articled to
a firm of solicitors at 6 Frederick's Place; in 1839, when he married, he moved
to 93 Park Lane; he died at 19 Curzon Street, which he had purchased in 1880.
His main home, however, was Hughenden Manor, Buckinghamshire, into
which he moved with his wife in 1848.

D'ISRAELI , Isaac (1766-1848). **6 Bloomsbury Square, WC1**
English scholar, writer and father of Benjamin Disraeli (q.v.); lived here 1818-
29. His works include *Curiosities of Literature* (1791-1834). *Duke of Bedford*

DOBSON, Frank (1886-1963). **14 Harley Gardens, SW10**
English sculptor; lived here. He was professor of sculpture at the Royal College
of Art until 1953 and was for many years associated with the 'London Group'.
English Heritage

Robert Donat, the English film and stage actor.

DOBSON, Henry Austin (1840-1921). **10 Redcliffe Street, SW10**
English poet and essayist; lived here. Between 1856 and 1901 he worked at the Board of Trade. His earliest poems were published in 1868, but he is more notable for his monographs of eighteenth-century figures. *London County Council*

DOCTORS' COMMONS, site of. Faraday Building, Queen Victoria Street, EC4
The colloquial name for the College of Advocates and Doctors of Law. From 1572 onwards it housed the ecclesiastical and Admiralty courts, together with the practising advocates. These advocates were required to hold doctorates of law awarded by the universities of Oxford or Cambridge. A description of the court and premises is given by Charles Dickens (q.v.) in *David Copperfield* (chapter 23). The premises were closed and demolished in 1867. *Corporation of the City of London*

DON, David (1800-41). See **BANKS, Sir Joseph**

DONAT, Robert (1905-58). **8 Meadway, NW11**
English film and stage actor; lived here. Having made his stage debut in 1921, he starred in several films, including *The Count of Monte Cristo* (1934), *The Thirty Nine Steps* (1935) and *Goodbye Mr Chips* (1939), for which he won an Academy Award. His final film was *Inn of the Sixth Happiness* (1958). *English Heritage*

DONOVAN, Terence (1936-96). **30 Bourdon Street, W1**
Photographer; born here. He was a leading fashion photographer in the 'Swinging Sixties'. *Westminster City Council*

DOOLITTLE, Hilda (1886-1961). **44 Mecklenburgh Square, WC1**
American-born poet and novelist (pen name 'H. D.'); lived here. She resided in London from 1911 and from 1937 in Switzerland. Her poetry includes 'Sea Garden' (1916), 'Flowering of the Rod' (1946) and 'Helen in Egypt' (1961). Among her many novels are *Hedylus* (1928) and *Bid Me to Live* (1960). *Private*

DORSET, Earl of. See **SACKVILLE, Charles**

DOUGLAS, Norman (1868-1952). **63 Albany Mansions, Albert Bridge Road, SW11**

Scottish novelist; lived here. Having worked at the Foreign Office and travelled extensively, he settled in Capri (1896). His writings mainly concerned his travels and acquaintances, who included Compton MacKenzie, Ouida (q.v.) and D. H. Lawrence (q.v.). *Greater London Council*

DOWSON, Ernest Christopher (1867-1900). **Dowson Court, Belmont Grove, SE13**
English poet of the 'decadent' school; lived in a house on this site. He spent most of his adult life in France and died of alcoholism. A second plaque at this address commemorates Edward Owen Greening (q.v.). *Borough of Lewisham*

DOYLE, Sir Arthur Conan (1859-1930). **12 Tennison Road, SE25** *Greater London Council;* **2 Upper Wimpole Street, W1** *Westminster City Council*
Scottish novelist; lived in Tennison Road 1891-4 and worked in Upper Wimpole Street 1891. He is famous as the creator of Sherlock Holmes (q.v.), who first appeared in *A Study in Scarlet* (1887) and subsequently in a number of stories. Other important novels were *Brigadier Gerard* (1896) and *The Lost World* (1912). Doyle served as a field physician in the second Boer War and in later years was interested in spiritualism.

The plaque at Tennison Road, SE25.

D'OYLY CARTE, Richard. See **CARTE, Richard D'Oyly**

DRYDEN, John (1631-1700). **43 Gerrard Street, W1**
English poet and dramatist; lived in a house on this site 1686-1700. Educated at Westminster School and Cambridge, he afterwards settled in London, initially working for his cousin, Cromwell's chamberlain. He wrote verse in support of both parliamentarians and the Restoration. He was appointed Poet Laureate in 1668. Several of his comedies and dramas were adaptations of the work of Shakespeare and Milton. This plaque, now in poor condition, was erected in 1875 and is one of the oldest of the 'official' plaques in London. *Royal Society of Arts*

DRYSDALE, Dr Charles Vickery (1874-1961). **153a East Street, Walworth, SE17**
A founder of the Family Planning Association; opened his first birth control clinic here in 1921. *English Heritage*

DU BOULAY, William Thomas (1832-1921). **43 Gilston Road, SW10**
Vicar of the church of St Mary, The Boltons, 1868-1909; lived here. *Private*

DUFF, Peggy (1910-81). **11 Albert Street, NW1**
First general secretary of the Campaign for Nuclear Disarmament (CND); lived here. She was also a local councillor. *Camden Borough Council*

DUKES, Ashley (1885-1959). **Kensington Temple, Ladbroke Road, W11**
British author and playwright who married the ballerina Marie Rambert (q.v.) in 1918. This building stands on the site of the Mercury Theatre, which he founded in 1931 and which was demolished in 1987. *Private*

DU MAURIER, George Louis Palmella Busson (1834-96). **91 Great Russell Street, WC1** *London County Council;* **28 Hampstead Grove, NW3** *Private, adopted by London County Council 1959*

French-born artist and writer; lived at both addresses, 1863-8 and 1874-95 respectively. Born in Paris, he came to England in 1851. He made his name as an illustrator and worked for *Punch* magazine (1864-96), becoming a well-known satirist. He also wrote and illustrated three novels, the best-known being *Trilby* (published 1894).

DU MAURIER, Sir Gerald (1873-1934). **Cannon Hall, 14 Cannon Place, NW3**
British actor-manager; lived here from 1916 until his death. The son of George Du Maurier (q.v.), he made a reputation on the stage in criminal roles and became joint manager of Wyndham's Theatre (1910-25). He was also manager of St James's Theatre 1926-34. Du Maurier was knighted in 1922. *Greater London Council*

DUNCAN, Leyland Lewis (1862-1923). **8 Lingards Road, SE13**
English historian; lived here 1873-1923. A civil servant by profession, he wrote the standard history of Lewisham and histories of the local church and school. *Lewisham Borough Council*

DUNDONALD, Tenth Earl of. See **COCHRANE, Thomas**

DU PRÉ, Jacqueline (1945-87). **27 Upper Montague Street, W1** *Private;* **5a Pilgrim's Lane, Hampstead, NW3** *Heath and Old Hampstead Society*
English cellist; lived at both addresses 1967-71 and 1970-5 respectively. She commenced her concert career at the age of sixteen and studied under Casals and Rostropovich. While married to the pianist Daniel Barenboim she developed multiple sclerosis and spent the last fourteen years of her life teaching from a wheelchair.

DYSON, Sir Frank Watson (1868-1939). **6 Vanbrugh Hill, Blackheath, SE3**
English astronomer; lived here 1894-1906. He was Astronomer Royal for Scotland (1905-10) and for England (1910-33). *English Heritage*

This plaque can be found in Upper Montague Street, W1.

E

EAGLE TAVERN, Shepherdess Walk, N1
The Grecian Theatre pleasure grounds, Grecian Saloon and Olympic Theatre stood here 1825-99, and Marie Lloyd (q.v.) gave her first public performance here in 1885. The Eagle is also the tavern mentioned in the song 'Pop Goes the Weasel'. *Borough of Hackney*

EARNSHAW, Thomas (1749-1829). **119 High Holborn, WC1**
Noted watch and chronometer maker and designer; site of his business premises. *London County Council*

EASTLAKE, Sir Charles Lock (1793-1865). **7 Fitzroy Square, W1**
English historical painter; lived here. He was the first director of the National Gallery (1855) and was noted for two full-length pictures of Napoleon and for his views of the countryside around Rome. *Greater London Council*

EDDINGTON, Sir Arthur Stanley (1882-1944). **4 Bennett Park, Blackheath, SE3**
English physicist; lived here. He was a leading exponent of Einstein's theory of relativity, which he explained to a wider circle by means of several publications in the 1920s and 1930s. *Greater London Council*

EDGWARE TURNPIKE, site of (*c.*1711-1871). **Corner of Deansbrook Road and Edgware Road, Edgware**
A toll was collected for the upkeep of the road until responsibility was finally passed to the council. This impressive blue plaque is noticed by drivers waiting at the traffic lights. *Hendon Corporation*

EDWARDS, John Passmore (1823-1911). **51 Netherhall Gardens, NW3** *English Heritage;* **Vernon Hall, Vernon Road, E3** *Borough of Tower Hamlets*
Journalist, editor and builder of free public libraries; lived in Netherhall Gardens; the plaque at Vernon Hall commemorates the old Passmore Edwards Library.

EISENHOWER, Dwight David (1890-1969). **31 St James's Square, SW1** *US Department of Defense;* **20 Grosvenor Square, W1** *US Department of Defense;* **Corner of Kingston Hill and Warren Road, Kingston-upon-Thames** *Borough of Kingston-upon-Thames*
US Army general and thirty-fourth president of the USA (1953-60); directed the Allied invasion from the first address; had his headquarters at the second; lived in a property near the third site. He commanded Allied forces in North

The United States of America recognizes the selfless service and manifold contributions of General Dwight David Eisenhower, Supreme Allied Commander, 1944-1945. At this site, General Eisenhower, on behalf of freedom loving peoples throughout the World, directed the Allied Expeditionary Forces against Fortress Europe, 6 June 1944.

This plaque was dedicated by a United States Department of Defense delegation and the Eisenhower family on 4 June 1990 during the Centennial year of his birth and the 46th Anniversary of Operation OVERLORD.

The commemorative plaque in St James's Square, SW1, to Dwight David Eisenhower.

Africa and Italy 1942-3, and the Allied invasion of Europe in 1944. A West Point graduate (1915), he resigned from the army in 1952 to stand for the presidency and was twice elected to that office.

ELDON, John Scott, First Earl of (1751-1838). **6 Bedford Square, WC1**
English lawyer and politician; lived here 1798-1818. He became an MP in 1782, Solicitor-General in 1788, Attorney-General in 1793 and Lord Chancellor (1801-27). *London County Council*

ELEN, Gus (1862-1940). **3 Thurleigh Avenue, SW12**
Cockney music-hall comedian; lived here the last six years of his life. *Greater London Council*

ELGAR, Sir Edward (1857-1934). **51 Avonmore Road, W14** *London County Council;* **42 Netherhall Gardens, NW3** *Heath and Old Hampstead Society;* **Abbey Studios, Abbey Road, NW8** *Westminster City Council*
English composer; lived at the first address 1890-1 and on the site of the second 1911-21; opened and recorded in Abbey Studios in 1931. His *Enigma Variations* (1899) and *The Dream of Gerontius* (1900) won him international recognition and his many other works include two symphonies, a much-loved cello concerto and the *Pomp and Circumstance* marches. He was Master of the King's Musick from 1924. The plaque in Netherhall Gardens should have been placed on the house next door, as this would have been nearer to the entrance of the original house.

ELIA. See **LAMB, Charles**

ELIOT, George (1819-80). **4 Cheyne Walk, SW3** *London County Council;* **Holly Lodge, 31 Wimbledon Park Road, SW18** *London County Council*
Pen name of Mary Ann Evans, English

Edward Elgar's plaque in Netherhall Gardens, NW3.

novelist; lived in Wimbledon Park Road; died in Cheyne Walk. Educated at home, she exhibited formidable intellectual powers. She was acquainted with Thomas Carlyle (q.v.), Herbert Spencer (q.v.) and George Henry Lewes, with whom she had a relationship until his death in 1878. In 1880 she married John Walter Ross (died 1924). Her works include *Adam Bede* (1859), *The Mill on the Floss* (1860), *Silas Marner* (1861) and *Middlemarch* (published serially 1871-2). She is considered one of the greatest authors of her time.

ELIOT, T. S. (Thomas Stearns) (1888-1965). **24 Russell Square, WC1** *Camden Borough Council;* **3 Kensington Court Gardens, W8** *English Heritage*
American-born British poet, critic and dramatist; worked at the first address; lived and died at the second. He lived in England from 1911 and worked as a teacher and a bank clerk, before moving into publishing, later to become a director of Faber & Faber. His most notable poems are *The Waste Land* (1922) and *Four Quartets* (1944); his most famous play is *Murder in the Cathedral* (1935). Eliot was a member of the Bloomsbury Group (q.v.) and was awarded the Nobel prize for literature in 1948.

ELIZABETH II, Her Majesty Queen (born 1926). **17 Bruton Street, W1**
The plaque (placed in 1977) reads: 'This plaque was dedicated in the silver jubilee year of her reign to Her Majesty The Queen, who was born here on April 21st 1926'. *Private*

ELLIS, Henry Havelock (1859-1939). **14 Dover Mansions, Canterbury Crescent, SW9**
English physician and writer; lived here. His *Studies in the Psychology of Sex* (seven volumes, 1897-1928) was very controversial and for some time banned in Britain. One of his female followers was Olive Schreiner (q.v.). *Greater London Council*

ENGELS, Friedrich (1820-95). **121 Regents Park Road, NW1**
German socialist and political philosopher; lived here 1870-94. He was a friend of Karl Marx (q.v.), with whom he produced *The Communist Manifesto* (1848). After Marx's death in 1883 he continued editing and translating his writings, including *Das Kapital. Greater London Council*

EPSTEIN, Sir Jacob (1880-1959). **18 Hyde Park Gate, SW7** *Private;* **Deerhurst, 50 Baldwins Hill, Loughton** *Loughton Town Council*
American-born British sculptor; lived at both addresses; died at Hyde Park Gate. His symbolic studies and his muscular nude figures, such as his eighteen statues produced for the British Medical Association, led to accusations

The plaque to Epstein at Loughton

of indecency. One of his most celebrated works is *St Michael and the Devil* (1958) at Coventry Cathedral. His bronze portrait heads of celebrities and children are of exceptional quality. The dates on the two plaques differ.

ESSEX STREET. Essex Hall, Essex Street, WC2
The plaque states: 'Essex Street was laid out in the grounds of Essex House by Nicholas Barbon [q.v.] in 1675. Among many famous lawyers who lived here were Sir Orlando Bridgeman [q.v.] (*c*.1606-74), Lord Keeper; Henry Fielding [q.v.] (1707-54), novelist; and Brass Crosby [q.v.] (1725-93), lord mayor of London. James Savage (1779-1852), architect, had his office here. Prince Charles Edward Stuart stayed at a house in the street secretly in 1750. The Revd Theophilus Lindsey [q.v.] (1723-1808), Unitarian minister, founded Essex Street Chapel here in 1774. Dr Samuel Johnson [q.v.] established an evening club at the 'Essex Head' in 1783.' The plaque was erected at 7 Essex Street in 1962 and re-erected at Essex Hall in 1964. *London County Council*

ETTY, William (1787-1849). **14 Buckingham Street, WC2**
English artist, lived here. Etty specialised in painting the female form, also mythological and historical subjects. The plaque is shared with Samuel Pepys (q.v.), Robert Harley (q.v.) and Clarkson Stanfield (q.v.).

EVANS, Dame Edith (1888-1976). **109 Ebury Street, SW1**
English actress; lived here. She appeared in many Shakespeare and Shaw plays in both London and New York; also, during later life, in several films. She is best remembered for her characterisation of Lady Bracknell in *The Importance of Being Earnest* by Oscar Wilde (q.v.). *English Heritage*

EVANS, Sir Geraint Llewellyn (1922-92). **34 Birchwood Road, Petts Wood**
Welsh opera singer and producer; lived here. He sang at Covent Garden from 1948 to 1984 and was known worldwide from his many appearances on tours. *Borough of Bromley*

EVANS, Mary Ann. See **ELIOT, George**

EVERETT, Sir Percy (1870-1952). **Schopwick, Elstree High Street**
County commissioner for Hertfordshire and Deputy Chief Scout under Lord Baden-Powell (q.v.); lived here. *Private*

EWART, William (1798-1869). **16 Eaton Place, SW1** *London County Council;* **Hampton Branch Library, Rose Hill, Hampton** *English Heritage*
English politician and reformer; lived at both addresses. He entered Parliament in 1828 and proposed many reforms, including the abolition of capital punishment for minor offences. He also introduced the Free Libraries Bill in 1850 and was the first to propose the erection of official commemorative plaques in London. The plaque at Hampton is shared with John Beard (q.v.).

FABIAN SOCIETY. White House, Osnaburgh Street, NW1

A small left-wing group; formed in 1884 in a house on this site. It took its name from the Roman general Fabius Cunctator, who was noted for his cautious military strategy, and adopts a gradual approach towards social reform. Past members include H. G. Wells (q.v.), George Bernard Shaw (q.v.), Sidney and Beatrice Webb (q.v.) and Edith Nesbit (q.v.). *Greater London Council*

FARADAY, Michael (1791-1867). **Faraday House, Hampton Court Road, Hampton** *Private;* **48 Blandford Street, W1** *Royal Society of Arts;* **Walworth Road, SE17** (south-west corner of shopping mall) *Borough of Southwark*

English chemist and physicist; born in Walworth Road; apprenticed in Blandford Street; lived in Hampton 1858-67. His experiments in the field of electricity resulted in the inventions of the dynamo, the transformer and, in 1831, the electric motor. He was a professor of chemistry at the Royal Institution from 1833 and one of the greatest experimental physicists of all time.

The plaque at Blandford Street, W1.

FARYNER, Thomas. Pudding Lane, EC3

The 'King's baker' and owner of the baker's shop where the Great Fire of London started in 1666. A Frenchman named Robert Hubert confessed to having started the fire and was hanged for it at Tyburn (q.v.). *Presented by the Worshipful Company of Bakers to mark the five hundredth anniversary of their charter, granted by Henry VII in 1486.*

NEAR THIS SITE STOOD THE SHOP BELONGING TO THOMAS FARYNER. THE KING'S BAKER. IN WHICH THE GREAT FIRE OF SEPTEMBER 1666 BEGAN.

PRESENTED BY THE WORSHIPFUL COMPANY OF BAKERS TO MARK THE 500th ANNIVERSARY OF THEIR CHARTER GRANTED BY KING HENRY VII IN 1486

FAWCETT, Dame Millicent Garrett (1847-1929). **2 Gower Street, WC1**
English suffragette and sister of Elizabeth Garrett Anderson (q.v.); lived and died here. She was the president of the National Union of Women's Suffrage Societies (1897-1919) but opposed militancy for the cause. *London County Council*

FENTON, Roger (1819-69). **2 Albert Terrace, Primrose Hill, NW1**
English photographer; lived here. He founded the Royal Photographic Society in 1853 and was the first war photographer, in the Crimea (1855). *English Heritage*

FERRIER, Kathleen (1912-53). **97 Frognal, NW3**
English contralto singer and pianist; lived at this address from 1942 until her early death. She trained after winning an amateur competition at a festival in 1937 and moved to London in 1942. On account of her fine voice and her personality, she was a much-loved performer, noted for her role in Gluck's *Orfeo,* among others. *Greater London Council*

FIELDING, Henry (1707-54). **Milbourne House, Barnes Green, SW13.** See also **BOW STREET** and **ESSEX STREET**
English novelist and dramatist; lived here. He wrote several light comedies, dramas, operas and burlesques, the best-known being *The History of Tom Jones, a Foundling* (1749). Fielding was made a Justice of the Peace in 1748 and assisted his half brother Sir John Fielding in the formation of the Bow Street Runners, an early form of police force. Ill health plagued him in his latter years. *Greater London Council.*

FIELDING, Sir John (1721-80). See **BOW STREET**

FIELDS, Dame Gracie (1898-1979). **20 Frognal Way, Hampstead, NW3**
Stage name of Grace Stansfield, Lancashire-born comedienne and singer; had this house designed and built as her home, 1934. She began as a child performer and became a music-hall favourite. Her films included *Sally in Our Alley* (1931) and *Sing As We Go* (1934). She went on to receive a television award for her performance in *The Old Lady Shows Her Medals* (1956). She eventually retired to the island of Capri. *Heath and Old Hampstead Society*

FIENNES, Celia (1662-1741). **Well Street, E9**
English traveller and diarist; lived in a house near this site from 1738 and died here. Between 1685 and 1702 she undertook a series of journeys, mostly on horseback, with a few servants. Her diary records the events and her impressions of the many houses, towns and places of interest found in her travels. In 1698

alone, she travelled more than a thousand miles. *Borough of Hackney*

FILDES, **Sir Samuel Luke** (1844-1927). **31 Melbury Road, W14**
English artist and illustrator; lived here 1878-1927. He is known for his woodcut illustrations, particularly those produced for Dickens's *Edwin Drood* (1870). This house was designed for him by R. Norman Shaw (q.v.). *London County Council.*

FISHER, John Arbuthnot, First Baron Fisher of Kilverstone (1841-1920). **16 Queen Anne's Gate, SW1**
British admiral; lived here 1904-10. He entered the navy in 1854 and served in the China wars (1859-60) and in Egypt (1882). He was Lord of the Admiralty 1892-7 and First Sea Lord 1904-10. *Greater London Council*

FITZROY, Admiral Robert (1805-65). **38 Onslow Square, SW7**
English hydrographer and meteorologist; lived here 1854-65. He commanded the *Beagle* on a survey of South America (1828-30) and also on a circumnavigation of the globe (1831-6) with Charles Darwin (q.v.). He became governor of New Zealand (1843-5) and was afterwards put in charge of the newly formed Meteorological Office by the Admiralty. *Greater London Council*

FLANAGAN, Bud (1896-1968). **12 Hanbury Street, E1**
Stage name of Robert Winthrop, comedian; born here. He performed on stage, screen and radio. Partnered by Chesney Allen in most of his stage appearances, he had several hit songs and was leader of the 'Crazy Gang' for over thirty years. *English Heritage*

FLAXMAN, John (1755-1826). **7 Greenwell Street, W1**
English sculptor; lived and died in a house on this site. He worked as a designer for Josiah Wedgwood 1775-94, directing their studio in Rome for the last six years. He was appointed first professor of sculpture at the Royal Academy of Arts (1810). His works, in a serene neoclassical style, include the monuments to Robert Burns in Westminster Abbey and Lord Nelson (q.v.) in St Paul's Cathedral. *Royal Society of Arts*

FLECKER, James Elroy (1884-1915). **9 Gilmore Road, SE13**
English poet and dramatist; born here. He wrote several volumes of verse while serving in the consular service, including *The Bridge of Fire* (1907), *The Golden Journey to Samarkand* (1913) and *The Old Ships* (1915). *Greater London Council*

The plaque to Alexander Fleming on St Mary's Hospital, Praed Street, W2.

FLEISCHMANN, Dr Arthur (1896-1990). **92 Carlton Hill, NW8**
Medical practitioner and sculptor; lived and worked here 1958-90. Born in Bratislava, he was probably the only sculptor who made portrait busts of four popes. Among his other well-known sitters were Kathleen Ferrier (q.v.), Lord Robens and the actor Trevor Howard. During the 1950s he began to experiment with perspex, producing outstanding results. Although based in England, he spent ten years of his life in Australia and travelled extensively. *Westminster City Council*

FLEMING, Sir Alexander (1881-1955). **20a Danvers Street, SW3** *Greater London Council;* **St Mary's Hospital, Praed Street, W2** *Private*
Scottish bacteriologist and discoverer of penicillin (1928); lived in Danvers Street; discovered penicillin in the second-storey room of the hospital above the plaque. He shared the Nobel prize for medicine in 1945 and spent most of his career at St Mary's Hospital.

FLEMING, Ian Lancaster (1908-64). **22 Ebury Street, SW1**
English novelist; lived here. Educated at Eton and Sandhurst, he worked as a foreign correspondent in Moscow (1929-33) and then (1933-9) as a banker and stockbroker. A naval intelligence officer during the Second World War, he later became foreign manager with the *Sunday Times* (1945-59). His novels featuring the suave secret agent James Bond were a huge success and have been made into highly successful films. *English Heritage*

FLEMING, Sir John Ambrose (1849-1945). **9 Clifton Gardens, W9**
English electrical physicist and engineer; lived here. He was the inventor of the thermionic valve (1904) and a pioneer in the widespread use of electricity. *Greater London Council*

FLINDERS, Captain Matthew (1774-1814). **56 Fitzroy Street, W1**
English naval officer and explorer; lived here. He surveyed the coast of New South Wales (1795-1800) and circumnavigated Australia (1801-3). A range of mountains, an island and a river are named after him. *London County Council*

Peel Cottage

Sir William Russell Flint
R.A..P.R.W.S.
Artist

Born 1880
Died 1969

Lived here
1925—1969

FLINT, Sir William Russell (1880-1969). **80 Peel Street, W8**
Scottish watercolour artist and illustrator; lived here 1925-69. He was president of the Royal Society of Painters in Watercolours 1936-56. *Private*

FLYING BOMB, first. Railway Bridge, Grove Road, Bow, E3
The first flying bomb, V1, to fall on London fell here on 13th June 1944. *English Heritage*

FORBES, Vivian (1891-1937). **Lansdowne House, 80 Lansdowne Road, W11.** See also **Ricketts, Charles**
English artist; lived and worked here. The plaque is shared with five other artists. *Greater London Council*

FORBES-ROBERTSON, Sir Johnston (1853-1937). **22 Bedford Square, W1**
English actor; lived here. He first performed on the London stage in 1874. He became manager of the Lyceum Theatre in 1895, where he performed to much acclaim as Hamlet two years later. *Duke of Bedford*

FORD, Ford Madox (1873-1939). **80 Campden Hill Road, W8**
Pen name of Ford Hermann Hueffer, English novelist and editor; lived here. A grandson of Ford Madox Brown (q.v.) he wrote some eighty books and edited two magazines with well-known contributors. His best-known novels are *The Fifth Queen* (1906), *The Good Soldier* (1915) and *Parade's End* (1924). *Greater London Council*

FORESTER, C. S. (Cecil Scott) (1899-1966). **58 Underhill Road, SE22**
English novelist; lived here. Born in Egypt, he became famous for his series of books about an eighteenth-century naval captain, Horatio Hornblower. He was also the author of *The African Queen* (1935), later made into a film starring Humphrey Bogart and Katherine Hepburn. *English Heritage*

FORSTER, E. M. (Edward Morgan) (1879-1970). **9 Arlington Park Mansions, Sutton Lane, W4**
English novelist and critic; lived here. His novels include *Where Angels Fear to Tread* (1905), *A Room with a View* (1908), *Howards End* (1910) and *A Passage to India* (1924). The last named was written after his many years in India, some spent as secretary to the Maharajah of Dewas. *Greater London Council*

FORTUNE, Robert (1812-80). **9 Gilston Road, SW10**
Scottish horticulturist; lived here. He travelled extensively for the London Botanical Society and introduced many previously unknown plants into Britain. *English Heritage*

FORTUNE THEATRE. Fortune Street, EC1
Opened on a site near here in 1600. Built for Edward Alleyn (1566-1626) and Philip Henslowe (died 1616), it was burnt down in 1621 and rebuilt. When the Puritans banned playhouse entertainment it continued in illicit use before being dismantled in 1649 and demolished in 1661. *Private*

FOSCOLO, Ugo (1778-1827). **19 Edwardes Square, W8**
Italian author and poet; lived here 1817-18. He came to London in 1814 when the Austrians occupied part of Italy. His last few years were spent in poverty. *English Heritage*

FOUNDERS' HALL. Founders' Court, EC2
Founders' Hall was built in 1531 and, having been rebuilt after the Great Fire of London, survived here until 1845. The Founders had the authority to examine all copper and brassware produced in the City of London. *Corporation of the City of London*

FOX, Charles James (1749-1806). **46 Clarges Street, W1**
English Whig politician; lived here 1803-4. He entered Parliament at the age of nineteen, later becoming Secretary of State. A great debater, he was leader of the coalition government with Lord North and leader of the opposition at the time of William Pitt (q.v.). He is buried in Westminster Abbey. *London County Council*

FRAMPTON, Sir George James (1860-1928). **32 Queen's Grove, St John's Wood, NW8**
English sculptor; lived and worked here 1894-1908. His works include the statue of Peter Pan in Kensington Gardens and the Edith Cavell memorial. He was joint first principal with William Lethaby (q.v.) of the Central School of Arts and Crafts. *Greater London Council*

FRANKLIN, Benjamin (1706-90). **36 Craven Street, WC2**
American statesman and scientist; lived in this house 1757-70, during which time he briefly returned to America. His experiments in the field of electricity resulted in many discoveries and inventions. Franklin was active in the negotiations resulting in American independence and was thrice president of the state of Pennsylvania. *London County Council*

Benjamin Franklin

FRANKLIN, Rosalind Elsie (1920-58). **Donovan Court, Drayton Gardens, SW10**
Pioneer in the study of molecular structures; lived here 1951-8. By applying x-ray diffraction to DNA she contributed to Crick and Watson's later discovery of its precise structure. *English Heritage*

FREAKE, Sir Charles James (1814-84). **21 Cromwell Road, SW7**
Builder and patron of the arts; lived here from 1860. He built the Royal College of Organists at his own expense. *Greater London Council*

FRENCH PROTESTANT CHURCH, site of. 2 Aldersgate Street, EC1
Built in the early sixteenth century for the French Protestants who fled to England, it was demolished in 1888. *Corporation of the City of London*

FREUD, Sigmund (1856-1939). **20 Maresfield Gardens, NW3**
Austrian neurologist and psychoanalyst; lived here 1938-9. He studied and published several works on human behaviour and sexuality resulting from childhood experiences. His studies, often using hypnosis, caused great controversy but have had a huge influence on the study of psychology. Freud escaped the Nazis in 1938 and settled in this house until his death. It is now a museum open to the public. *London County Council*

FRITH, William Powell (1819-1909). **114 Clifton Hill, NW8**
English artist; lived and died here. He painted large detailed contemporary pictures, such as *Ramsgate Sands* (1851), bought by Queen Victoria for Buckingham Palace and now in the Tate Gallery, *Derby Day* (1856-8) and *The Railway Station* (1862). *Greater London Council*

FROBISHER, Sir Martin. See **WILLOUGHBY, Sir Hugh**

FROUDE, James Anthony (1818-94). **5 Onslow Gardens, SW7**
English historian and man of letters; lived here 1873-92. His major work, completed in 1869, was the twelve-volume *History of England from the Fall of Wolsey to the Defeat of the Spanish Armada.* Froude was literary executor to Thomas Carlyle (q.v.). *London County Council*

FRY, C. B. (Charles Burgess) (1872-1956). **8 Moreland Court, Finchley Road, NW2**
English sportsman and journalist; lived here 1950-6. Known mainly as a cricketer, he also represented his country in athletics and soccer. He held a record of six successive centuries in first-class cricket. Fry was also a well-known broadcaster and represented India at the League of Nations. He was once offered (and refused) the throne of Albania. *Hendon Corporation*

Elizabeth Fry (left) and the plaque at St Mildred's Court, Poultry (above).

FRY, Elizabeth (1780-1845). **St Mildred's Court, Poultry, EC2** *Corporation of the City of London;* **195 Mare Street, Hackney, E8** *Borough of Hackney*

English Quaker philanthropist and reformer; lived at St Mildred's Court 1800-9; Mare Street was an Elizabeth Fry Refuge 1849-1913. She devoted her life to prison and asylum reform, having discovered the appalling conditions at Newgate prison. She founded many hostels and charity organisations.

FURNIVAL'S INN. Prudential Buildings, High Holborn, EC1

An inn of Chancery attached to Lincoln's Inn, once belonging to Sir William Furnival; demolished 1897. Charles Dickens (q.v) wrote *The Pickwick Papers* here in 1836. *Corporation of the City of London*

FUSELI, Henry (1741-1825). **37 Foley Street, W1**

Swiss-born British artist; lived here 1788-1803. His work, such as *The Nightmare* (1781), was typical of the brooding drama of Romanticism. His paintings included illustrations to Shakespeare's and Milton's works. In 1799 he became professor of painting at the Royal Academy. *London County Council*

GAGE, Thomas (1721-87). **41 Portland Place, W1**
English soldier; lived here. He served as military governor of Montreal (1760), commander-in-chief of the British forces in America (1763-72) and governor of Massachusetts (1774). He was relieved after the battle of Bunker Hill, which marked the commencement of the American War of Independence (1775). *English Heritage*

GAINSBOROUGH, Thomas (1727-88). **82 Pall Mall, SW1**
English landscape and portrait painter; lived here 1774-88. Born in Suffolk, he settled in Bath in 1759, where he painted many portraits. Coming to London in 1774 he established himself as a court painter, exhibiting regularly at the Royal Academy. As a portrait painter he was the arch-rival of Sir Joshua Reynolds (q.v.). Without losing the likeness, he was able to imbue his portraits with a charm and grace that made them very popular. Among his most famous paintings are *The Blue Boy* (1770), *The Morning Walk* (1780) and *Mrs Siddons* (1785). *London County Council*

GAINSBOROUGH FILM STUDIOS. Poole Street, N1
The studios (1924-49) made many outstanding films during their twenty-five years; their trademark was an introductory scene of a lady in a large hat in the style of a Gainsborough painting. Among those who worked here were Alfred Hitchcock (q.v.), Ivor Novello (q.v.) and Gracie Fields (q.v.). *Borough of Hackney*

GAITSKELL, Hugh Todd Naylor (1906-63). **18 Frognal Gardens, NW3**
English socialist politician; lived here. He first entered Parliament in 1945 and was Minister of Fuel and Power (1947), Chancellor of the Exchequer (1950-1) and Leader of the Opposition (1955-63). A second plaque at this address commemorates Sir Walter Besant (q.v.). *Greater London Council*

GALSWORTHY, John (1867-1933). **Grove Lodge, Admiral's Walk, NW3.**
See also **ADAM, Robert**
English novelist and playwright; lived here 1918-33. The author of *The Forsyte Saga* (1922) and its sequels, he was also a life-long friend of Joseph Conrad (q.v.) and was awarded the Nobel prize for literature in 1932. *London County Council*

GALTON, Sir Francis (1822-1911). **42 Rutland Gate, SW7**
English scientist, traveller and explorer; lived here for fifty years. He explored unknown territory in South Africa, publishing his findings. His study of heredity

The plaque to Mahatma Gandhi in Baron's Court Road, W14.

led to the science of eugenics, and he was also responsible for the early system of fingerprint identification. The privately erected stone plaque was adopted by London County Council in 1959. *London County Council*

GANDHI, Mahatma (Mohandas Karamchand) (1869-1948). **Kingsley Hall, Powis Road, E3** *London County Council;* **20 Baron's Court Road, W14** *Greater London Council*

Indian leader; lived in Baron's Court Road while a student; stayed in Kingsley Hall in 1931. He studied law in London but settled in South Africa, where he led the Indian community against racial discrimination until the outbreak of the First World War. Returning to India as leader of the National Congress, Gandhi successfully campaigned for independence. He was gaoled many times by the British and underwent repeated hunger strikes during his pacifist resistance. He was assassinated by dissident Hindus.

GARRETT, Millicent. See **FAWCETT, Dame Millicent**

GARRETT ANDERSON, Elizabeth. See **ANDERSON, Elizabeth Garrett**

GARRICK, David (1717-79). **Garrick's Villa, Hampton Court Road, Richmond** *Greater London Council;* **27 Southampton Street, WC2** *Duke of Bedford (1900).* See also **ADELPHI TERRACE**

This detailed plaque commemorating David Garrick can be found at 27 Southampton Street, WC2.

British actor and theatre manager; lived at both addresses (Southampton Street 1750-72). He studied under Samuel Johnson (q.v.) but took up acting in 1741. He established himself at Drury Lane until 1776, as both actor and manager, and was buried in Westminster Abbey.

GARTH, Susan. Red Lion Antique Arcade, Portobello Road, W11
The plaque states: 'On this site Susan Garth launched London's first antiques market, making the Portobello Road an international institution.' The erection of this plaque in 1975 was strongly opposed by other market traders, as it was put up during her lifetime, and many felt that she should not be credited with this achievement, as there had been antique stalls in the area since the end of the Second World War. *Private*

GARTHWAITE, Anna Maria (1690-1763). **2 Princelet Street, Spitalfields, E1**
Designer of Spitalfields silks; lived and worked here. *English Heritage*

GARVEY, Marcus (Moziah) (1887-1940). **2 Beaumont Crescent, W14**
Jamaican-born political leader; lived here for a short time. He founded the Universal Negro Improvement Association in 1914, aiming to achieve human rights for black Americans. Garvey lived mainly in the USA, and a park is named after him on Manhattan Island, New York. He is considered one of the first militant black nationalists. *Private*

GASKELL, Mrs Elizabeth Cleghorn (1810-65). **93 Cheyne Walk, SW10**
British novelist; born here. Like Dickens (q.v.), to whose journal, *Household Words,* she contributed, she used her novels as a means of exposing social injustice, examples being *Mary Barton* (1848), *Ruth* (1853) and *North and South* (1855). Her other most notable works are *Cranford* (1853), *The Life of Charlotte Bronte* (1857) and *Wives and Daughters* (1865). *London County Council*

GAUDIER-BRZESKA, Henri (1891-1915). **454 Fulham Road, SW6**
French sculptor; worked here. He settled in London in 1911 and with Percy Wyndham Lewis (q.v.) and C. R. W. Nevinson (1889-1946) started the Vorticist movement of modern sculpture. He was killed in action during the First World War. *Greater London Council*

GENERAL LETTER OFFICE. Princes Street, EC2
The General Letter Office stood near this spot in Post House Yard in 1653-66. The first postmarks in the world were struck here in 1661. *Corporation of the City of London*

GEORGE, Sir Ernest (1839-1922). **17 Bartholomew Street, SE1**
English architect; lived here. He received the Royal Academy of Arts gold medal for architecture (1859) and later became president of the Royal Institute of British Architects (1908-9). George was responsible for many designs and much restoration work in London and the home counties. He was knighted in 1907. *Southwark Council*

GEORGE III. See WHITBREAD, Samuel

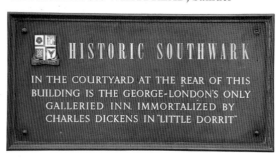

GEORGE INN. 73 Borough High Street, SE1
In the courtyard at the rear of this building is the George, London's only surviving galleried inn. It was immortalised by Charles Dickens (q.v.) in *Little Dorrit*. *Southwark Council*

GERALD ROAD POLICE STATION, site of. Gerald Road, SW1
The police station stood on this site 1846-1993. This blue plaque was unveiled by the Metropolitan Police Commissioner Paul Condon in 1993. *Private*

GERTLER, Mark (1891-1939). **32 Elder Street, E1** *Greater London Council;* **1 Well Mount Studios, Well Mount, NW3** *Hampstead Plaque Fund;* **Penn Studio, 13a Rudall Crescent, NW3** *Hampstead Plaque Fund*
English artist; lived at Elder Street; lived and worked at Penn Studio 1915-32; lived and worked at Well Mount Studios 1932-3. Of Polish Jewish background, he worked in an individual style that showed the influences of post-Impressionism and folk art. A conscientious objector in the First World War, he suffered from depression and eventually committed suicide.

GIBBON, Edward (1737-94). **7 Bentinck Street, W1**
British historian; lived in a house on this site 1773-83. He was the author of the six-volume *History of the Decline and Fall of the Roman Empire* (1776-88). *London County Council*

GIBBONS, Grinling (1648-1721). See **BOW STREET**
British woodcarver and sculptor, born in Rotterdam. He is noted for his exquisite carvings of natural objects, including birds, flowers and fruit etc. His work can be seen in St Paul's Cathedral, Hampton Court and many great historic houses.

GILBERT, Sir W. S. (William Schwenck) (1836-1911). **39 Harrington Gardens, SW7** *London County Council;* **Grim's Dyke, Old Redding, Harrow Weald** *Greater London Council* and *Harrow Heritage Trust*
English humorist and librettist; lived at the first address 1894-8; lived and died at the second. He worked in close collaboration with Sir Arthur Sullivan to produce a succession of popular light operettas, the best-loved of which include *HMS Pinafore* (1878), *The Pirates of Penzance* (1880) and *The Mikado* (1885). He met his death at Grim's Dyke, where he drowned in the lake. The GLC plaque there also commemorates R. Norman Shaw (q.v.) and Frederick Goodall (q.v.).

GILLIES, Sir Harold (1882-1960). **71 Frognal, Hampstead, NW3**
British surgeon; lived here. He specialised in plastic and reconstructive work and was also a cousin of the noted plastic surgeon Sir Archibald McIndoe (1900-60). *English Heritage*

GILPIN, William (1724-1804). **Tabor Court, High Street, Cheam**
English clergyman, writer, artist and headmaster of Cheam school (1752-77), on the site of which this plaque has been erected. From 1777 he was the vicar of Boldre in Hampshire. He wrote and illustrated several books on the scenery of Britain and was satirised by William Combe and Thomas Rowlandson (q.v.) as Dr Syntax. *Borough of Sutton*

GILTSPUR STREET COMPTER, site of. 2 Giltspur Street, EC1
This was a debtors' prison demolished in 1854. It was named after the gilt spurs worn by medieval knights who rode down the street on their way to tournaments at nearby Smithfield. *Corporation of the City of London*

W. E. Gladstone

GISSING, George Robert (1857-1903). **33 Oakley Gardens, SW3**
English novelist; lived here 1882-4. His books give graphic accounts of Victorian poverty, which he himself experienced in early life. They include *The Emancipated* (1890), *New Grub Street* (1891) and *The Private Papers of Henry Ryecroft* (1902). Owing to ill health, Gissing spent his final years in the south of France. *Greater London Council*

GLADSTONE, William Ewart (1809-98). **11 Carlton House Terrace, SW1** *London County Council;* **Eglington Road School, Plumstead, SE18** *Private;* **73 Harley Street, W1** *London County Council;* **10 St James's Square, SW1**

81

British Liberal prime minister 1868-74, 1880-5, 1886 and 1892-4; lived in Carlton House Terrace and St James's Square; lived in a house on the Harley Street site; delivered his last speech to his constituents in Plumstead. Gladstone entered Parliament in 1833 as a Conservative and twice held the office of Chancellor of the Exchequer. His achievements included the introduction of elementary education (1870) and voting by secret ballot (1872) as well as many other reforms. He is buried in Westminster Abbey. The Harley Street plaque is shared with Sir Charles Lyell, the St James's Square one with Pitt (q.v.) and Derby (q.v.).

GLAISHER, James (1809-1903). **20 Dartmouth Hill, SE10**
English astronomer, meteorologist and pioneer of weather forecasting; lived here. He joined the Ordnance Survey in 1829, later becoming the chief meteorologist at Greenwich. *Greater London Council*

GLOBE PLAYHOUSE, site of (1598-1613). **Park Street, SE1**
The bronze plaque, with a bust of William Shakespeare and a panoramic view of the Globe and the Thames, is inscribed 'Commemorated by the Shakespeare Reading Society of London and by subscribers in the United Kingdom and India'. In the 1990s a complete replica of the Globe, initiated by Sam Wanamaker, was built on a nearby riverside site.

GODLEY, John Robert (1814-61). **48 Gloucester Place, W1**
Founder of Canterbury, New Zealand; lived and died here. *London County Council*

GODLEY, Sidney Frank, VC (1889-1957). **Sidney Godley House, Digby Street, E2**
The plaque reads: 'This block is named Sidney Godley to commemorate the heroism of private Sidney Frank Godley VC (4th Battalion Royal Fusiliers), who was awarded the Victoria Cross for outstanding gallantry in Belgium during the First World War 1914-18. The official citation records 'In defence of a railway bridge near Nimy, 23rd August 1914, Private Godley of B Company showed particular heroism in his management of the machine guns. His commanding officer having been severely wounded and each machine gunner in turn shot, Private Godley was called to the firing line on the bridge, and under an extremely heavy fire he had to remove three dead bodies and proceed to an advanced machine gun position under a sustained enemy fire. He

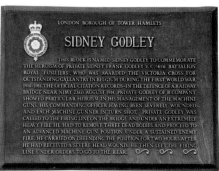

carried on defending the position for two hours after he had received a severe head wound. He then left the firing line under orders to go to the rear.' *Borough of Tower Hamlets*

GODWIN, George (1813-88). **24 Alexander Square, SW3**
Architect, journalist and social reformer; lived here. He was editor of *The Builder* journal (1884) and a gold medallist of the Institute of Architects (1881). He

erected many buildings in Bristol and was an active member of the Royal Commission on Housing of Working Classes. Godwin wrote several books on architecture, including *The Churches of London* (1838). *Greater London Council*

GOLDSCHMIDT, Madame. See **LIND, Jenny**

GOODALL, Frederick (1822-1904). **Grim's Dyke, Old Redding, Harrow Weald**
English painter; owned this house, which was built for him. He is best known for his subject pictures, including *Cranmer at the Traitors Gate* (1856). Commemorated on the same plaque are R. Norman Shaw (q.v.) and W. S. Gilbert (q.v.). *Greater London Council*

GOOSSENS Family. 70 Edith Road, W14
Home of the musical family. Eugene Goossens (1867-1958), violinist and conductor, and his sons Sir Eugene (1893-1962), composer and conductor, Leon (1897-1988), oboist, and their two sisters Marie and Sidonie, both well-known harpists. *English Heritage*

GOSSE, Philip Henry (1810-88). **56 Mortimer Road, N1**
English novelist and zoologist; lived here. He was particularly interested in marine biology. He published several works including *Romance of Natural History* (1860-2). His son **Sir Edmund Gosse** (1849-1928), who was born here, is also commemorated on the same plaque. A prolific writer and poet, Edmund was also librarian to the House of Lords. *Greater London Council*

GOUNOD, Charles François (1818-93). **17 Morden Road, SE23**
French composer; stayed here in 1870 to avoid the Franco-Prussian war. His operas include *Faust* (1859) and *Roméo et Juliette* (1867). He was also popular as a song writer. *London County Council*

GRACE, W. G. (William Gilbert) (1848-1915). **7 Lawrie Park Road, SE26** *Lewisham Council;* **Fairmount, Mottingham Lane, SE9** *London County Council*
English cricketer and physician; lived in a house on the first site; also lived at 'Fairmount'. He played for his county (Gloucestershire) at the age of sixteen. Grace scored 2739 runs in 1871 and made 152 in his first test match. In 1876 he scored 344 runs in an innings for the Marylebone Cricket Club (MCC). During his cricketing career of forty-four years he made a total of 54,896 runs and took 2864 wickets, playing in twenty-two test matches for England.

GRAHAM, George (1673-1751). **69 Fleet Street, EC4**
English clockmaker; lived on this site. A Fellow of the Royal Society, he was buried in Westminster Abbey. He shares a plaque with another clockmaker, Thomas Tompion (q.v.). *Private*

The plaque at 7 Lawrie Park Road, SE26.

GRAHAME, Kenneth (1859-1932). **16 Phillimore Place, W8**
Scottish author of children's books; lived here 1901-8. His best-known work is *The Wind in the Willows* (1908), which was later dramatised by A. A. Milne (q.v.) as *Toad of Toad Hall* (1929). *London County Council*

GRAINGER, Percy Aldridge (1882-1961). **31 King's Road, SW3**
Australian-born composer and pianist; lived here. His popular works, reviving the English folk-song tradition, include *The Floral Dance*. From 1914 he lived mainly in America. *Greater London Council*

GRAVES, Robert (Von Ranke) (1895-1985). **1 Lauriston Road, Wimbledon, SW19**
English novelist and poet; born here. He was wounded in the First World War, during which his first poems were composed. His best poetic work was written between 1928 and 1943. Graves's novels *I Claudius* (1934) and *Claudius the God* (1934) were later adapted for television. *English Heritage*

GRAY, Henry (1827-61). **8 Wilton Street, SW1**
English anatomist; lived here. His famous work *Anatomy* was published in 1853 and has remained the standard textbook for medical students. Gray's life was cut short by smallpox. This brown plaque is out of keeping with the normal LCC blue style. *London County Council*

GRAY, Thomas (1716-71). **39 Cornhill, EC3**
English poet; born in a house on this site. He was the leading poet of his time and a friend of Horace Walpole (q.v.), with whom he went on a thirty-month Grand Tour of France and Italy. His *Elegy Written in a Country Churchyard* (1751) is the most memorable of his works. The bronze plaque bears his bust and the first words of his immortal poem: 'The curfew tolls the knell of parting day'. *Private*

GREAT EASTERN, SS. **Westferry Road, E14**
The largest steamship of the nineteenth century. Built here by I. K. Brunel (q.v.) and J. Scott Russell (q.v.), it was launched in 1858. *London County Council*

GREAT HOUSE, site of the. 536-42 High Road, Leyton, E10
Built by Sir Fisher Tench and Thomas Oliver between 1700 and 1720. Thomas Oliver (q.v.) lived here 1750-1803. *Leyton Urban District Ratepayers Association*

GREATER LONDON COUNCIL. See COUNTY HALL

GREAVES, Walter (1846-1930). **104 Cheyne Walk, SW10**
Artist; lived here 1855-97. The house bears a second plaque to Hilaire Belloc (q.v.), who lived here three years later. *Greater London Council*

GREEN, John Richard (1837-83). **St Philip's Vicarage, Newark Street E1**
London County Council; **4 Beaumont Street, W1** *London County Council*
English historian; lived in Newark Street 1866-9 and in a house on the Beaumont Street site 1869-76. He was the author of *A Short History of the English People* (1874), *A History of the English People* (1877-80), *The Making of England* (1881) and *The Conquest of England* (1883).

GREENAWAY, Kate (Catherine) (1846-1901). **147 Upper Street, N1** *Borough of Islington;* **39 Frognal, NW3** *London County Council;* **Sylvia Court, Cavendish Street, N1** *Borough of Hackney*
English artist and book illustrator; born at 1 Cavendish Street (where Sylvia Court now stands); lived at Upper Street; lived and died at Frognal. She illustrated a series of children's books, including *Mother Goose* (1881), and also designed Christmas cards. She exhibited at the Royal Academy in 1877 and was also distinguished, surprisingly, by the praise of John Ruskin (q.v.). There is an annual Kate Greenaway Award for the best children's book illustrator. (Photograph, page 87)

GREENING, Edward Owen (1836-1923). **Dowson Court, Belmont Grove, Lee, SE13**
Founder of co-operative movements and campaigner against slavery; lived in a house on this site 1893-1923. A second plaque at this address commemorates the poet Edward Christopher Dowson (q.v.). *Lewisham Council*

GREET, Sir Phillip Benjamin (1857-1936). **160 Lambeth Road, SE1**
Actor-manager; lived here 1920-36. A life-long bachelor, he worked with Lilian Baylis (q.v.) at the Old Vic from 1914. He was knighted in 1929. *London County Council*

GRESHAM, Sir Thomas (1519-79). **International Finance Centre, Old Broad Street, EC2**
English merchant, financier and philanthropist; lived in a house on this site. He founded and built the Royal Exchange and Gresham College. In his will he bequeathed money for almshouses. *Corporation of the City of London*

GRESLEY, Sir (Herbert) Nigel (1876-1941). **West Offices, King's Cross Station, NW1**
Scottish-born locomotive engineer; had his office here 1923-41. He was the foremost designer of British classic trains, including the *Mallard,* which held the world steam train speed record of 126 mph (203 km/h) from 1938. *English Heritage*

GREY, Sir Edward, First Viscount Grey of Falloden (1862-1933). **3 Queen Anne's Gate, SW1**
British Liberal statesman; lived here 1906-12. He served as Foreign Secretary 1905-16 and ambassador to the USA 1919-20. *Greater London Council*

GREY FRIARS MONASTERY, site of. 106 Newgate Street, EC1
During the three centuries of its existence (1225-1538) the monastery was considerably extended. Richard Whittington (q.v.) is known to have been one of its benefactors. It was destroyed, with other monasteries, during the reign of Henry VIII. *Corporation of the City of London*

GRIMALDI, Joseph (1779-1837). **Finchley Memorial Hospital, Granville Road, N12** *Borough of Barnet;* **56 Exmouth Market, EC1** *English Heritage*

The plaque to Joseph Grimaldi at 56 Exmouth Market, SE1.

London-born pantomime clown; lived on a site in Granville Road and at 56 Exmouth Market 1818-28. Of Italian descent, he first appeared on stage at the age of two. He regularly appeared at Sadler's Wells and Drury Lane, and his name, 'Joey', was later used by clowns worldwide.

GROOM, John (1845-1919). **8 Seckforde Street, EC1**

English philanthropist; lived here. In 1866 he founded the Watercress and Flower Girls' Christian Mission, which afterwards became known as John Groom's Crippleage, the forerunner of the present-day homes for elderly and disabled people. His home here was near to his first institution. He died at Clacton-on-Sea. *English Heritage*

GROSER, the Reverend St John (1890-1966). **Royal Foundation of St Katherine, 2 Butcher Row, E14**
Priest and social reformer; lived here. *English Heritage*

GROSSMITH, George (1847-1912). **28 Dorset Square, NW1**
English comedy actor and entertainer; lived here. He took leading parts in Gilbert and Sullivan operettas (1877-89) and with his brother Weedon wrote *Diary of a Nobody* (1892). *London County Council*

GROSSMITH, George (1874-1935). **3 Spanish Place, W1**
English comedy actor-manager; lived here. The son of the above named George Grossmith, he was a musical comedy actor, a songwriter and the manager of the Gaiety Theatre. A plaque to Captain Frederick Marryat (q.v.) can be found at this same address. *London County Council*

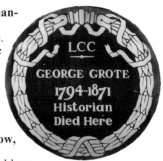

GROTE, George (1794-1871). **12 Savile Row, W1**
English politician, banker and historian; died here.
He was MP for the City of London 1832-41. His historical works include a *History of Greece* (1846-56), *Plato and the Other Companions of Socrates* (1865) and *Fragments on Ethical Subjects* (1876). He is buried in Westminster Abbey. *London County Council*

GROVE, Sir George (1820-1900). **208 Sydenham Road, SE26**
English civil engineer and expert on music; lived in a house on this site 1860-1900. A director of the Crystal Palace Company, he edited the *Dictionary of Music and Musicians* (1878-89), which is still the foremost reference work on music. He was knighted in 1883 when he became the first director of the Royal College of Music. *Lewisham Council*

GUNPOWDER PLOT. 244-78 Crondall Street, N1
The plaque states: 'In a house near this site on the 12th October 1605 Lord Monteagle received a letter unmasking the plot led by Guy Fawkes to blow up the Houses of Parliament.' *Borough of Hackney*

GUY, Thomas (*c.*1644-1724). **1 Cornhill, EC3**
Founder of Guy's Hospital (1722); had his home and bookshop on this site 1668-1724. In addition to founding and endowing Guy's Hospital, he also built and furnished three wards at St Thomas's Hospital (1707) and built several almshouses. *Private*

GWYNNE, Nell (Eleanor) (*c.*1650-87). **80 Pall Mall, SW1**
English actress and mistress of Charles II; lived in a house on this site 1671-87. Born of humble parentage, she sold oranges before going on the stage at Drury Lane. As a result of her affair with the King she bore a son, Charles Beauclerk, Duke of St Albans. She is buried at St Martin-in-the-Fields. *Private*

This colourful plaque to Kate Greenaway (pictured right) can be found at 39 Frognal, NW3.

HADEN-GUEST, Leslie Haden, First Baron Haden-Guest of Saling (1877-1960). **38 Tite Street, SW3**
Author, journalist and physician; lived here. He was a socialist MP 1923-7 and 1937-50. He served in both world wars and was a founder of the Anglo-French Companions of the Red Cross Society and of the Order of St John. He was created a baron in 1950 and served as a lord-in-waiting to the king in 1951. *Private*

HAGEDORN, Elisabeth (1892-1945). **15 Ravenshaw Street, NW6**
The heart-shaped plaque built into the brick-work of this house was erected by her two daughters, who considered her an exceptional mother. *Private*

HAGGARD, Sir Henry Rider (1856-1925). **69 Gunterstone Road, W14**
English novelist; lived here 1885-8. He was the author of *King Solomon's Mines* (1885), *She* (1887), *Allan Quartermain* (1887) and many other adventure stories. *Greater London Council*

HALDANE, Richard Burdon, First Viscount Haldane (1856-1928). **28 Queen Anne's Gate, SW1**
Statesman, lawyer and philosopher; lived here from 1907. He entered Parliament as a Liberal MP in 1879. As Secretary of State for War (1905-12), he founded the Territorial Army. He was Lord Chancellor 1912-15 and Minister of Labour in 1924 under the Labour government. Haldane was also an eminent judge and published three philosophical treatises. *London County Council*

HALIFAX, Edward Frederick Lindley Wood, First Earl of Halifax (1881-1959). **86 Eaton Square, SW1**
English Tory statesman; lived here. Halifax served as Viceroy of India (1926-31), Foreign Secretary (1938-40) and ambassador to the USA (1941-6). He was created an earl in 1944. *English Heritage*

HALL, Henry, CBE (1898-1989). **8 Randolph Mews, W9**
English band leader, composer, arranger and

Henry Hall, CBE, the band leader and broadcaster.

broadcaster; lived here 1959-81. His popular 'Guest Night' broadcasts started in 1932, with a signature tune 'Here's to the next time', that he composed himself. After the Second World War he became an impresario, staging several West End shows. In the 1950s he hosted the television show *Face the Music* and is best remembered by his catch phrase 'This *is* Henry Hall speaking'. *English Heritage*

HALL, Keith Clifford (1910-64). **140 Park Lane, W1**
Pioneer in the fitting of contact lenses; practised here 1945-64. *Westminster City Council*

HALL, Marguerite Radclyffe (1880-1943). **37 Holland Street, W8**
English novelist and poet; lived here from 1924 to 1929. She wrote four volumes of poetry before the appearance of her first book in 1924. Her novel *The Well of Loneliness* (1928) was controversial owing to its sympathetic approach to lesbianism. *English Heritage*

HALL, Newman (1816-1902). **8 Hampstead Square, NW3**
English clergyman and author. The plaque reads: 'Homes for the aged, given by his widow.' He was the founder of Christ Church, Lambeth (1876), built at a cost of £64,000; the first pastor of Albion Congregational church, Hull (1842-54); and the pastor of Surrey Chapel, London, 1854-76. He was also the brother of John Vine Hall, captain of the *Great Eastern* (q.v.). He travelled extensively and had many religious works published. Hall lived at nearby Vine House at the time of his death. *Private*

HALLAM, Henry (1777-1859). **67 Wimpole Street, W1**
English historian; lived here. He was called to the bar in 1802. Private means enabled him to pursue his historical interests and his *Constitutional History of England from Henry VIII to George II* (1827) established his reputation. It was followed by other detailed works. *London County Council*

HAMILTON, Charles. See **RICHARDS, Frank**

HAMMOND, John Lawrence le Breton (1872-1949), and his wife **Lucy Barbara** (1873-1961). **Hollycot, Vale of Health, NW3**
English social historians; lived here 1906-13. Married in 1901, they worked together revealing the harshness of English social conditions and publishing many works between 1911 and 1938. *Greater London Council*

HANCOCK, Tony (Anthony John) (1924-68). **10 Grey Close, NW11** *The Dead Comics Society;* **Teddington Studios, Broom Road, Teddington** *Comic Heritage*
English comedian; lived in Grey Close for a short time during 1947-8; worked at the studios. He is best remembered for his performances as a lugubrious misfit in *Hancock's Half Hour* on radio (1954) and later television (1956-61).

HANDEL, George Frideric (1685-1759). **St Lawrence Church, Whitchurch Lane, Edgware** *Harrow Heritage Trust;* **25 Brook Street, W1** *London County Council*
German-born composer; was composer-in-residence at St Lawrence's; lived

George Frideric Handel

and died in Brook Street. His first opera *Almira* (1705) was performed in Hamburg. He settled in England and enjoyed royal patronage, writing the *Water Music* for George I (former Elector of Hanover). His masterpiece, *Messiah,* was first performed in Dublin in 1742. In all he composed forty-six operas, thirty-two oratorios and many cantatas, orchestral, instrumental, vocal and sacred pieces. He is buried in Westminster Abbey at Poets' Corner.

HANDL, Irene (1901-87). **Teddington Studios, Broom Road, Teddington**
English comedy actress of stage, radio and television; worked at these studios. She first appeared on stage in 1937 and performed in numerous roles. Her films include *The Italian Job, I'm All Right Jack* and *Two Way Stretch.* She was best known on television for her starring role in the series *For the Love of Ada. Comic Heritage*

HANDLEY, Tommy (Thomas Reginald) (1892-1949). **34 Craven Road, W2**
English comedian and regular broadcaster; lived here. His weekly radio programme, *ITMA (It's That Man Again)*, was loved by millions from 1939 until his death in 1949 and did much to boost public morale during the difficult days of the Second World War. *Greater London Council*

HANSOM, Joseph Aloysius (1803-82). **27 Sumner Place, SW7**
British architect and inventor; lived here 1873-7. He designed Birmingham Town Hall (1831) and the Roman Catholic Cathedral at Plymouth. He was also the founder-editor of *The Builder* journal but is best remembered for designing the Hansom cab (1834). *Greater London Council*

Teddington Studios in Broom Road, Teddington, where a whole line of plaques can be seen to the many different people who have worked there, including one to Irene Handl.

HARDY, Thomas (1840-1928). **16 Westbourne Park Villas, W2** *Private;* **172 Trinity Road, Tooting, SW17** *London County Council.* See also **ADELPHI TERRACE**

English poet, novelist and dramatist; lived at both addresses 1863-74 and 1878-81 respectively. His novels include *Far from the Madding Crowd* (1874), *The Mayor of Casterbridge* (1886), *The Woodlanders* (1887) and *Tess of the d'Urbervilles* (1891), which have been adapted for cinema and television. His poems include *Wessex Poems* (1898), the verse drama *The Dynasts* (1904-8), *Winter Words* (1928) and several volumes of lyrics.

Thomas Hardy

HARLEY, Robert, First Earl of Oxford (1661-1724). **14 Buckingham Street, WC2**
English statesman; lived in a house on this site. He was Speaker of the House of Commons (1701), Secretary of State (1704) and chief minister to Queen Anne (1711-14). The plaque is shared with Samuel Pepys (q.v.), William Etty (q.v.) and Clarkson Stansfield (q.v.). *London County Council*

HARMSWORTH, Alfred Charles William, First Viscount Northcliffe (1865-1922). **32 Pandora Road, NW6**
Irish newspaper magnate; lived here. He founded the *Daily Mail* (1896) and the *Daily Mirror* (1903) and became proprietor of *The Times* in 1908. *Greater London Council*

HARRISON, John (1693-1776). **Summit House, Red Lion Square, WC1**
English horologist; lived and died in a house on this site. He invented and constructed five highly accurate marine chronometers to determine longitude. For many years the Board of Longitude was reluctant to acknowledge his achievement, believing that only astronomy could afford a solution worthy of the longitude prize (available to the solver of the longitude problem). Eventually, however, his life's work was recognised. *London County Council*

HARTE, Francis Brett (1836-1902). **74 Lancaster Gate, W2**
American author and poet; lived and died here. Harte founded the *Overland Monthly* (1868), to which he contributed many items, including *The Luck of*

This plaque to the film director Alfred Hitchcock can be found at 517 Leytonstone High Road, E11.

Roaring Camp and *The Outcasts of Poker Flat* (1870). He was United States consul in Glasgow 1880-5 before settling in Lancaster Gate. *Greater London Council*

HISTORIC SOUTHWARK

THE 'QUEEN'S HEAD INN' OWNED BY THE FAMILY OF JOHN HARVARD, FOUNDER OF HARVARD UNIVERSITY, FORMERLY STOOD HERE

HARVARD, John (1607-38). **103 Borough High Street, SE1**
Founder of Harvard University; on this site stood the Queen's Head inn owned by the Harvard family. John, who became a nonconformist preacher, was educated at Emmanuel College, Cambridge, and emigrated to America. He married in 1637 but died from consumption a year later. Harvard bequeathed his library of around three hundred books and £779 to the college in Cambridge, Massachusetts, which later took his name. *Borough of Southwark*

HAWTHORNE, Nathaniel (1804-64). **4 Pond Road, Blackheath, SE3**
American novelist; stayed here 1856. His works include *The Scarlet Letter* (1850), *The House of Seven Gables* (1851) and *Tanglewood Tales* (1853). *London County Council*

HAYDON, Benjamin Robert (1786-1846). **116 Lisson Grove, NW1**
British historical artist; lived here 1817-22. He painted many huge canvases including *Christ's Entry into Jerusalem* (1820) and *The Raising of Lazarus* (1823). Although he experienced some success, he lived in poverty and finally shot himself. The plaque also commemorates the sculptor Charles Rossi (q.v.). *London County Council*

HAYNES, Arthur (1914-66). **72 Gunnersbury Avenue, W5**
Stage and radio comedian; lived and died here 1963-6. He became known through the wartime radio show *Stand Easy* accompanying Charlie Chester. The television show *Strike a New Note* brought him to a wider audience in the 1950s, and he had offers from America. In 1961 he received a Variety Club award and was named television personality of the year. *The Dead Comics Society*

HAZLITT, William (1778-1830). **6 Bouverie Street, EC4** *Corporation of the City of London;* **6 Frith Street, W1** *London County Council*
English essayist and critic; lived in a house on the Bouverie Street site; died in Frith Street. Hazlitt wrote and lectured on *Characters of Shakespeare's Plays*, *English Poets*, *English Writers* and other topics. His work is characterised by invective, irony and a gift for epigram.

HEARNE, Thomas (1744-1817). **6 Meard Street, W1**
English topographical draughtsman and watercolourist; lived here. He is best known for his work with the engraver William Byrne (1743-1805) on *The Antiquities of Great Britain* (1786), for which he made fifty-two drawings. *Private*

HEATH ROBINSON. See **ROBINSON, W. Heath**

HEINE, Heinrich (1797-1856). **32 Craven Street, WC2**
German poet and essayist; lived here 1827. He had works published in his own country and in France.

92

Two plaques can be seen on this building in Brook Street, W1; the one on the left is to Jimi Hendrix and the one on the right is to George Frideric Handel.

For the last eight years of his life he was confined to bed, suffering a severe spinal condition. The plaque mistakenly gives his birthdate as 1799. *London County Council*

HENDERSON, Arthur (1863-1935). **13 Rodenhurst Road, Clapham, SW4**
Scottish socialist politician; lived here. He was chairman of the Labour party three times between 1908 and 1932 and served as Home Secretary (1924) and Foreign Secretary (1929-31). He was a strong supporter of disarmament. *Greater London Council*

HENDRIX, Jimi (James Marshall) (1942-70). **23 Brook Street, W1**
American rock guitarist and singer; lived here 1968-9. He came to England in 1966 when at the height of his career, and his early death was the result of a mix of drugs and alcohol. Objections were initially raised to the erection of this plaque as it happens to be next door to that of Handel (q.v.). *English Heritage*

HENRY VIII (1491-1547). **23 Cheyne Walk, SW3** *Borough of Kensington and Chelsea;* **Cheyne Studios, Cheyne Gardens, SW3** *Private*
The Cheyne Walk plaque reads: 'King Henry VIII's manor house stood here until 1753 when it was demolished after the death of its last occupant, Sir Hans Sloane. Nos. 19 to 26 Cheyne Walk were built on its site in 1759-65. The old manor house garden still lies beyond the end wall of Cheyne Mews and contains

some mulberry trees said to have been planted by Queen Elizabeth I.' The circular blue plaque in Cheyne Gardens also refers to the manor house, noting that part of its boundary wall adjoins Cheyne Studios.

HENTY, G. A. (George Alfred) (1832-1902). **33 Lavender Gardens, SW11**
English novelist and war

correspondent; lived here. He wrote a large number of historical adventure stories for children, including *With Clive in India* (1884), *With Moore at Corunna* (1898) and *With the Allies at Peking* (1904). *London County Council*

HEPWORTH, Cecil (1874-1953). **17 Somerset Gardens, SE13**
English pioneer film maker; born here. The most notable of his films was *Rescued by Rover,* made in 1905, featuring a faithful dog rescuing a baby. Despite leaving the industry in the 1920s he made a few films for the Ministry of Agriculture during the Second World War. *British Film Institute*

HERBERT, Sir Alan Patrick (1890-1971). **12 Hammersmith Terrace, W6**
English author, humorist and politician; lived and died here. Having established himself as a comic-verse writer with *Punch* magazine, he turned to writing libretti for musicals in the 1930s and 1940s. He also wrote several successful novels and was an independent MP for Oxford University 1935-50. *English Heritage*

HERFORD, Robert Travers (1860-1950). **Dr Williams's Library, 14 Gordon Square, WC1**
Unitarian minister, scholar and interpreter of Judaism; lived and worked here. *English Heritage*

HERTZ, Joseph Herman (1872-1946). **103 Hamilton Terrace, NW8**
Chief Rabbi of the United Hebrew Congregation of the British Empire 1913-46, during which time he lived in this house. Born in Hungary, he studied in New York and was a Chief Rabbi and a professor of philosophy in South Africa before coming to Britain. *Westminster City Council*

HERZEN, Alexander (1812-70). **1 Orsett Terrace, W2**
Russian political thinker and writer; lived here 1860-3. He was imprisoned in 1834 and exiled within Russia, leaving for Paris in 1847. By 1851 he had settled in London. Through his novels and treatises, he continued to propound his socialist ideals in his homeland. *Greater London Council*

HESELTINE, Philip Arnold. See WARLOCK, Peter

HESS, Dame Myra (1890-1965). **48 Wildwood Road, NW11**
English concert pianist; lived here. She was famed both in America and in Britain and was awarded the DBE in 1941 in recognition of her wartime concerts at the National Gallery. *English Heritage*

HIGHBURY BARN. Highbury Barn Tavern, Highbury Grove, N5
The plaque commemorates the period 1861-71 when old buildings on this site were demolished and a licence was given to Edward Giovanelli to lay out a lavish pleasure ground, including an open-air theatre. This he did, but the many petty criminals

Right: *The plaque to William Hogarth on the house named after him in Hogarth Lane, W4.*

WILLIAM
HOGARTH
Painter & Engraver
1697 - 1764
LIVED AND WORKED
HERE FOR 15 YEARS

COUNTY OF   MIDDLESEX

Below: *This plaque to the Pre-Raphaelite artist Arthur Hughes can be seen at 284 London Road, Wallington.*

HERITAGE IN SUTTON

SUTTON
LEISURE SERVICES

ARTHUR HUGHES (1832-1915)

WANDLE BANK WAS, FROM 1876-1891, THE HOME OF ARTHUR HUGHES. AN ASSOCIATE OF THE PRE-RAPHAELITES, HE WAS A PORTRAIT PAINTER AND ILLUSTRATOR, WHOSE WORK APPEARS IN MANY GALLERIES. HIS MOST FAMOUS PAINTING APRIL LOVE NOW HANGS IN THE TATE GALLERY. HUGHES ADDED THE STUDIO TO BE SEEN AT THE RIGHT OF THE HOUSE.

Below: *The plaque to the biologist Julian Huxley at 31 Pond Street, Hampstead, NW3.*

who came to the area disturbed the local residents, and the gardens were finally closed in 1871. *Islington Borough Council*

HILL, Benny (Alfred Hawthorne).
(1924-92). 1 and 2 Queen's Gate, SW7
The Dead Comics Society; **Teddington**
Studios, Broom Road, Teddington *Comic Heritage*
English comedian; lived at Queen's Gate 1960-86; worked at the studios. During the Second World War he appeared in *Stars in Battledress*, and later became a touring comedian. Appearing on television from 1949, he received the 'personality of the year award' in 1954. His national and American popularity came from his television series *The Benny Hill Show*. He also appeared in films.

BENNY
HILL

1925 ~ 1992
Comedian

COMIC HERITAGE

One of two plaques to the comedian Benny Hill. This one can be seen at Teddington Studios.

HILL, Octavia (1838-1912). **2 Garbutt Place, W1**
English social reformer, who improved housing conditions for the poor and co-founded the National Trust in 1895; began her work here. *English Heritage*

The plaque at Cartwright Gardens, WC1.

HILL, Sir Rowland (1795-1879). **Orbit House, 197 Blackfriars Road, SE1** *Borough of Southwark;* **Cartwright Gardens, WC1** *Camden Borough Council;* **1 Orme Square, W2** *London County Council*
English preacher and postal pioneer. The three plaques commemorate respectively: the site of Surrey Chapel (Hill's headquarters as an itinerant preacher, where the first Sunday School was held); the site where he wrote a pamphlet leading to the foundation of the postal service; one of his homes. He was the originator of the postage stamp and introduced the penny post (1840) and successive postal reforms.

HILTON, James (1900-54). **42 Oak Hill Gardens, Woodford Green**
English novelist and scriptwriter; lived here. Many of his novels were filmed, including *Lost Horizon* (1933), *Goodbye Mr Chips* (1934) and *Random Harvest* (1941). *English Heritage*

HITCHCOCK, Sir Alfred Joseph (1899-1980). **517 Leytonstone High Road, E11**
English-born film director; born near this site. His early films, noted for their air of mystery and suspense, include *Blackmail* (1929), *The Thirty-Nine Steps* (1935) and *The Lady Vanishes* (1939). He went to Hollywood in 1940 and received US citizenship in 1955. In Hollywood he enjoyed a string of successes. Hitchcock also hosted two television shows. (Photograph, page 91) *Borough of Waltham Forest*

HOARE, John Gurney (1810-75). **The Hill, North End Way, NW3**
Banker; born in a house near this site. The plaque states: 'He was the prime mover in the battle to save Hampstead Heath from development.' *Hampstead Plaque Fund*

HOBBS, Sir Jack (John Berry) (1882-1963). **17 Englewood Road, SW12**
English cricketer; lived here. A great Surrey batsman (1905-35), he played in sixty-one test matches for England and in his career scored 61,237 runs, including 197 centuries. He was the first cricketer to be knighted (1953). *Greater London Council*

HO CHI MINH (Nguyen Van Thann) (1890-1969). **New Zealand House, Haymarket, SW1**
Communist leader of North Vietnam; worked in 1913 at the Carlton Hotel on this site. He became prime minister of North Vietnam and the president in 1954 and 1960. He led the war against the French (1946-54) and US-backed South Vietnam (1954-75). *Britain Vietnam Association*

HODGKIN, Thomas (1798-1866). **35 Bedford Square, WC1**
English physician and pathologist; lived here. He held

35 Bedford Square, WC1, which has plaques to Thomas Hodgkin and Thomas Wakley.

various positions at Guy's Hospital and identified the disease named after him. A second plaque at this address commemorates Thomas Wakley (q.v.). *Greater London Council*

HOFMANN, August Wilhelm von (1818-92). **9 Fitzroy Square, W1**
German scientist; lived here. He became director of the Royal College of Chemistry in 1845 and chemist to the Royal Mint 1856-65, after which he returned to Berlin. He studied coal tar derivatives, discovering many organic compounds, including formaldehyde. *English Heritage*

HOGARTH, William (1697-1764). **Hogarth House, Hogarth Lane, W4**
English painter and engraver; lived and worked here for fifteen years. He is best known for his satirical paintings depicting moral corruption, as in the series *The Rake's Progress* (c.1732) and *Marriage à la Mode* (1743-5). His mastery of human expression and characterisation was outstanding and is exhibited in many works, including a portrait study of six of his servants (1750-5). He opened his own gallery in St Martin's Lane (1735). Hogarth House is open to the public. (Photograph, page 95) *County of Middlesex*

HOGG, Quintin (1845-1903). **5 Cavendish Square, W1**
British philanthropist who founded the Regent Street Polytechnic in 1882; lived here 1885-98. *London County Council*

HOLMES, Sherlock. 221b Baker Street, W1
Fictional detective created by Sir Arthur Conan Doyle (q.v.). The address given in Conan Doyle's books, 221b Baker Street, is a private museum, frequented by Holmes lovers from around the world. *Private*

HOLST, Gustav Theodore (von) (1874-1934). **9 The Terrace, Barnes, SW13**
Swedish-born English composer; lived here 1908-13. He wrote operas, ballets, choral works and orchestral suites, notably *The Planets* (1917). A friend of Ralph Vaughan Williams (q.v.), he shared his interest in English folk music. *Private*

HOLTBY, Winifred (1898-1935). **58 Doughty Street, WC1**
English novelist, journalist and feminist; lived here. Her best-known novel was *South Riding* (1936). The plaque is shared by Vera Brittain (q.v.). *English Heritage*

HOLY TRINITY, site of the priory of the. Mitre Square, EC3
Founded 1108 and built by the Canons of Augustine. The church of St Katherine Cree was built in its grounds. The priory was dissolved by Henry VIII, and the parishioners of the church later decided to demolish it. *Corporation of the City of London*

HOLYWELL PRIORY. 98 Curtain Road, EC2
The priory, which was indeed named after a holy well, was founded on this site around 1152-8 and flourished until the dissolution of the monasteries in 1539. The plaque gives details of its boundaries. *Borough of Hackney*

HOOD, Thomas (1799-1845). **Midland Bank, Poultry, EC2** *Corporation of the City of London;* **59 Vicar's Moor Lane, Winchmore Hill, N21** *Borough of Enfield.* See also **ADAM, Robert**
English poet and humorist; born in a house on the Poultry site; lived in Rose Cottage on the second site. After an apprenticeship as an engraver he joined the *London Magazine,* where he met such persons as De Quincey (q.v.), Hazlitt (q.v.) and Lamb (q.v.), and published many works. In 1829 he moved to Vicar's Moor Lane, where he began his 'comic annuals'. From 1835 he lived in Europe but returned to London in 1840 and died at a house in Finchley Road, where a London County Council plaque was in place for many years.

The plaque at Muswell Hill, N21.

HOPE, Anthony (Sir Anthony Hope Hawkins) (1863-1933). **41 Bedford Square, WC1**
English novelist; lived here 1903-17. He is best remembered for *The Prisoner of Zenda* (1894) and its sequel, *Rupert of Henzau* (1898). *Greater London Council*

HOPE, Bob (born 1903). **44 Craigton Road, Eltham, SE9**
Stage name of Leslie Townes Hope, British-born American comedian; born in this house. At the age of four he was taken to America. He worked in vaudeville as a comedian and dancer and made his first film appearance in 1934. Hope went on to become a popular broadcaster with his own regular show and partnered Bing Crosby in a series of 'Road' films between 1940 and 1961. *British Film Institute*

HOPKINS, Gerard Manley (1844-89). **Manresa House, Holybourne Avenue, SW15** *Greater London Council;* **9 Oak Hill Park, NW3** *Hampstead Plaque Fund*
English poet; lived and studied in Manresa House; lived in Oak Hill Park 1852-63. He was ordained a Roman Catholic priest in 1877. None of his writings was published in his lifetime, but his great friend Robert Bridges published a full edition of his poems in 1918. Perhaps his most popular poem is 'Pied Beauty'. His correspondence was published in 1935.

The plaque at 9 Oak Hill Park, NW3.

HOPPE, Emil Otto (1878-1972). **7 Cromwell Place, SW7**
German-born photographer; lived here. He travelled extensively and lived mainly in London and New York. He wrote many articles for periodicals and published several books on the subject of photography. The plaque is shared with Millais (q.v.) and Bacon (q.v.). *National Art Collections Fund*

HORE-BELISHA, Leslie, First Baron Hore-Belisha (1893-1957). **16 Stafford Place, SW1**
British Liberal politician; lived here. He was Minister of Transport 1934-7 and is remembered for the introduction of 'Belisha' beacons at road crossings. He also held the post of War Minister 1937-40. *Greater London Council*

HORNIMAN, John (1803-93), and **Frederick John** (1835-1906). **The Horniman Museum, London Road, SE23** *Greater London Council;* **Coombe Cliff Centre, Coombe Road, Croydon** *Greater London Council*
Tea merchants, collectors and public benefactors. They both lived in Coombe Road. Their extensive collection from worldwide travels is housed in the Horniman Museum, which was presented to the people of London by Frederick John (who lived near this site) in 1901.

This plaque to John and Frederick John Horniman can be seen in Coombe Road, Croydon.

HOUSMAN, A. E. (Alfred Edward) (1859-1936). **17 North Road, Highgate, N6**
English poet and scholar; wrote *A Shropshire Lad* while living here. It was published 1896. Other volumes include *Last Poems* (1922) and *More Poems* (1936). He was professor of Latin at University College London, and later at Cambridge. *Greater London Council*

HOWARD, Sir Ebenezer (1850-1929). **50 Durley Road, N16** *English Heritage;* **Moor House, 119 London Wall, EC2** *Corporation of the City of London*

English town planner and reformer; born in a house on the London Wall site; lived in Durley Road. His book *Tomorrow* (1898), republished as *Garden Cities of Tomorrow* (1902), led to the building of the first garden cities, Letchworth (1903) and Welwyn (1919).

HOWARD, John (1726-90). **23 Great Ormond Street, WC1** *London County Council;* **157-9 Lower Clapton Road, E5** *Borough of Hackney*
English philanthropist and prison reformer; born near the Lower Clapton Road site; lived in Great Ormond Street 1777-89. As high sheriff of Bedfordshire in 1773 he undertook a tour of British prisons and was appalled at the conditions. This led to two Acts of Parliament for improvement. He afterwards travelled widely and published works on prison conditions and reform. The Howard League for Prison Reform (1866) was named after him.

John Howard.

HOWERD, Frankie (Francis Alick Howard) (1922-92). **27 Edwardes Square, W8**
English comedian; lived here 1966-92. As a stand-up comic he performed regularly on radio and television shows. One of his most notable appearances was in *A Funny Thing Happened on the Way to the Forum* (1963). His later television series *Up Pompeii* resulted in a film of the same name (1971). This plaque mistakenly gives his birthdate as 1917. *Dead Comics Society*

HUDSON, William Henry (1841-1922). **40 St Luke's Road, W11**
Argentine-born British author and naturalist; lived and died here. He arrived in England in 1869 and was naturalised in 1900. He wrote several books on natural history and birds and also about his rambles in the New Forest. There are two plaques at the address: one placed by Hudson's Friends Society of Quilmes, near Buenos Aires, adopted by *London County Council* and a second to commemorate the 150th anniversary of his birth, by the *Anglo-Argentine Society.*

HUGHES, Arthur (1832-1915). **22 Kew Green, Richmond** *English Heritage;* **284 London Road, Wallington** *Borough of Sutton*
Pre-Raphaelite artist; lived and worked at Wallington 1876-91; lived and died in Richmond. Born in London, he was a member of the Pre-Raphaelite movement and is best known for his painting *April Love* (1856). He also pursued a career as an illustrator and worked with Christina Rossetti (q.v.). In later life he was reclusive. (Photograph, page 95)

HUGHES, David Edward (1831-1900). **4 Great Portland Street, W1**
London-born inventor; lived and worked here. Brought up in Kentucky, USA, he invented a telegraph typewriter (1855) and the microphone (1878). In his will he left a large sum of money to London hospitals. *English Heritage*

HUGHES, Hugh Price (1847-1902). **8 Taviton Street, WC1**
Welsh Methodist preacher; lived and died here. He founded the *Methodist Times* (1885) and pioneered the West London Mission. *English Heritage*

HUGHES, Mary (1860-1941). **71 Vallance Road, E2**
Described on the plaque as a 'friend of all in need'; lived and worked here 1926-41. Financially independent, she devoted her life to helping the poor, taking in lodgers and holding socialist meetings twice weekly. *London County Council*

HUGHES, William Morris (1864-1952). **7 Moreton Place, SW1**
Australian prime minister 1915-23; born in this house. He emigrated to Australia in 1884. After serving as prime minister he held several cabinet posts between 1934 and 1941. *Commonwealth of Australia*

HUNT, James Leigh (1784-1859). **Vale of Health, NW3** *Private;* **22 Upper Cheyne Row, SW3** *London County Council*
English poet and essayist; lived in a cottage on the first site 1816-21; lived at the second address. He edited *The Examiner* 1808-21, which produced association with Byron, Moore (q.v.), Shelley (q.v.), Lamb (q.v.) and Keats (q.v.), among others. He was imprisoned with his brother (co-editor) in 1813-15 for libelling the Prince Regent and lived abroad 1822-5 with Shelley and Byron.

HUNT, William Holman (1827-1910). **18 Melbury Road, W14**
English painter; lived and died here. A co-founder of the Pre-Raphaelite Brotherhood, together with Millais (q.v.), Rossetti (q.v.) and other artists, he pursued realistic detail and truth to nature in his often deeply symbolic paintings such as *The Scapegoat* (1854). From 1854 he travelled extensively in the Middle East, and this is reflected in his work. *London County Council*

HUNTER, John (1728-93). **31 Golden Square, W1**
Scottish surgeon and anatomist; lived in a house on this site. He pioneered many surgical operations and built up a huge collection of specimens from his

many experiments. He was the brother of William Hunter (q.v.). There is a weathered stone bust of John in Leicester Square. *London County Council*

HUNTER, Robert (1823-97). **Forest Villa, 7 Staples Road, Loughton**
English lexicographer, naturalist and missionary; lived here. He was a colleague of Stephen Hislop at the Free Church Mission, Nagpore, central India 1846-55 and a resident tutor of the Presbyterian church of England in London 1864-6. Hunter edited *Lloyd's Encyclopaedic Dictionary,* published in 1889. *Loughton Town Council*

HUNTER, William (1718-83). **Rear of Lyric Theatre, Great Windmill Street, W1**
Scottish anatomist and obstetrician; lived here. He was the first professor of anatomy to the

Royal Academy (1768). His collection was bequeathed to Glasgow University. John Hunter (q.v.) was his brother. *London County Council*

HUSKISSON, William (1770-1830). **28 St James's Place, SW1**
English statesman; lived here. He was a supporter of William Pitt (q.v.) and became Secretary of the Treasury (1804-9), President of the Board of Trade and Treasurer of the Navy (1823) and Colonial Secretary (1827). He was the first person in Britain to be killed by a train (at the opening of the Liverpool & Manchester Railway). *London County Council*

HUTCHINSON, Sir Jonathan (1828-1913). **15 Cavendish Square, W1**
English surgeon; lived here 1874-1913. He worked at the London Hospital (1863-83) and was professor of surgery at the Royal College of Surgeons. *Greater London Council*

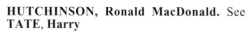

HUTCHINSON, Ronald MacDonald. See **TATE**, **Harry**

HUXLEY, Aldous Leonard (1894-1963). **16 Bracknell Gardens, NW3**
English novelist and essayist; lived here. He was the son of Leonard Huxley (q.v.), the brother of Sir Julian Sorell Huxley (q.v.) and the grandson of Thomas Henry Huxley (q.v.). From his early works in the 1920s he veered towards science fiction, most notably in *Brave New World* (1932), in which he created a disconcerting world of scientifically bred humans. Other novels include *Eyeless in Gaza* (1936), *After Many a Summer* (1939) and *Time Must Have a Stop* (1944). The plaque is shared with his father and brother. *English Heritage*

HUXLEY, Sir Julian Sorell (1887-1975). **31 Pond Street, Hampstead, NW3**
Private; **16 Bracknell Gardens, NW3** *English Heritage*
English biologist and first director-general of UNESCO (1946-8); lived in
Bracknell Gardens and in Pond Street 1943-75. He was professor of zoology at
King's College London (1925-7) and secretary of the Zoological Society of
London (1935-42) before becoming director-general of UNESCO. He pub-
lished many humanitarian and biological works. Sir Julian shares the Bracknell
Gardens plaque with his father Leonard Huxley (q.v.) and his brother Aldous
Huxley (q.v.). (Photograph, page 95)

HUXLEY, Leonard (1860-1933). **16 Bracknell Gardens, NW3**
The son of Thomas Henry Huxley (q.v.), he was a teacher at Charterhouse
School (1884-1901) and went on to become assistant editor (1901-16) and
editor (1916-33) of the *Cornhill Magazine*. The plaque is shared with his sons.
English Heritage

HUXLEY, Thomas Henry (1825-95). **38 Marlborough Place, NW8**
English biologist and humanist; lived here 1872-90. Having studied medicine,
he served in the Royal Navy, where he collected and studied marine life. He
became professor of natural history at the Royal School of Mines (1854-85). An
ardent supporter of Charles Darwin's (q.v.) theory of evolution, he wrote
several scientific and humanitarian works. He was the originator of the word
'agnostic', to describe his own religious attitude. *London County Council*

HYNDMAN, Henry Mayers (1842-1921). **13 Well Walk, NW3**
Socialist leader; lived here 1916-21 and died here. A dedicated follower of Karl
Marx's (q.v.) principles, he established the Socialist Democratic Federation
(1884) and influenced the Labour movement in Britain. This house was previously home to the poet and novelist John Masefield. *Greater London Council*

INNER LONDON EDUCATION SERVICE. Main entrance, County Hall, SE1

Based here from 1922, the ILES, sucessor to the London School Board (1870-1904), later became the Inner London Education Authority, taking on the responsibility from London County Council (1904-65). *Greater London Council*

INNES, John (1829-1904). Rutlish School, Watery Lane, SW20

Posthumous founder of the John Innes Horticultural Institution (1909-46); lived here from 1867. He bequeathed the bulk of his considerable fortune for the promotion of horticultural instruction and research. *Greater London Council*

IRELAND, John (1879-1962). 14 Gunter Grove, SW10

English composer; lived here. His varied works include song settings of poems by Hardy (q.v.), Housman (q.v.) and Masefield, piano and violin sonatas and orchestral preludes. *English Heritage*

IRVING, Edward (1792-1834). 4 Claremont Square, N1

Scottish clergyman; lived here. He began preaching in 1822, having first trained as a schoolmaster. Irving founded the Catholic Apostolic Church, after being convicted of heresy by the London presbytery in 1830. *Greater London Council*

IRVING, Sir Henry (John Henry Brodribb) (1838-1905). 15a Grafton Street, W1

English actor; lived here 1872-99. He first appeared on stage in Sunderland (1856), reaching London ten years later. By 1871 he had established himself at the Lyceum Theatre, where he became manager in 1878. He staged a series of Shakespearian productions, many with Ellen Terry (q.v.) as his leading lady. Irving was considered to be the greatest actor of his time and was the first to receive a knighthood. *London County Council*

Sir Henry Irving

IRVING, Washington (1783-1859). **8 Argyll Street, W1**
American short-story writer and essayist; lived here. His first published volume was *A History of New York* (1809), written under a pseudonym. *The Sketch Book* (1819-20) contained such tales as *Rip Van Winkle* and *The Legend of Sleepy Hollow*. He travelled extensively in Europe and was for a short time secretary to the US legation in London. He was also American ambassador to Spain 1842-6. *Greater London Council*

ISAACS, Rufus Daniel, First Marquess of Reading (1860-1935). **32 Curzon Street, W1**
English lawyer and statesman; lived and died here. He entered Parliament in 1904, becoming Solicitor-General in 1910, Lord Chief Justice 1913, British ambassador to the USA 1918-21, Viceroy of India 1921-6 and Foreign Secretary 1931. Isaacs was created a Marquess in 1926 and after retirement from politics pursued a business career, which included the presidency of ICI Ltd and the chairmanship of United Newspapers Ltd. *Greater London Council*

IVES, Charles Edward (1874-1954). **17 Half Moon Street, W1**
American composer; stayed here 1934. He composed five symphonies, including the *Holiday Symphony*, chamber music and many songs. He was awarded the Pulitzer prize in 1947. *Private*

JACKSON, John Hughlings (1835-1911). **3 Manchester Square, W1**
English surgeon and neurologist; lived here. He worked at the London Hospital 1874-94 and at the National Hospital for the Paralysed and Epileptic until 1906. *London County Council*

JACOBS, William Wymark (1863-1943). **Corner of Lower Road and Goldings Road, Loughton** *Loughton Town Council;* **15a Gloucester Gate, NW1** *English Heritage*

London-born short-story writer; lived on the Loughton site and at the Gloucester Gate address. His best-known tale is probably *The Monkey's Paw* (1902). In more recent times this was adapted for radio.

The plaque at Goldings Road, Loughton.

JACQUES, Hattie (Josephine Edwina Jacques) (1924-80). **67 Eardley Crescent, Earls Court, SW5**
English comic actress; lived here 1945-80. She first appeared on stage at the Players' Theatre in 1944, and her first film appearance was in *Green for Danger* in 1946. On radio she appeared in *ITMA* (1948-9) and *Educating Archie* (1950-4). A veteran of fourteen 'Carry On' films, she also appeared in a long-running series on television, co-starring with Eric Sykes. *Comic Heritage*

JAMES, Henry (1843-1916). **34 De Vere Gardens, W8**
American novelist; lived here 1886-1902. He lived in Europe from 1875. His many novels include *Washington Square* (1880), *Portrait of a Lady* (1881), *The Bostonians* (1886), *The Spoils of Poynton* (1897), *The Wings of a Dove* (1902), *The Ambassadors* (1903) and *The Golden Bowl* (1904). James became a British subject shortly before his death. This rectangular plaque is an unusual design for the LCC. *London County Council*

JAMES, Sid (Sidney) (1913-76). **35 Gunnersbury Avenue, Ealing, W5** *The British Comedy Society;* **Teddington Studios, Broom Road, Teddington** *Comic Heritage*
South African-born comedy actor; lived at the first address 1956-63; worked at the second. Resident in Britain from 1946, he appeared in many films, including most of the

The plaque in Ealing, W5.

'Carry On' series, and on television, first partnering Tony Hancock (q.v.) and later in *Citizen James* and *Bless This House* (1971-5).

JEFFERIES, Richard (1848-87). **20 Sydenham Park Road, SE26** *Lewisham Council;* **59 Footscray Road, Eltham, SE29** *Greater London Council*
English naturalist and writer; lived at both addresses. His books include *Wood Magic* (1881) and *Bevis* (1882).

JELLICOE, John Rushworth, First Earl (1859-1935). **25 Draycott Place, SW3**
British admiral and commander-in-chief of the Grand Fleet in the First World War; lived here. He fought at the battle of Jutland (1916) and became First Sea Lord (1916-17) and governor of New Zealand (1920-4). He was created an earl in 1925 and is buried in St Paul's Cathedral. *Greater London Council*

JEROME, Jerome K. (Klapka) (1859-1927). **91-4 Chelsea Gardens, Chelsea Bridge Road, SW1**
English humorist and writer; wrote *Three Men in a Boat* here, his best-known work (1889). Other works include *The Idle Thoughts of an Idle Fellow* (1889), *Three Men on the Bummel* (1900) and a play, *The Passing of the Third Floor Back* (1907). He also wrote his autobiography, *My Life and Times,* in 1926. *English Heritage*

JESSOP, G. L. (Gilbert Laird) (1874-1955). **3 Sunnydale Gardens, NW7**
English cricketer; lived here 1924-36. He played for Gloucestershire 1894-1914, during which time he captained the team for twelve years. Jessop appeared in seven test series, including two Australian tours. In 1907 he hit 191 runs in ninety minutes at the Hastings Festival. *Hendon Corporation*

JEWEL, Jimmy (1909-95). **Teddington Studios, Broom Road, Teddington**
English comedian and actor; worked here. His original music-hall act was in partnership with Ben Warriss (q.v.). In later life he appeared as a serious actor in many television plays. *Comic Heritage*

JINNAH, Mohammed Ali (Quaid i Azam) (1876-1948). **35 Russell Road, W14**
Statesman and founder of Pakistan; stayed here 1895. He studied at Lincoln's Inn and was called to the bar in 1897. Returning to India, he built a large practice. He joined the Indian National Congress and became president of the Indian Muslim League in 1913. He strongly advocated a separate Muslim state, opposing Gandhi's (q.v.) view, and when for this reason independence was given to Pakistan in 1947 Jinnah became the first governor-general. *London County Council*

JOHN, Augustus (Edwin) (1878-1961). **28 Mallord Street, SW3**
Welsh painter; had this house built. He studied in London and Paris. He is known chiefly for his portraits – many of his wife – and is remarkable for his fine draughtsmanship and characterisation, free handling and acute

responsiveness to beauty. *Greater London Council*

JOHNSON, Amy (1903-41). **Vernon Court, Hendon Way, NW2**
English aviator; lived here. She gained her pilot's licence in 1929 and was the first woman to fly alone from England to Australia (1930). She flew to Japan and back in 1931 and, alone, to Cape Town and back in 1932. The next year she crossed the Atlantic with her husband in thirty-nine hours. During the Second World War she joined the Air Transport Auxiliary and was probably shot down by 'friendly fire' over the Thames estuary. *English Heritage*

JOHNSON, Denis (*c*.1760-1833). **Acre House, 69-76 Long Acre, WC2**
Bicycle pioneer. In 1819 Denis Johnson made and sold the first 'Hobby-Horse' bicycle at premises formerly on this site. His invention was the forerunner of the modern bicycle. *Westminster City Council*

JOHNSON, Dr Samuel (1709-84). **8 Russell Street, WC2** *Greater London Council;* **17 Gough Square, EC4** *Royal Society of Arts;* **Johnson's Court, Fleet Street, EC4** *Corporation of the City of London;* **9 Gerrard Street, W1** *Westminster City Council.* See also **ESSEX STREET**
English lexicographer, critic, writer, wit and conversationalist. The four plaques respectively denote: the house where Johnson met Boswell (q.v.) in 1763; his home; the site of another home 1765-7; the address where he and Reynolds (q.v.) founded The Club. In 1735 he married a widow twenty years his senior, and they opened a school near Lichfield. This venture not being successful, they moved to London, with one of their pupils, David Garrick (q.v.), joining them (1737). Johnson earned his living by writing for *The Gentleman's Magazine* and published the poem *London* in 1738. Other works followed, and his famous *Dictionary* was published in 1755. He became the dominant figure in eighteenth-century London literary circles and in 1764 founded The Club (later the Literary Club) with his friends Sir Joshua Reynolds (q.v.), Oliver Goldsmith, Edmund Burke (q.v.), Charles James Fox (q.v.), David Garrick (q.v.) and James Boswell (q.v.), who was to become his biographer. The house in Gough Square is now a museum open to the public.

This plaque to Dr Samuel Johnson can be seen in Fleet Street, EC4.

JOHNSTON, Edward (1872-1944). **3 Hammersmith Terrace, W6**
Master calligrapher; lived here 1905-12. He taught at the Central School of Fine Arts and Crafts and at the Royal College of Art (1899-1912). His books were highly significant in the development of calligraphy. *Greater London Council*

JOINERS AND CEILERS, Worshipful Company of. Upper Thames Street, EC4
The hall of the Worshipful Company of Joiners and Ceilers stood on this site 1603-1796. *Corporation of the City of London*

JONES, Dr Ernest (1879-1958). **19 York Ter-race East, NW1**
Welsh psychoanalyst; lived here. A follower and friend of Sigmund Freud (q.v.), he founded the British Psycho-Analytical Society in 1913 and edited a journal of psychoanalysis 1920-33. He also wrote numerous works on the subject as well as a biography of Freud. *Greater London Council*

JORDAN, Dorothy (née Bland) (1762-1816). **30 Cadogan Place, SW1** *Greater London Council;* **Ashberry Cottage, Honor Oak Road, SE23** *Private*
Irish-born actress; lived at both addresses. In 1790 she became the mistress of the Duke of Clarence (later William IV; q.v.) and the affair lasted until 1811. During this time she bore him ten children. She retired from the stage in 1815.

JOYCE, James Augustine Aloysius (1882-1941). **28b Campden Grove, W8**
Irish-born novelist; stayed here in 1931. His most famous works are *Dubliners* (1914), *Portrait of the Artist as a Young Man* (1916), *Ulysses* (1922) and *Finnegan's Wake* (1939). Joyce lived mainly in Paris after the First World War. *English Heritage*

KALVOS, Andreas (1792-1869). 182 Sutherland Avenue, W9

Greek poet and patriot; lived here. He spent most of his life in Italy and England. He was secretary to Ugo Foscolo (q.v.), who greatly influenced his writings. Kalvos founded his own private school in Corfu and published twenty patriotic odes. His last years were spent in England. *English Heritage*

KARLOFF, Boris (1887-1969). 36 Forest Hill Road, SE23

Stage name of William Henry Pratt; born and spent his early years at this address. Karloff went to North America in 1908 and took up acting. After ten years in repertory and appearing in several silent films, he made his name as the monster in *Frankenstein* (1931). He afterwards appeared in many horror films and continued with stage appearances until his death. *English Heritage*

KARSAVINA, Tamara Platonovna (1885-1978). 108 Frognal, Hampstead, NW3

Russian-born ballerina; lived here. One of the original members of Diaghilev's company, she came to London in 1918 with her English husband. She became vice-president of the Royal Academy of Dancing (until 1955) and also wrote several books on ballet. *English Heritage*

KEATS, John (1795-1821). 87 Moorgate, EC2 *Corporation of the City of London;* Enfield Town station, booking hall *Private;* 7 Keats Parade, Church Street, Edmonton, N9 *Edmonton Council;* Keats House, Keats Grove, Hampstead, NW3 *Royal Society of Arts*

English poet. The four plaques denote, respectively, the site of his birthplace; the site of the house where he went to school; the site of the cottage where he

was apprentice to Thomas Hammod, surgeon; his home. He had his first sonnets published (1816) in *The Examiner.* By 1819-20 he had published *Lamia and Other Poems,* including 'To a Nightingale' and 'Ode on a Grecian Urn'. He sailed to Italy in 1820 but died from consumption in Rome at the age of twenty-five. His house in Hampstead is open to the public as a museum.

This plaque to John Keats is in Church Street, Edmonton, N9.

KEDLESTON, Marquess of. See **CURZON, George Nathaniel**

KEEPING, Charles (1924-88). **16 Church Road, Shortlands**
Artist and book illustrator; lived here. His pictures are to be found in a large range of books, particularly children's, including *Black Beauty*. He lived in this house from 1961 until his death. *Borough of Bromley*

KEITH, Sir Arthur (1866-1955). **17 Aubert Park, N5**
Scottish physiologist and anthropologist; lived here 1908-33. He wrote *Introduction to the Study of Anthropoid Apes* and works on human embryology and the theory of evolution. *Borough of Islington*

KELLY, Sir Gerald (Festus) (1879-1972). **117 Gloucester Place, W1**
British portrait painter; lived here 1916-72. He was a member of the Royal Fine Art Commission (1938-43), painted state portraits of the king and queen (1945) and received many European as well as British honours. *English Heritage*

KELVIN, William Thomson, First Baron (1824-1907). **15 Eaton Place, SW1**
Irish-born physicist; lived here. He introduced the absolute temperature scale, known as the Kelvin scale. He also invented and improved many electrical and telegraphic instruments, supervised the laying of the trans-Atlantic cable and improved ships' compasses. He was created a baron in 1892 and was buried in Westminster Abbey. *English Heritage*

KEMPE, Charles Eamer (1837-1907). **37 Nottingham Place, W1**
Stained-glass artist and manufacturer; lived and worked here. Much of Kempe's work (sometimes signed with a wheatsheaf) is in the fifteenth-century style. His facial drawing, intricate detail and use of pale and dark green are distinctive. *English Heritage*

KEMP-WELCH, Lucy (1869-1958). **20 High Street, Bushey**
English artist; lived here. She painted animals, especially horses, exhibited

The house where Lucy Kemp-Welch used to live in the High Street in Bushey.

annually at the Royal Academy from 1894 and was president of the Society of Animal Painters, formed in 1914. Her paintings can be found in galleries throughout the world, and her large wall panel entitled *Women at Work during the War* can be seen in the Royal Exchange. *Private*

KENNEDY, John Fitzgerald (1917-63). **14 Princes Gate, SW7**
Thirty-fifth president of the USA (1961-3); lived here as a young man. He studied in London after leaving Harvard and worked at the US embassy. The first Roman Catholic and the youngest person to be elected president, he sanctioned the unsuccessful Bay of Pigs invasion of Cuba (April 1961) and obtained the withdrawal of Russian missiles from the island (October 1962). He was assassinated while on a visit to Dallas. *Private*

KEYNES, John Maynard, First Baron Keynes (1883-1946). **46 Gordon Square, WC1**
English economist; lived here 1916-46. He was a member of the Bloomsbury Group (q.v.) and an advisor to the Treasury in both world wars. He led the British delegation that set up the International Monetary Fund (1944) and was one of the most influential economists of the twentieth century. His ideas shaped the post-war economy worldwide. *Greater London Council*

KHAN, Sir Syed Ahmed (1817-98). **21 Mecklenburgh Square, WC1**
Muslim reformer and scholar; lived here 1869-70. He obtained a grant from Britain in 1875 enabling him to found a college, which later became Aligarh University. As a result Muslims were able to receive the education required for the political administration of Pakistan. A second plaque here commemorates Richard Henry Tawney (q.v.). *English Heritage*

KING'S ARMS TAVERN. See MARINE SOCIETY

KING'S WARDROBE, site of the. 5 Wardrobe Place, EC4
Built in the fourteenth century as a private house and sold to Edward III to house his ceremonial robes, the establishment was later extended to hold the robes of all the king's ministers and Knights of the Garter. After its destruction in 1666 the wardrobe was re-established in the Savoy and later in Buckingham Street. *Corporation of the City of London*

KINGSLEY, Charles (1819-75). **56 Old Church Street, SW3**
English author and clergyman; lived here. His best-known novels are *Westward Ho!* (1855), *The Water Babies* (1863) and *Hereward the Wake* (1866). He was professor of modern history at Cambridge (from 1860) and chaplain to Queen Victoria (from 1873). The plaque, situated by the front door of the house, is not easily seen, owing to the high surrounding wall. *Greater London Council*

KINGSLEY, Mary Henrietta (1862-1900). **22 Southwood Lane, N6**
English traveller and ethnologist; lived here as a child. Niece of Charles Kingsley (q.v.), she travelled extensively in West Africa (1893-5) and published *Travels in West Africa* (1899) and *West African Studies* (1899), based on her experiences. She died of a fever while serving as a nurse in the second Boer War. *Greater London Council*

KIPLING, Rudyard (1865-1936). **43 Villiers Street, WC2**
English writer and poet; lived here 1889-91. Born in Bombay, he was educated in England, returned to India 1880-9 and, apart from a few years in America, lived mainly in England. His works, the most famous of which were for children, include *The Jungle Books* (1894-5), *Kim* (1901), *Just So Stories* (1902) and *Puck of Pook's Hill* (1906). He was awarded the Nobel prize for literature in 1907. *London County Council*

KIRK, Sir John (1847-1922). **32 John Street, WC1**
English philanthropist; lived here. Born in Leicestershire, he organised several charitable funds. He was known as the 'children's friend' because of his assistance to needy children, particularly those crippled. *Private*

KITCHENER, Horatio Herbert, First Earl Kitchener of Khartoum (1850-1916). **2 Carlton Gardens, SW1**
Irish-born soldier and statesman; lived here 1914-15. He served in the Sudan (1883-5), which he regained for Egypt by defeating the Dervishes at Omdurman (1898) and re-occupying Khartoum. He was chief-of-staff in South Africa (1900-2) during the Boer War, after which he was made a peer. Appointed Secretary for War in 1914, he was lost two years later aboard HMS *Hampshire*, which was mined off the Orkney islands. *London County Council*

KLEIN, Melanie (1882-1960). **42 Clifton Hill, NW8**
Austrian-born psychoanalyst; lived here. Influenced by Sigmund Freud (q.v.), she pioneered child psychoanalysis, making some surprising discoveries, and later extended her studies to adults. Her first paper was published in 1919, but her two main

Earl Kitchener of Khartoum.

113

works were not published until the end of her life. *Greater London Council*

KNEE, Frederick (1868-1914). **24 Sugden Road, SW11**
London Labour Party pioneer and housing reformer; lived here 1898-1901. He was born in Somerset but from 1890 worked in the printing trade in London. He wrote many articles for publication. *Greater London Council*

KNIGHT, John Peake (1828-86). **12 Bridge Street, SW1**
Inventor of the world's first traffic lights, erected here in 1868. He worked for the railway, becoming manager of the London, Brighton & South Coast Railway. In 1868 he was called in as an expert on railway signalling to erect the first road traffic signals at this junction. These were gaslit and, when unfortunately a fault occurred, the resulting explosion caused the death of a policeman. *Westminster City Council*

KNIGHT, Dame Laura (1877-1970) and **Harold** (1874-1961). **16 Langford Place, NW8**
English artists; lived here. Dame Laura specialised in oil paintings of ballet, circus and gypsy scenes, as well as watercolour landscapes. Harold was a portrait painter. *Greater London Council*

KNOX, Edmund (George) Valpy (1881-1971). **110 Frognal, Hampstead, NW3**
English humorous writer and poet, whose pen name was Evoe; lived here from 1945 until his death. He joined *Punch* magazine in 1921 and was editor 1932-49. He was also the author of a number of books. *Private*

KOKOSCHKA, Oskar (1886-1980). **Eyre Court, Finchley Road, NW8**
Austrian-born, naturalised British painter; lived here. He taught at the Dresden Academy of Art (1919-24) and travelled widely but settled in London in 1938 to escape the Nazis. His final years were spent in Switzerland. Kokoschka painted in a highly imaginative expressionist style and is noted for his portraits, landscapes and allegorical pictures. *English Heritage*

KOSSUTH, Louis (Lajos) (1802-94). **39 Chepstow Villas, W11**
Hungarian nationalist; stayed here. He was appointed provisional governor of Hungary after the overthrow of the Habsburg dynasty (1849). He fled to Turkey after defeat by Austria and Russia, afterwards moving to London and finally Turin, Italy. *London County Council*

KRISHNA MENON, Vengalil Krishnan (1896-1974). **57 Camden Square, NW1** Indian politician; lived here 1924-47. He came to Britain in 1924 and practised as a barrister. He was secretary of the India League from 1929, Indian High Commissioner in London from 1947, Indian delegate at the United Nations from 1952 and Indian defence minister 1957-62. During his last ten years in this house he was a St Pancras borough councillor. *Camden Borough Council*

KROPOTKIN, Prince Peter (1842-1921). **6 Crescent Road, Bromley** Russian anarchist, revolutionary and geographer; lived here. His geographical studies took him to Siberia, Finland and Sweden, but in 1872 he joined the extremist arm of a working men's association and was imprisoned. He escaped to England in 1876 and later moved to Switzerland and France. At Lyon he was again imprisoned for anarchism (1883-6). Returning to England, he settled until the Russian Revolution of 1917, when he returned to Moscow and retired from politics. Kropotkin published several works on anarchism, the French Revolution and other subjects. *English Heritage*

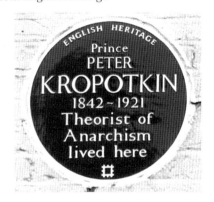

LABOUR PARTY. Caroone House, Farringdon Street, EC4
Site of the Congregational memorial hall, where the Labour Party was founded
on 27th February 1900. *Greater London Council*

LADYWELL MINERAL SPRING, site of. 148 Ladywell Road, SE13
This spring ran dry as a result of sewage works in the middle of the nineteenth
century. The water was regarded by local inhabit-
ants as especially helpful to persons with poor
eyes. *Lewisham Council*

LAMB, Charles (1775-1834). **2 Crown Of-
fice Row, Temple, EC4** *Private;* **64 Duncan
Terrace, N1** *London County Council;*
**Clarendon Cottage, 85 Chase Side, En-
field** *Private;* **Westwood Cottage, 89 Chase
Side, Enfield,** *Private;* **Lamb's Cottage,
Church Street, Edmonton, N9** *Private*

English essayist and critic. The five plaques
denote, respectively: the site of his birthplace; his
home; his home 1827-9; his home 1829-33; his
final home. He was born and grew up in the Inner Temple because his father
worked there as a clerk. A friend of Coleridge (q.v.), whom he met at Christ's
Hospital, he lived most of his life with his sister Mary, who in a fit of insanity
stabbed and killed their mother in 1796. For much of his life he worked at the
East India Company. His best-known essays were published under the pseudonym 'Elia' and appeared in book form in 1823. He and his sister are buried in
Edmonton churchyard.

*The unusual-shaped plaque to
Charles Lamb at 89 Chase Side,
Enfield.*

LAMBERT, Constant (1905-51). **197 Albany Street, NW1**
English composer, conductor, lyricist and critic; lived here 1947-51. For several years he worked as a conductor and composer for ballet, particularly at Sadler's Wells. Among his many compositions are the ballets *Romeo and Juliet* (1926), *Pomona* (1927), *Horoscope* (1938), the jazz composition *The Rio Grande* (1929) and the concerto *Summer's Last Will and Testament* (1936). He also published several books on music. *English Heritage*

LAMERIE, Paul de (1688-1751). **40 Gerrard Street, W1**
The king's silversmith; lived and worked in a house on this site 1738-51. *Westminster City Council*

LANE, Sir Hugh Percy (1876-1915). **8 South Bolton Gardens, SW5**
Director of the National Gallery of Ireland, 1914-15; lived here. He founded Dublin's first modern art collection and encouraged the artists Jack Butler Yeats (q.v.) and Sir William Orpen (q.v.). A year after becoming director of the National Gallery of Ireland he was drowned when the *Lusitania* went down. The house also has a plaque to Sir William Orpen. *Private*

LANG, Andrew (1844-1912). **1 Marloes Road, W8**
Scottish writer, historian and man of letters; lived here from 1876 until his death. His works include *Custom and Myth* (1884), *Myth, Ritual and Religion* (1887) and *The Making of Religion* (1898). He also wrote a *History of Scotland* (1899-1904), several books of verse and fairy stories for children. *London County Council*

LANGTRY, Lillie (Emilie Charlotte, née Le Breton) (1853-1929). **Cadogan Hotel, 21 Pont Street, SW1** *Greater London Council;* **8 Wilton Place, SW1** *Private*
British actress and society beauty; lived at both addresses. She was mistress to the Prince of Wales, later Edward VII. Lillie Langtry first appeared on stage in 1881, when she became known as the 'Jersey Lily', after her birthplace and a famous portrait of her by Millais (q.v.). In later life she was a noted racehorse owner. Married twice, she died at Monte Carlo. Both plaques show her birthdate as 1852 although record books give it as a year later. *Private*

LANSBURY, George (1859-1940). **39 Bow Road, E3**
English statesman; lived for twenty-three years in a house formerly on this site. He was a Poplar borough councillor 1903-40 and mayor of Poplar, an MP, minister and a privy councillor. *Bow Heritage*

LASKI, Harold Joseph (1893-1950). **5 Addison Bridge Place, W14**
British socialist and political theorist; lived

The plaque at Wilton Place, SW1, to Lillie Langtry.

The plaque on this wall in EC4 commemorates Laurence Pountney Church and Corpus Christi College, which were destroyed in the Great Fire of London.

here 1926-50. After lecturing in the USA he became professor of political science at the London School of Economics (1926) and chairman of the Labour Party 1945-6. He published *A Grammar of Politics* (1925), *The American Presidency* (1940) and other works. *Greater London Council*

LAUDER, Sir Harry (1870-1950). **46 Longley Road, Tooting, SW17**
Stage name of Hugh MacLennon, Scottish music-hall singer and comedian; lived here 1903-11. He was popular on the London stage and worldwide. His songs 'Roamin' in the Gloamin'' and 'I Belong to Glasgow' were his trademarks, the former being taken as a title for his memoirs (1928). Lauder was knighted in 1919. *Greater London Council*

LAUGHTON, Charles (1899-1962). **15 Percy Street, W1**
English-born stage and film actor; lived here 1928-31. After mainly Shakespearian stage performances, he turned to films, his most notable roles being the title part in *Henry VIII* (1932), for which he received an Oscar, Captain Bligh in *Mutiny on the Bounty* (1935) and Quasimodo in *The Hunchback of Notre Dame* (1939). He became an American citizen in 1950. *English Heritage*

LAURENCE POUNTNEY CHURCH AND CORPUS CHRISTI COLLEGE. Laurence Pountney Hill, EC4
This church and college were destroyed in the Great Fire of 1666 and never rebuilt. Sir John de Poulteney, who was four times lord mayor of London, lived near here in the fourteenth century, and the name was probably derived from this family association. *Corporation of the City of London*

LAVERY, Sir John (1856-1941). **5 Cromwell Place, SW7**
British artist; lived here 1899-1940. Born in Belfast, he was a popular Edward-

ian society portrait painter. *Greater London Council*

LAW, Andrew Bonar (1858-1923). **24 Onslow Gardens, SW7**
Canadian-born British statesman; lived here. He made a fortune in Scotland
before entering Parliament. He succeeded Balfour (q.v.) as Unionist leader in
1911 and became Colonial Secretary 1915-6, Chancellor of the Exchequer
1916-18 and Lord Privy Seal 1919-21 in Lloyd George's (q.v.) coalition.
Bonar Law was prime minister October 1922 to May 1923 but retired through
ill health. *London County Council*

LAWRENCE, (Arabella) Susan (1871-1947). **44 Westbourne Terrace, W2**
Social reformer and politician; lived here. She was a Labour MP 1923-4 and
1926-31, parliamentary secretary to the Ministry of Health 1929-31 and
chairman of the Labour Party from 1930. A member of the London County
Council 1910-28, she served as deputy chairman 1925-6. *English Heritage*

LAWRENCE, D. H. (David Herbert) (1885-1930). **1 Byron Villas, Vale of
Health, NW3**
English novelist and poet; lived here 1915. As many of his books were
sexually explicit, his publishers were constantly coming into conflict with the
obscenity laws. His first success was *Sons and Lovers* (1913). Later novels
included *Women in Love* (1921) and *Lady Chatterley's Lover* (1928), the last
not being published in unexpurgated form in the United Kingdom until 1960.
Greater London Council

**LAWRENCE, John Laird Mair,
First Baron** (1811-79). **Southgate
House, Michenden School, High
Street, N14**
English administrator; lived here 1861-
3. Appointed lieutenant-governor of
the Punjab, he successfully put down a
rebellion and recaptured Delhi. He was
appointed governor-general of India
in 1864 until his return to England five
years later. He was chairman of the
London School Board 1870-3, and re-
mained in parliament until his death. He was buried in Westminster Abbey.
Private

LAWRENCE, Philip (1949-95). **St George's School, Maida Vale, W9**
Headmaster of St George's School. While attempting to defend one of his
pupils from an attacker he was stabbed to death in the playground. *Private*

LAWRENCE, T. E. (Thomas Edward) (1888-1935). **14 Barton Street,
SW1**
British soldier, adventurer and writer; lived here. After leaving Oxford he
worked as a member of the British Museum archaeological team (1911-14)
under Sir Flinders Petrie (q.v.) in Egypt. During the First World War he was
with army intelligence in North Africa and joined the Arab revolt against the
Turks, leading guerrilla operations and earning his nickname 'Lawrence of
Arabia'. His book *The Seven Pillars of Wisdom* (1926) described his experiences. Turning his back on public acclaim, he joined the RAF in 1922 under an
assumed name. He died in a motorcycle accident. A film was made of his life,
starring Peter O'Toole. *Greater London Council*

LEAR, Edward (1812-88). **Bowman's Mews, Seven Sisters Road, N1**
Borough of Islington; **30 Seymour Street, W1** *London County Council*
English humorist and artist; was born and lived near Bowman's Mews; lived in
Seymour Street. He travelled extensively, making sketches and paintings of
birds, animals and landscapes, which he published in travel books. His 'nonsense' verses were first published anonymously in 1846 under the title *A Book
of Nonsense.* Later 'nonsense' books were published 1870-6. His last years
were spent in Italy.

LECKY, William Edward Hartpole (1838-1903). **38 Onslow Gardens,
SW7**
Irish historian and essayist; lived and died here. His work *A History of the Rise
and Influence of the Spirit of Rationalism in Europe* (1865) argued that rationalism and tolerance were essential elements in a civilised society. It made him
famous and was followed by other works, including *A History of England in the
Eighteenth Century* (1878-90) and the essay collections *Democracy and Liberty* (1896) and *The Map of Life* (1899). He was MP for Dublin University
(1895) and a privy councillor in 1897. *London County Council*

LEE, Richard Nelson (1806-72). **67 Shrubland Road,
Hackney, E8**
Actor, theatre manager and pantomime writer; lived
here between 1851 and 1872. He is credited with
having written over two hundred pantomimes.
Borough of Hackney

LEIGH, Vivien (1913-67). **54 Eaton Square,
SW1**
Stage name of Vivien Mary Hartley, English actress and film star; lived here. She received Oscars
for her performances in the films *Gone with the Wind*
(1939) and *A Streetcar Named Desire* (1951). Among
her other films were starring roles in *Lady Hamilton* (1941) and *Anna Karenina*
(1948). On stage she appeared frequently with Laurence Olivier (to whom she was
married 1940-60), particularly in Shakespearian dramas. *English Heritage*

LEIGHTON, Frederic, First Baron Leighton of Stretton (1830-96). **12
Holland Park Road, W14**
English painter and sculptor; lived and died here. He travelled extensively
in Europe and specialised in classical Greek subjects. Many of his paintings were reproduced and became bestsellers in Victorian Britain. Made
president of the Royal Academy of Arts in 1878, he became a peer in 1896.
His home, Leighton House, is now a museum open to
the public. *London County Council*

LE MESURIER, John (1912-83). **Barons
Keep, Hammersmith, W14**
English comedy actor; lived here 1966-77. Born
in Bedford, he trained for the stage and worked
in repertory, later appearing in countless films.
His most notable part was in television, as Ser-
geant Wilson in the *Dad's Army* comedy series,
which ran for nine years from 1968. He was
married twice, his first wife being the comedy
actress Hattie Jacques (q.v.). *The Dead Comics Society*

LENIN, Vladimir Ilyich Ulyanov (1870-1924). **Site of 16 Percy Circus, WC1**
Russian revolutionary leader; stayed at 16 Percy Circus 1905. A follower of Karl Marx (q.v.) and Friedrich Engels (q.v.), he became the first leader of the USSR. He was sent to Siberia for spreading revolutionary propaganda 1895-1900 and was active in the unsuccessful 1905 revolution. Prior to settling in Switzerland, he stayed at this address in London. Upon returning to Russia in 1917, he became leader of the revolution that installed communism in what became known as the Soviet Union or USSR. After his death his embalmed

body was placed for public view in a specially built mausoleum in Red Square, Moscow. *Private*

LENO, Dan (1860-1904). **56 Akerman Road, SW9**
Stage name of George Galvin, English comedian and music-hall celebrity; lived here 1898-1901. He began his career at the age of four, singing in public houses, and graduated to clog dancing before being invited into pantomime some ten years later. He is best remembered for his performances as pantomime 'dames'. *London County Council*

LETHABY, William Richard (1857-1931). **20 Calthorpe Street, WC1** *Greater London Council;* **Central School of Arts and Crafts, Southampton Row, WC1** *London County Council*
English architect and teacher; lived in Calthorpe Street 1880-91; was principal of the art school 1896-1911. He worked 1877-87 for R. Norman Shaw (q.v.). In 1891 he became associated with Philip Webb (q.v.) and the Society for the Protection of Ancient Buildings. With George Frampton (q.v.) he founded, and became joint first principal of, the Central School of Arts and Crafts (1896).

LEWIS, John and **John Spedan. Grange Gardens, Templewood Avenue, NW3**
Respectively, silk mercer and founder of the John Lewis partnership; lived 1888-1929 in Spedan Tower, formerly on this site. John Spedan Lewis was the elder son of John Lewis. *Hampstead Plaque Fund*

LEWIS, Percy Wyndham (1882-1957). **61 Palace Gardens Terrace, W8**
English artist and writer; lived here. He was a pioneer of Vorticism (a modernistic style of painting) with Gaudier-Brzeska (q.v.) and C. R. W. Nevinson (1889-1946). His literary works include the novels *Tarr* (1918) and *The*

Childermass (1928), autobiographies and essays. He was editor of *Blast*, the literary and artistic magazine. *Greater London Council*

LEYBOURNE, George (1842-84). **136 Englefield Road, N1**
Stage name of Joseph Saunders, music-hall artist; lived and died here. He became extremely popular through his songs 'Champagne Charlie' (which became his nickname) and 'The Daring Young Man on the Flying Trapeze'. He introduced his daughter, Florrie, to the stage, and she later married Albert Chevalier (q.v.). *Greater London Council*

LINACRE, Thomas (*c*.1460-1524). **Private road (rear of GPO)**, **Knightrider Street, EC4**
English physician to kings Henry VII and VIII; lived in a house on this site. He was the founder and first president of the Royal College of Physicians (1518). The plaque, in a poor condition, is not easily accessible. *Corporation of the City of London*

LIND, Jenny (Madame Goldschmidt) (1820-87). **189 Brompton Road, SW7**
Swedish soprano; lived here 1876-86. She was nicknamed the 'Swedish Nightingale' and was internationally popular. In later life she founded and endowed many musical scholarships in both England and Sweden. *London County Council*

LINDSEY, Reverend Thomas Theophilus (1723-1808). See **ESSEX STREET**

LINNAEAN SOCIETY (1820-57). See **BANKS, Sir Joseph**
A society of botanists, taking its name from the Swedish botanist Carl Linnaeus (1707-78).

LINNELL, John (1792-1882). **Old Wyldes, North End, Hampstead, NW3** *Greater London Council;* **37 Woolstone Road, SE23** *Greater London Council*
English artist, engraver and sculptor; lived at both addresses. A patron of William Blake (q.v.), who is commemorated on the same plaques, he painted portraits of many well-known persons and particularly excelled at landscapes, mainly of Surrey scenes. He was also a friend of Samuel Palmer (q.v.). The two oval plaques are similar in design.

LIPTON, Sir Thomas Johnstone (1850-1931). **Oakdale, Osidge, East Barnet, N14**
Scottish entrepreneur and philanthropist; lived here. In his youth he worked on plantations in the USA. Back in Scotland, he opened his first grocery shop in 1870, rapidly expanding the business into a chain and becoming a millionaire by the age of thirty. In connection with his business, he purchased tea plantations and rubber estates and was benevolent in his management of them. A keen yachtsman, he made several unsuccessful attempts to win the 'America's Cup'. *Borough of Barnet*

LISTER, Lord Joseph (1827-1912). **12 Park Crescent, W1**
English surgeon; lived here. He was the founder of antiseptic surgery (1867) and a professor of surgery in both Glasgow (1859) and Edinburgh (1869). He later became professor of clinical surgery at King's College Hospital, London (1895-1900), and president of the Royal Society during the same period. A statue of him can be found in nearby Portland Place. *London County Council*

LISZT, Franz (Ferenc) (1811-86). **18 Great Marlborough Street, W1**
Hungarian composer and pianist; stayed in a house on this site, 1840 and 1841. A child prodigy, he was sent to study in Vienna, after which he toured Europe, settling in Paris (1823). In 1848 he went to Weimar, where he directed operas and concerts, and he subsequently divided his time between Weimar, Rome and Budapest. He was a virtuoso pianist with many admirers, especially women (the child of one of his liaisons, Cosima, married Richard Wagner). During his career he visited London several times. His compositions include many orchestral pieces, symphonies and masses. *The Liszt Society*

LITTLE TICH. See **RELPH, Harry**

LIVINGSTONE, David (1813-73). **Livingstone Cottage, Hadley Green, Barnet**
Scottish-born explorer; lived here 1857. Working as a missionary from 1840 in Bechuanaland, he travelled further north (1852-6), discovering Lake Ngami and the Victoria Falls. In 1858 the British government sent him on an expedition to explore the Zambesi. He made many discoveries, but his wife died on the trip. Returning again to Africa in 1866, he searched for the source of the Nile and, amid many hardships, made further discoveries. Henry Morton Stanley (q.v.) searched for and finally met him in Ujiji in 1871. During his travels, Livingstone charted much of the then unknown areas of central Africa and did much to foster trade. He died in what is now Zambia but was brought home and is buried in Westminster Abbey. *Private*

15 Lombard Street, EC3, where a plaque commemorates the site of Lloyds Coffee House.

LLOYD, Edward (1815-90). **William Morris Gallery, Forest Road, E17**
English newspaper publisher; lived here 1857-85. He issued *Lloyd's Weekly London Newspaper* from 1842 and bought the *Daily Chronicle* in 1876. The plaque is shared with William Morris (q.v.), who lived here before him. *Borough of Walthamstow*

LLOYD, Marie (1870-1922). **55 Graham Road, E8**
Stage name of Matilda Alice Victoria Wood, English music-hall entertainer; lived here. Her famous songs include 'Oh Mr Porter'. 'My Old Man Said Follow the Van' and 'I'm One of the Ruins that Cromwell Knocked About a Bit'. *Greater London Council*

LLOYD-GEORGE OF DWYFOR, David, First Earl (1863-1945). **3 Routh Road, SW18**
Welsh Liberal politician; lived here. He was Chancellor of the Exchequer 1908-15 and prime minister 1916-22. He introduced old-age pensions, health and unemployment benefits and played a major role in the Versailles peace treaty after the First World War. *English Heritage*

LLOYDS COFFEE HOUSE, site of. 15 Lombard Street, EC3
Established by Edward Lloyd; stood here 1691-1785. It became a meeting place for businessmen, some of whom developed an insurance company devoted to shipping. Over the years this expanded to become the present Lloyds insurance company (underwritten by the Lloyds' 'names') and bank. *Corporation of the City of London*

LONDON AND GREENWICH RAILWAY. Deptford Station, Deptford High Street, SE8
The plaque commemorates the first railway line in London, opened in 1836. This is also the oldest London station still in use. *Private*

LONDON COUNTY COUNCIL. See **COUNTY HALL**

A nineteenth-century engraving of the London & Greenwich Railway.

LONDON HOUSE. 171 Aldersgate Street, EC1
The home of the Bishops of London after the Restoration; destroyed by fire 1766. *Corporation of the City of London*

LONDON SALVAGE CORPS. 61 Watling Street, EC4
Set up in 1866; had its headquarters here 1907-60. In 1866 the responsibility for fighting fires in London was in the hands of the Metropolitan Board of Works, who gave insurance companies the right to establish a separate salvage force to attend fires. When first founded, the London Salvage Corps had its office in Watling Street. From 1961 it was in Aldersgate Street until disbanded in 1984, its duties being continued by the London Fire Brigade. *Private*

LOPEZ-PUMAREJO, Alfonso (1886-1959). 33 Wilton Crescent, SW1
Colombian statesman; lived and died here. Twice president of Colombia, he lived here whilst ambassador to the Court of St James's. *Private*

LORD, Thomas (1755-1832). Dorset Square, NW1
English sportsman; laid out his first cricket ground in Dorset Square 1787. The site became the home of the Marylebone Cricket Club (MCC). The present site in St John's Wood was established in 1814. A second plaque, commemorating the

Dorset Square, NW1, was the original site of Thomas Lord's cricket ground, home of the Marylebone Cricket Club. The left-hand plaque commemorates the MCC; the right-hand one is to Lord.

bicentenary of the MCC, was placed alongside in 1987. *Marylebone Cricket Club*

LOUDON, John Claudius (1783-1843), and his wife **Jane** (1807-59). **3 Porchester Terrace, W2**
Scottish horticulturists and writers; lived here. The plaque states that 'their horticultural work gave new beauty to London squares'. J. C. Loudon founded the *Gardener's Magazine* (1826-43) and the *Architectural Magazine* (1834) and compiled an *Encyclopaedia of Gardening* (1822) and an *Encyclopaedia of Cottage, Farm and Villa Architecture and Furniture* (1833). His wife's publications, however, were to save them from their creditors. In addition to writing for women on the subject of gardening, she was the first editor of *The Ladies' Companion; At Home and Abroad.* Whilst living here, J. C. Loudon designed the prototype semi-detached house. *London County Council*

LOVELACE, Augusta Ada, Countess of (1815-52). **12 St James's Square, SW1**
English mathematician and writer; lived here. The daughter of Lord Byron, she became a friend of the computer pioneer, Charles Babbage (q.v.). Her translation of L. F. Menabree's article on Babbage's 'Analytical Engine' contains many useful explanatory notes she wrote herself. The computer language 'ADA' is named after her. *English Heritage*

LOW, Sir David (1891-1963). **Melbury Court, Kensington High Street, W8**
British political cartoonist; lived here. Born in New Zealand, he joined the *Evening Standard* in 1927, having previously worked on *The Star*. From 1950 he worked for the *Daily Herald* and from 1953 for *The Guardian*. His cartoon character 'Colonel Blimp' made him world-famous. *English Heritage*

LOWE, Arthur (1915-82). **2 Maida Avenue, W2**
English comedy actor; lived here 1969-82. He was best known for the part of Captain Mainwaring in the television series *Dad's Army* (1968-77). He made

his first stage appearance in 1945 after serving with the entertainment division in the services. His film debut was in 1948, and he appeared in various stage shows during the 1950s. Television was his forte, and he appeared in many episodes of *Coronation Street* before *Dad's Army* went into production. *The Dead Comics Society*

LUBBOCK, Sir John. See **AVEBURY, Baron**

LUCAN, Arthur (1887-1954). **11 Forty Lane, Wembley**
Stage name of the comedian and entertainer Arthur Towle; lived here. He characterised 'Old Mother Riley' and with his wife, Kitty McShane, appeared on stage, screen and radio. Their popularity resulted in a series of films, but after the Second World War the partnership broke up, and Lucan continued performing alone. *Greater London Council*

LUDGATE, site of. Ludgate Hill, EC4
The original London gate was near this spot. Rebuilt in the early thirteenth century, it was finally demolished in 1760. *Corporation of the City of London*

LUGARD, Baron Frederick John Dealtry (1858-1945). **51 Rutland Gate, Hyde Park, SW7**
British colonial administrator; lived here 1912-19. After serving in the army (1878-89), he worked in Uganda, facilitating its conversion to a protectorate (1890). He was high commissioner for Northern Nigeria (1900-7) and governor of Hong Kong (1907-12). Returning to Nigeria he was governor-general 1914-19. During the period 1922-36 he served on the permanent mandate commission of the League of Nations. *Greater London Council*

LUTYENS, Sir Edwin Landseer (1869-1944). **13 Mansfield Street, W1**
English architect; lived here from 1923. His style showed Renaissance, classical and vernacular influences, and his work includes the Cenotaph in London, the Viceroy's House, New Delhi, the fountains in Trafalgar Square and country houses in the Arts and Crafts style, such as Castle Drogo, Devon (1910-30). The plaque is shared with J. L. Pearson (q.v.), who lived here before him. *London County Council*

LYELL, Sir Charles (1797-1875). **73 Harley Street, W1**
Scottish geologist; lived in a house on this site 1854-75. His *Principles of Geology* (1830-3) changed the discipline of geology by suggesting that the forces that created the landscape might still be in operation – a theory later expounded by Charles Darwin (q.v.). The plaque is shared with W. E. Gladstone (q.v.). *London County Council*

LYNCH, Bradley (1972-88). **Bradley Lynch Court, Morpeth Street, E2**

The plaque reads: 'Bradley Lynch was a local youth who died at the age of sixteen years from cancer. Before his death he worked selflessly and very hard to raise funds for the fight against the disease from which he was suffering. His courage and sacrifice for others are an inspiration to all people, especially the young.' *Camden Town Neighbourhood*

MACAULAY, Dame (Emilie) Rose (1881-1958). **Hinde House, 11-14 Hinde Street, W1**
English novelist; lived and died here. Between 1906 and 1918 she published nine novels, largely Victorian in style. Her *Potterism* (1920) established her form, and she produced many more successful novels in the following years. Her last and best-known book was the award-winning *The Towers of Trebizond* (1956). She also published travel books. *English Heritage*

MACAULAY, Thomas Babington, First Baron Macaulay (1800-59). **Atkins Buildings, Queen Elizabeth College, Campden Hill, W8** *London County Council;* **The Pavement, Clapham Common, SW4** *London County Council*
English historian, poet and politician; lived in Clapham; died in Campden Hill. He was Secretary of War 1839-41. His five-volume *History of England* was published 1848-61, and he was a contributor to the *Edinburgh Review* for nearly twenty years. He shares the Clapham plaque with his father Zachary (q.v.).

The plaque at Campden Hill, W8.

MACAULAY, Zachary (1768-1838). **5 The Pavement, Clapham Common, SW4**
English philanthropist; lived here. He was governor of Sierra Leone 1793-9 and secretary to the Sierra Leone Company 1799-1808. The editor of the *Christian Observer* (1802-16), a paper devoted to the abolition of the slave trade, he also helped form an anti-slavery society and did much for the abolitionist cause. He was the father of Thomas Babington Macaulay (q.v.), with whom he shares this plaque. *London County Council*

MacCOLL, Ewan (1915-89). **35 Stanley Avenue, Beckenham**
Pseudonym of James Miller, English songwriter, singer, playwright and socialist; lived here. He worked with Joan Littlewood in the establishment of the theatre workshop and was influential in the British folk-music revival. *Borough of Bromley*

MACDONALD, George (1824-1905). **25 Upper Mall, Hammersmith, W6**
Scottish poet and novelist; lived here 1867-77. Professor at Bedford College, London, he was the author of the poetry collections *Within and Without* (1856) and *Poems* (1857) and of the novels *David Elginbrod* (1863) and *Lilith* (1895). He is

best known for his children's books, which include *The Princess and the Goblin* (1872) and *The Princess and Curdie* (1883). *Private*

MACDONALD, James Ramsay (1866-1937). **103 Frognal, Hampstead, NW3** *Hampstead Plaque Fund;* **9 Howitt Road, Hampstead, NW3** *London County Council*
Scottish politician; lived at both addresses (Howitt Road 1916-25 and Frognal 1925-37). He became leader of the Labour Party (1911-14 and 1922-31) and Britain's first Labour prime minister (January-October 1924 and 1929-35 – from 1931 as leader of the coalition government). The plaque in Frognal is shared with Donald Ogden Stewart (q.v.).

MacDOWELL, Patrick (1799-1870). **34 Wood Lane, N6**
British sculptor; lived here. He was elected to the Royal Academy of Arts in 1846. Among his most notable works are *Girl Going to the Bath* (1841) and the *Europa* group on the Albert Memorial. *Private*

MacFARREN, Sir George Alexander (1813-87). **20 Hamilton Terrace, NW8**
English composer and teacher; lived and died here. He was a professor at the Royal Academy of Music, becoming principal in 1876. His works include the overture *Chevy Chase* (1836), the cantatas *Lenora* (1851), *May Day* (1856) and *Christmas* (1859), and several operas. Failing eyesight led to his eventual blindness, but he continued to compose by dictation and also to lecture at the Royal and London Institutions. He was knighted in 1883. Another plaque commemorating William Strang (q.v.) can be found at this same address. *Incorporated Society of Musicians*

MACKENZIE, Sir James, FRS (1853-1925). **17 Bentinck Street, W1**
Scottish physician and cardiologist; lived here 1907-11. He moved to London in 1907, having qualified as a doctor in Edinburgh in 1882. Mackenzie published two works on his studies of heart disease, which, coincidentally, was to be the cause of his own death. *College of General Practitioners*

MACKENZIE, Sir Morell (1837-92). **742 High Road, Leytonstone, E11** *Leyton Urban District Ratepayers Association;* **32 Golden Square, W1** *Westminster City Council*
English physician and throat specialist; born in Leytonstone. He founded the first throat hospital in Golden Square in 1865 and was knighted in 1887.

MACKLIN, Charles (*c.*1697-1797). **See BOW STREET**
Irish actor who first appeared in London at Drury Lane in 1773. One of the finest actors of his day, he was at his best in his portrayal of Shylock in *The Merchant of Venice.* He wrote several farces and comedies, but not all of these were published. He last performed at Covent Garden in 1789.

MacMILLAN, Douglas (1884-1969). **15 Ranelagh Road, SW1**
Founder of Macmillan Cancer Relief; lived here. Macmillan nurses tend and support cancer patients and their families. *English Heritage*

MacNEICE, Louis (1907-63). **52 Canonbury Park South, N1**
Irish poet; lived here 1947-52. He was a left-wing poet, a contemporary of Sir Stephen Spender and W. H. Auden. His volumes of poetry include *Blind Fireworks* (1929), *Autumn Journal* (1939), *Collected Poems* (1949) and *Autumn Sequel* (1954). He also wrote several plays for radio, notably *The Dark Tower* (1947) and a verse translation of Goethe's *Faust*. *English Heritage*

MADOX BROWN, Ford. See **BROWN, Ford Madox**

MADOX FORD, Ford. See **FORD, Ford Madox**

MALLARMÉ, Stéphane (1842-98). **6 Brompton Square, SW3**
French poet of the Symbolist group; stayed here 1863. He visited England on several occasions and taught English in Paris. He translated Poe's *The Raven* (1875) into French, and his own work inspired composers and artists, including Debussy and Manet. *London County Council*

MALLON, Dr James Joseph, CH (1874-1961). **Toynbee Hall, Commercial Street, E1**
Social reformer; lived here. He was the warden of Toynbee Hall 1919-54, served on numerous committees during peace and wartime and was on the board of governors of the BBC 1937-9 and 1941-6. He published several booklets and contributed to newspapers. *Greater London Council*

MALONE, Edmond (1741-1812). **40 Langham Street, W1**
Irish writer and editor of *Shakespeare* periodical; lived here 1779 -1812. He edited an eleven-volume Shakespeare edition (1790). *London County Council*

MANBY, Charles (1804-84). **60 Westbourne Terrace, W2**
English civil engineer; lived here 1870-6. He and his father, George (1765-1854), designed and supervised the building of the first iron sea-going steamship (1822). Charles settled in London in 1835. Among his achievements were the planning of the Suez Canal and involvement in the staging of the Great Exhibition of 1851. He was also business manager of the Haymarket and Adelphi theatres. *London County Council*

MANNING, Cardinal Henry Edward (1808-92). **22 Carlisle Place, SW1**
English Roman Catholic priest; lived here. Archdeacon of Chichester (1840), he converted to Rome in 1851, becoming Archbishop of Westminster in 1865 and cardinal in 1875. He was prominent in the movements of temperance and benevolence. *London County Council*

MANSBRIDGE, Albert (1876-1952). **198 Windsor Road, Ilford**
English educationalist; lived here. He was active in the promotion of adult education. In addition to being the founder (1903) and general secretary (1905) of the Workers' Educational Association, he was a founder of the National Central Library (1916) and the author of a biography of Margaret McMillan (q.v.). *Greater London Council*

MANSFIELD, Katherine (Katherine Mansfield Beauchamp) (1888-1923). **17 East Heath Road, NW3**
New Zealand-born novelist and short-story writer; lived here. She lived a bohemian lifestyle, and her three-week relationship with her first husband and subsequent miscarriage of another man's child are recalled in *In a German Pension* (1911). She and her second husband, John Middleton Murry (q.v.), inspired the two central characters of D. H. Lawrence's (q.v.) *Women in Love.* Her notable works include *Prelude* (1917) and *Bliss and Other Stories* (1920). Her letters were published posthumously. The plaque is shared with her second husband. *Greater London Council*

MANSON, Sir Patrick (1844-1922). **50 Welbeck Street, W1**
Scottish-born doctor; lived here. He is noted for his pioneering work with Sir Ronald Ross (q.v.), including the discovery that the malaria parasite is carried by the mosquito (1877). He worked for many years in China and Hong Kong, where he founded a school of medicine, and he co-founded the London School of Tropical Medicine (1899). *Greater London Council*

MARCONI, Guglielmo Marchese (1874-1937). **71 Hereford Road, W2** *London County Council;* **British Telecom Building, Newgate Street, EC1** *Private*

Italian physicist and inventor; lived in Hereford Road; made his first public wireless trasmission from the second site (1896). He was the pioneer of radio. His first successful transmission was in Italy in 1895 and in 1898 he transmitted signals across the English Channel. By 1901 he had established radio communication across the Atlantic Ocean. Marconi shared the Nobel prize for physics in 1909.

The plaque on the British Telecom Building in EC1.

MARINE SOCIETY. Change Alley, EC3
The Marine Society was founded in 1756 in the King's Arms Tavern, on this site. The society, which still operates from Lambeth, was formed to promote careers at sea for boys, especially those living in needy circumstances. *Private*

This plaque in Change Alley, EC3, commemorates the Marine Society, founded on this site in 1756.

131

MARRYAT, Captain Frederick (1792-1848). **3 Spanish Place, W1**
English naval officer and novelist; lived here towards the end of his life. He commenced his naval career as a midshipman in 1806 and rose to command several vessels, retiring in 1830. Among his many novels are *Frank Mildmay* (1829), *Peter Simple* (1834) and *Mr Midshipman Easy* (1836), but his best-known work is perhaps his children's book *Children of the New Forest* (1847). A plaque to George Grossmith (q.v.) can be found at the same address. *London County Council*

MARSDEN, William (1796-1867). **65 Lincoln's Inn Fields, WC2**
English surgeon; lived here. He was the founder of the Royal Free and Royal Marsden hospitals and the Brompton Cancer Hospital. *Greater London Council*

JOHN MARSHALL
founder of Marshall's Charity lived at his mansion house near this spot until his death in 1631 as did his father before him
Marshall's Charity had its offices here until 1967

MARSHALL, John (died 1631). **Mollison House, 9 Newcomen Street, SE1**
English philanthropist; lived near this site. A wealthy English land-owner, he bequeathed land and property which formed the basis of Marshall's Charity. Still in existence, it provides for the restoration of churches and had its offices on this site until 1967. *Private*

MARVELL, Andrew (1621-78). **Outside wall, Waterlow Park, High Street, Highgate, N6**
English poet; lived on this site. This hundred-year old, worn rectangular copper plaque reads: 'Four feet below this spot is the stone step formerly the entrance to the cottage in which lived Andrew Marvel, poet, wit and satirist, colleague with John Milton in the foreign or Latin secretaryship during the Commonwealth, and for about twenty years MP for Hull. Born at Winestead, Yorkshire, 31st March 1621. Died in London, 18th August 1678, and buried in the church of St Giles-in-the-Fields.' *London County Council*

Andrew Marvell

MARX, Karl (1818-83). **28 Dean Street, W1** *Greater London Council;* **101-8 Maitland Park Road, NW3**, *Camden Borough Council*
German social, economic and political theorist; lived in Dean Street 1850-6, lived and died in a house on the second site 1875-83. His *Das Kapital* (1867-95) was the most influential work in the development of communism. Marx was a life-long friend of Friedrich Engels (q.v.), with whom he worked in London, having been expelled from Prussia in 1849. Together, Marx and Engels wrote *The Communist Manifesto* (1848). Marx's imposing tombstone can be seen in Highgate Cemetery.

ERECTED BY CAMDEN LONDON BOROUGH COUNCIL
KARL MARX
1818-1883
PHILOSOPHER
Lived and Died in a House on this Site
1875-1883

MARYLEBONE CRICKET CLUB (MCC). Dorset Square, NW1
This plaque was unveiled on the 1st June 1987 to

The plaque in Maitland Park Road, NW3.

mark the bicentenary of the first cricket match played at Dorset Fields. A second plaque commemorates Thomas Lord (q.v.). *Private*

MASARYK, Thomas Garrigue (1850-1937). **21 Platts Lane, NW3** Czechoslovak president and nationalist leader; lived and worked here during the First World War. With Eduard Beneš (q.v.), he founded the new republic of Czechoslovakia in 1918 and became its first president, retiring in 1935. *Czechoslovak Colony*

MATCH GIRLS' STRIKE, site of.
Fairfield Works, Fairfield Road, E3
In 1888, at the former Bryant & May factory on this site (1861-1979), the working girls made their protest against their working conditions. *Historic Buildings of Bow*

MATCH TAX ABANDONMENT. 149-51 Bow Road, E3
The plaque states: 'Near this spot stood the testimonial fountain erected by public subscription in 1872 to commemorate the part played by Bryant & May and their work people in securing the abandonment of the proposed match tax.' *Bow Council*

MATTHAY, Tobias (1858-1945). **21 Arkwright Road, NW3**
Pianist and piano teacher; lived here. He published *The Art of Touch* (1903), and among his pupils were Myra Hess (q.v.) and Harriet Cohen. *Greater London Council*

MATTHEWS, Jessie (1907-81). **22 Berwick Street, W1**
English actress and dancer; born near here. She made her stage debut at the age of ten and was extremely popular in the musical revues of the 1920s. In the following decade she enjoyed success in musical films, after which she faded from the limelight. In later life she took the role of Mrs Dale in the popular daily radio serial *Mrs Dale's Diary. Westminster City Council*

MAUGHAM, W. (William) Somerset (1874-1965). **6 Chesterfield Street, W1**
English novelist and short-story writer; lived here 1911-19. Born in Paris, he qualified as a doctor but turned instead to writing. Among his novels are *Of Human Bondage* (1915), *The Moon and Sixpence* (1919), *Cakes and Ale* (1930) and *The Razor's Edge* (1945). He also wrote several plays and in 1908 had four running in London. Many of his stories were filmed, including the collections *Quartet* (1949) and *Trio* (1950). Maugham served as a secret agent in both world wars, and some of his works are based on his experiences. *Greater London Council*

MAURICE, (John) Frederick Denison (1805-72). **2 Upper Harley Street, NW1**
English Anglican cleric and writer; lived here 1862-6. He was chaplain to Guy's Hospital (1837) and later to Lincoln's Inn. He lost his professorship of theology at King's College, London, as a result of the publication of his

Theological Essays (1853). He later (1866) became professor of moral philosophy at Cambridge. With Charles Kingsley (q.v.) he founded the Christian socialist movement. *Greater London Council*

MAXIM, Sir Hiram Stevens (1840-1916). **57d Hatton Garden, EC1**
American-born inventor and engineer; designed the Maxim gun here. He emigrated to England in 1881 and perfected his machine-gun two years later. He also designed a flying machine (1894) and many items for domestic use. *Greater London Council*

MAXWELL, James Clerk (1831-79). **16 Palace Gardens Terrace, W8**
Scottish-born physicist; lived here. A Cambridge mathematics graduate, he later set up the Cavendish laboratories there. He was an outstanding scientist, who contributed to the study of electromagnetic waves, optics, gases and colour photography. *London County Council*

MAY, Phil (Philip William) (1864-1903). **20 Holland Park Road, W14**
English caricaturist; lived and worked here. His cartoons in *Punch* and his own *Annual* established his reputation and were forerunners of the modern simple-line style of cartooning. *Greater London Council*

MAYER, Sir Robert (1879-1985). **2 Mansfield Street, W1**
British philanthropist and patron of music; lived here in flat number 31. He founded the Transatlantic Foundation Anglo-American scholarships and the Robert Mayer concerts for children. *English Heritage*

MAYFAIR, site of. 17 Trebeck Street, W1
From 1688 an annual fair, previously staged in the Haymarket, was held in the first two weeks of May in the area now called Shepherd's Market. During the eighteenth century the surrounding district became popular with the nobility and many classical-style buildings were erected, few of which have survived. The area now known as Mayfair is roughly bordered by Oxford Street, Park Lane, Piccadilly and Regent Street and includes some of London's finest hotels. *Private*

MAYFAIR'S OLDEST HOUSE. Hilton Mews Hotel, Stanhope Row, W1
The plaque reads: 'On this site, until destroyed by bombing during the winter of 1940, stood an archway and Mayfair's oldest house, "The Cottage, 1618 AD", from where a shepherd tended his flock whilst Tyburn idled nearby.' The plaque was erected at the instigation of the local residents' association as a permanent reminder of Mayfair's rural origins. *Westminster City Council*

MAYHEW, Henry (1812-87). **55 Albany Street, NW1**
English author and first joint editor of *Punch*; lived here. He wrote several successful novels, and some works in collaboration with his two brothers. He was the author of *London Labour and the London Poor* (1851-62). *London County Council*

MAZZINI, Giuseppe (1805-72) **183 North Gower Street, NW1** *London County Council;* **5 Hatton Garden, EC1** *Private;* **10 Laystall Street, EC1** *Private*

The plaque in Laystall Street, EC1.

Italian nationalist leader; lived in Gower Street 1837-40. His stormy career included expulsion and imprisonment but paved the way for Garibaldi and Cavour to establish the new united Italian kingdom. The two plaques in Hatton Garden and Laystall Street commemorate him for having inspired 'young Italy with the ideal of independence, unity and regeneration' and are very similar in design.

McBEY, James (1883-1959). **1 Holland Park Avenue, W11**
Scottish artist and etcher; lived here. Travelling extensively in Europe, Africa, America and the Middle East, he produced some of the finest etchings known in British printmaking. *Private*

McGILL, Donald (1875-1962). **5 Bennett Park, Blackheath, SE3**
English comic postcard cartoonist; lived here. He became famous for his postcard drawings of large ladies in bathing suits, usually with a weedy husband, accompanied by a humorous caption. Many of his postcards are now collectors' items. *Greater London Council*

McMILLAN, Margaret (1860-1931) and **Rachel** (1859-1917). **McMillan College, Creek Road, Deptford, SE8** *Greater London Council;* **127 George Lane, SE13** *Borough of Lewisham*
American-born social and educational reformers (sisters); both lived in George Lane, Margaret lived in Creek Road. Margaret first campaigned in the north of England and joined her sister in London in 1902. Together they opened the first school clinic (1908) and the first open-air nursery school (1914).

McNAIR, Squadron Leader Robin John, DFC & Bar (1918-96). **McNair Road, Southall**
English pilot and airline executive who was born in Rio de Janeiro. He had a very distinguished record with the RAF during the Second World War, completing four hundred sorties and seeing action in the Battle of Britain and the continued air strikes in Europe. As one of the leading fighter pilots, he commanded a squadron of Typhoon aircraft in the 'Death and Glory' raids over France and also a squadron of the first jet fighter planes. After the war McNair became a

We don't care if it snows - we're here

A Donald McGill postcard.

director of civil aviation companies and contributed greatly to the development of peacetime flying. He was honoured by the borough in which he lived for more than thirty-two years by having a street named after him, where this plaque is situated. *Borough of Ealing*

MEDTNER, Nicolas (Nikolai) (1880-1951). **69 Wentworth Road, NW11**
Russian composer and pianist; lived here from 1935 until his death. His compositions were mainly for piano and included three concertos. *Borough of Barnet*

MEE, Arthur (1875-1943). **27 Lanercost Road, Tulse Hill, SW2**
English journalist, writer and topographer; lived here. He produced a *Children's Encyclopaedia* (1908) and the *Children's Newspaper*. Among his many publications was a series of books about the English counties. *English Heritage*

MEEK, Joe (Joseph) (1929-67). **304 Holloway Road, N7**
Musician and composer; lived and worked here. He was born in Newent, Gloucestershire, where a similar plaque records the fact. During the 1950s and early 1960s he was Britain's leading independent record producer and was responsible for the success of many well-known popular singers and recording groups. Using modern techniques, his 'Telstar' was top of the record charts and became synonymous with his name. *Private*

MELBA, Dame Nellie (1861-1931). **Coombe House, Beverley Lane, Coombe Lane West, Kingston-upon-Thames**
Stage name of Helen Porter Mitchell, Australian soprano; lived here. She first appeared at Covent Garden in 1888. The peach melba dessert and melba toast were named after her. She was created DBE in 1927. *English Heritage*

MENDOZA, Daniel (1764-1836). **3 Paradise Row, E2**
English pugilist; lived here while writing *The Art of Boxing* (1789). He successfully united sparring with boxing. During his career he toured England and Ireland, retiring from the sport in 1820. *Tower Hamlets Environment Trust*

MENON. See **KRISHNA MENON**

MERCURY THEATRE. See **DUKES, Ashley**

MEREDITH, George (1829-1909). **7 Hobury Street, SW10**
English novelist and poet; lived here. His works include *The Ordeal of Richard Feverel* (1859), *Evan Harrington* (1860), *The Egoist* (1879) and *Diana of the Crossways* (1885). *Greater London Council*

George Meredith

METTERNICH, Prince Clemens Lothar Wenzel (1773-1859). **44 Eaton Square, SW1**
Austrian statesman; lived here 1848. He was ambassador in turn to Dresden, Berlin and Paris, Austrian foreign minister and Chancellor from 1821. He fled to England in 1848 at the time of the Austrian revolution, returning to his homeland in 1851. During his short stay in Eaton Square, he entertained many prominent statesmen, including the Duke of Wellington, who was a regular visitor. *Greater London Council*

MEYNELL, Alice Christiana Gertrude (née Thompson) (1847-1922). **47 Palace Court, W2**
English poet and essayist; lived here with her author husband Wilfred 1890-1905. Her poems include *Preludes* (1875) and a collection published in 1923 shortly after her death. Essays include *The Rhythm of Life* (1893), *The Colour of Life* (1896) and *Hearts of Controversy* (1917). *London County Council*

MILL, John Stuart (1806-73). **18 Kensington Square, W8**
English philosopher and economist; lived here 1837-51. Educated by his father, he worked for the East India Company, retiring in 1858.
His essays were first published in a newspaper in 1822, after which he wrote many works on the subjects of utilitarianism and political economy. His love of debate and discussion brought him into contact with Carlyle (q.v.), Coleridge (q.v.) and Tennyson (q.v.). *London County Council*

MILLAIS, Sir John Everett (1829-96). **Millais House, 7 Cromwell Place, SW7** *National Art Collections Fund;* **2 Palace Gate, W8** *London County Council*
British artist and painter; lived in Cromwell Place; lived and died in Palace Gate. With Dante Gabriel Rossetti (q.v.) and William Holman Hunt (q.v.), he

The plaque in Cromwell Place, SW7.

was a founder of the Pre-Raphaelite Brotherhood (q.v.). Among his most famous paintings are *Ophelia* (1852), *The Boyhood of Raleigh* (1870) and *Bubbles* (1886). One of the most popular artists of his day, he became president of the Royal Academy in 1896, the year of his death. The artists Emil Otto Hoppe (q.v.) and Francis Bacon (q.v.) are also recorded on the Cromwell Place plaque.

The view across the Thames from the site of Millbank prison.

MILLBANK PRISON, site of. Millbank, SW1
The plaque reads: 'Near this site stood Millbank Prison, which was opened in 1816 and closed in 1890. This buttress stood at the head of the river steps from which, until 1867, prisoners sentenced to transportation embarked on their journey to Australia.' *London County Council*

MILNE, A. A. (Alan Alexander) (1882-1956). **13 Mallord Street, SW3**
English writer; lived here. He was an assistant editor of *Punch* by the age of
twenty-four. His well-known children's stories include *Winnie-the-Pooh* (1926)
and *The House at Pooh Corner* (1928). Many of his characters were based on
the toys and childhood games of his son Christopher Robin. He also wrote,
among other plays, *Toad of Toad Hall* (1929), which was an adaptation of
Kenneth Grahame's (q.v.) *The Wind in the Willows. Greater London Council*

MILNER, Alfred, First Viscount Milner (1854-1925). **14 Manchester
Square, W1**
British statesman; lived here. He served as chairman of the Board of Inland
Revenue 1892-7, governor of the Cape Colony 1897-1901, governor of the
Transvaal and Orange River Colony 1901-5 and High Commissioner for South
Africa 1897-1905. He was a member of Lloyd George's (q.v.) war cabinet in
1916, Secretary for War 1918-19 and Colonial Secretary 1919-21. He became a
viscount in 1902. *Greater London Council*

MIRANDA, Francisco de (1750-
1816). **58 Grafton Way, W1**
Latin-American liberator; lived here
1802/3-10. He became the dictator
controlling the new republic of Venezuela in 1811 but was overthrown
one year later. During his period of
residence in this house he gathered
around him a circle of South American republican conspirators, including Simón Bolívar (q.v.). His statue
can be found nearby in Fitzroy Street.
The original plaque, set up by the
Borough of Camden, has been replaced by English Heritage, who also
commemorate Andres Bello (q.v.).
English Heritage

MITFORD, Nancy Freeman (1904-
73). **10 Curzon Street, W1**
English novelist and biographer;
worked here 1942-5. The daughter of
the Second Baron Redesdale and sister of Diana, Jessica and Unity Mitford, her
novels include *Pursuit of Love* (1945), *Love in a Cold Climate* (1949) and *The
Blessing* (1951). She also wrote biographies of Madame de Pompadour, Voltaire
and Frederick the Great. She edited *Noblesse Oblige,* the treatise that coined the
phrases 'U' and 'non-U', denoting upper- and lower-class manners and usage.
After the Second World War she lived in France.

MITRE TAVERN, site of. 37 Fleet Street, EC4
This was a favourite tavern of Dr Johnson (q.v.), his biographer James Boswell
(q.v.) and other members of his circle, including Oliver Goldsmith. It was
closed in 1865. *Corporation of the City of London*

MONDRIAN, Piet Cornelis (1872-1944). **60 Parkhill Road, NW3**
Dutch abstract artist; lived here. He resided in Paris 1919-38, having been
inspired by Cubism on an earlier visit. The succeeding two years were spent in
London, after which he settled in New York. His abstract paintings typically

consisted of horizontal and vertical black lines arranged according to ratios considered pleasing to the eye, with the resultant boxes filled in with white and primary colours. *Greater London Council*

MONOUX, George (1477-1543). **41 Billet Road, Walthamstow, E17**
Mayor of London; lived in a house on this site, called 'Moones'. Originally from Bristol, where he was mayor 1501-2, he came to London shortly afterwards, becoming an alderman and master of the Drapers' Company. He settled in Walthamstow, where he was a well-known local benefactor, and became mayor of London in 1514. *Borough of Walthamstow*

MONTEFIORE, Sir Moses Haim (1784-1885). **99 Park Lane, W1**
Italian-born British philanthropist and Jewish leader; lived here for sixty years. He became sheriff of London in 1837. He did much to support oppressed Jewish people in Europe and endowed a hospital in Jerusalem as well as a college in Ramsgate. *Greater London Council*

MONTGOMERY, Bernard Law, First Viscount Montgomery of Alamein (1887-1976). **Oval House, 52-4 Kennington Oval, SE11**
British field marshal; born here. He commanded the Eighth Army in North Africa in the Second World War, defeating the Axis forces at El Alamein (1942). This was the turning point of the war and led to the Allied advance into Tunisia and invasion of Sicily and Italy. Montgomery also commanded Allied forces at the invasion of France and received the German surrender on Luneburg Heath on 3rd May 1945. He was appointed chief of the Imperial General Staff (1946) and was Deputy Supreme Commander of Europe under Eisenhower (q.v.). *English Heritage*

MOODY, Dr Harold (1882-1947). **164 Queens Road, SE15**
Medical practitioner and campaigner for racial equality; lived and worked here. Born in Jamaica, he founded the League of Coloured Peoples in 1931. *English Heritage*

MOORE, George Augustus (1852-1933). **121 Ebury Street, SW1**
Irish writer; lived here from 1911 until his death. He spent some of his early years leading a bohemian lifestyle in London and Paris. Among his first works were *A Modern Lover* (1883), *A Mummer's Wife* (1885) and *Esther Waters* (1894), all of which reflected his own style of almost poverty-stricken living. His later novels and prose reflected his interest in theology, mythology and the arts. *London County Council*

MOORE, Thomas (1779-1852). **85 George Street, W1**
Irish poet; lived here. Following early travels in Bermuda and North America he married and settled in Wiltshire (1811). His *Lalla Rookh* was published in 1817 and *Irish Melodies* from 1807. The latter includes 'The Minstrel Boy' and 'The Last Rose of Summer', which were set to music by John Stevenson.

Moore also wrote biographies of Sheridan (q.v.) and his friend Lord Byron. *London County Council*

MOOR GATE (1515-1761). **72 Moorgate, EC2**
Moor Gate was built in London Wall as an exit route from the city to the moor nearby. This was drained in 1527, and the gate, having been improved in the seventeenth century, was demolished in 1761. *Corporation of the City of London*

MORDEN, John (1548-1625). **Hendon School, Golders Rise, NW4**
English cartographer; lived in a house on this site off Brent Street. He was official map-maker to Elizabeth I and was authorised to travel throughout Britain to chart the counties in detail. This resulted in his work *Speculum Britanniae* ('Mirror of Britain'). *Hendon Corporation*

MORE, Kenneth (1914-82). **27 Rumbold Road, SW6**
British film actor; lived and died here. He featured in many films including *Genevieve* (1953), *Doctor in the House* (1954) and *The Thirty-Nine Steps* (1959). *Private*

MORECAMBE, Eric (1926-84). **85 Torrington Park, N12** *Comic Heritage;* **Teddington Studios, Broom Road, Teddington** *Comic Heritage*
Stage name of Eric Bartholomew, English comedian; lived at the first address 1956-61, worked at the second. His birthplace was Morecambe, Lancashire. He teamed up with Ernie Wise in 1943 when they appeared in the review *Strike a New Note*. From 1947 they were billed as 'Morecambe and Wise' on stage, radio, film and their most successful medium – television. They were probably the most popular comic double act of their time.

The plaque on the front of Teddington Studios.

MORGAN, Charles Longbridge (1894-1958). **16 Campden Hill Square, W8**
English author and critic; lived and died here. He served in the navy before and during the First World War, then studied at Oxford 1918-21, where he published *The Gunroom* (1919). Afterwards joining *The Times* newspaper, he became drama critic (1926-39). He wrote the award-winning *Portrait in a Mirror* (1929), as well as *The Fountain* (1932), *The Voyage* (1940), plays and critical essays. *English Heritage*

MORRELL, Lady Ottoline (1873-1938). **10 Gower Street, WC1**
Literary hostess and patron of the arts; lived here. She was a half-sister of the sixth Duke of Portland. Her distinguished circle met at Garsington Manor, Oxfordshire, 1913-24 and afterwards at this address. *Greater London Council*

MORRIS, William (1834-96). **William Morris Gallery, Lloyd Park, Forest Road, E17** *Borough of Walthamstow;* **Fire Station, Forest Road, E17** *Borough of Walthamstow;* **17 Red Lion Square, WC1** *London County Council;* **Red House, Red House Lane, Bexleyheath** *Greater London Council;* **91-101 Worship Street, EC2** *Borough of Hackney*
English craftsman, designer, writer and poet born on a site opposite the second

The William Morris Gallery in Walthamstow, E17. The plaque commemorating Morris is on the right-hand side of the building between the ground-floor and first-floor windows.

A caricature of Morris in a characteristic pose, drawn by his lifelong friend Burne-Jones.

address cited above; he lived at Lloyd Park 1848-56, at Red Lion Square 1856-9 and at the Red House 1860-5; he is mentioned on the Worship Street plaque as Webb's co-founder of the Society for the Protection of Ancient Buildings (1877). At Oxford he formed a friendship with Edward Burne-Jones (q.v.) and together they made the acquaintance of Dante Gabriel Rossetti (q.v.), with whom they studied painting in Red Lion Square. Having married Jane Burden (who later had an affair with Rossetti) in 1859, Morris had the Red House (q.v.) built by his friend the architect Philip Webb (q.v.). In 1861 he founded a firm to design and produce furniture, wallpaper and carpets, which was highly influential on twentieth-century taste. He also published several volumes of verse romances, founded the Kelmscott Press in 1890 and was a committed socialist and social reformer. A museum of his work is housed at his childhood home in Forest Road, where the plaque is shared with Edward Lloyd (q.v.).

MORRISON, Herbert Stanley, Baron Morrison of Lambeth (1888-1965).
55 Archery Road, Eltham, SE9
English socialist politician; lived here 1929-60. In 1915 he became the founder and secretary of the London Labour Party. He was mayor of Hackney 1920-1 and joined the London County Council in 1922, becoming its leader in 1934. He was MP for South Hackney three times between 1923 and 1945, Minister of Transport 1929-31, Home Secretary in the wartime cabinet, Leader of the

House of Commons 1945-51 and Foreign Secretary for a short time during 1951. Later Deputy Leader of the Opposition, he was created a life peer in 1959. *Greater London Council*

MORSE, Samuel Finley Breese (1791-1872). **141 Cleveland Street, W1**
American inventor and artist; lived here 1812-15 while studying art. The first president of the National Academy of Design, New York (1826), he was also a professor at New York University from 1832. In 1837 he presented his idea for a magnetic telegraph to Congress, which later funded an experimental connection between Washington and Baltimore (1844). He invented the Morse Code for use with the telegraph. *London County Council*

MOSES, Miriam, OBE (1886-1965). **17 Princelet Street, E1**
Britain's first woman Jewish mayor; born here. She spent a lifetime fighting against poverty and slum housing and was a founder member of the League of Jewish Women and the Board of Deputies (q.v.). She was mayor of Stepney 1931-2. *Borough of Tower Hamlets*

MIRIAM MOSES
OBE JP
Social Reformer and First Woman Mayor of Stepney
1931 - 1932
was born here
in
1886

MOTOR ACCIDENT, first fatal. **Grove Hill, Harrow-on-the-Hill**
The first recorded fatal motor accident in Great Britain involving the death of the driver occurred here on 25th February 1899. The first involving the death of a pedestrian was at Crystal Palace. *Borough of Harrow*

TAKE HEED
THE FIRST RECORDED MOTOR ACCIDENT IN GREAT BRITAIN INVOLVING THE DEATH OF THE DRIVER OCCURRED ON GROVE HILL ON 25TH FEBRUARY 1899.
THIS PLAQUE WAS UNVEILED ON THE 70TH ANNIVERSARY BY THE MAYOR OF HARROW ALDERMAN CHARLES STENHOUSE

MOZART, Wolfgang Amadeus (1756-91). **180 Ebury Street, SW1** *London County Council;* **20 Frith Street, W1** *Royal Musical Association*
Austrian composer; lived and worked in a house on the Frith Street site 1764-5; composed his first symphony in Ebury Street 1764. His father, Leopold, took the young Mozart and his musician sister on a tour of Europe when Wolfgang was only six. During the tour they stayed for fifteen months in Ebury Street. After his marriage (1782) he lived mainly in Vienna. Failing in health, he died impoverished. His works include many symphonies, violin concertos, piano concertos , several operas and his *Requiem,* on which he was working when he died. These were catalogued by Ludwig von Köchel (1800-77) in 1862. 'K' numbers are still used to identify Mozart's works.

MUIRHEAD, Alexander (1848-1920). **20 Church Road, Shortlands, Bromley**
Electrical engineer; lived here. He was the inventor of duplex cables, which can send messages in different directions simultaneously. He established a factory for the manufacture of electrical instruments and lived nearby at this address until his death. Muirhead was made a Fellow of the Royal Society in 1904. *Greater London Council*

MUNNINGS, Sir Alfred (1878-1959). **96 Chelsea Park Gardens, SW3**
English artist; lived here 1920-59. He was well known for his paintings of horses and hunting scenes. As president of the Royal Academy (1944-9) he was outspoken in his criticism of modern art. *Private*

The right-hand plaque on this building at 180 Ebury Street commemorates Mozart; the left-hand one is to Vita Sackville-West and Harold Nicolson.

MURDER ON A TRAIN, first. 'Top o' the Morning' pub, Cadogan Terrace, E9

On 9th July 1864 Thomas Briggs was assaulted by Franz Muller, who attempted to steal his gold watch. When Briggs was found on the tracks in critical condition he was taken to this public house, where he died from his injuries. *Borough of Tower Hamlets*

MURRAY, Sir James Augustus Henry (1837-1915). Sunnyside, Hammers Lane, Mill Hill, NW7

Scottish-born philologist and lexicographer; lived here 1870-85. For many years a schoolmaster at Mill Hill School, he began work on the *New English Dictionary* (which became the *Oxford English Dictionary*) in 1879 and was responsible for the preparation of more than half of it. The *Dictionary* was first published in 1884 in Oxford, where he later lived. *Hendon Corporation*

MURRY, John Middleton (1889-1957). 17 East Heath Road, NW3

English writer and critic who married Katherine Mansfield (q.v.); lived with her in this house from 1918 until her premature death. His criticisms include studies of Keats (q.v.), Blake (q.v.), Shakespeare (q.v.) and D. H. Lawrence (q.v.), who was a personal friend. A pacifist, he became editor of *Peace News* (1940-6). The plaque is shared with Katherine Mansfield. *Greater London Council*

MUYBRIDGE, Eadweard (1830-1904). 2 Liverpool Road, Kingston.

Adopted name of Edward James Muggeridge, British photographer; lived here 1894-1904. He was a pioneer of motion photography. His sequences of photographs included one of Isadora Duncan dancing. Another series proved that when a horse gallops there are times when all its hooves are off the ground, contrary to the popular misconception of earlier artists. He also invented a machine for showing his photographs as moving pictures. There are two plaques to Muybridge at this address. *The Royal Photographic Society* and the *British Film Institute*

NABUCO, Joachim (1849-1910). **52 Cornwall Gardens, SW7**
Brazilian statesman and diplomat; lived at this address while Brazilian ambassador in London. He devoted his political life to the abolition of slavery in Brazil, the results of his efforts reaching fruition by 1888. *Brazilian Government*

NAPOLEON III (Charles Louis Napoleon Bonaparte) (1808-73). **1c King Street, St James's, SW1**
Emperor of France and nephew of Napoleon I; lived in this house during a temporary exile in 1848. The plaque, erected by the Royal Society of Arts in 1875, is one of the oldest surviving of its type. *Royal Society of Arts*

NASH, Paul (1889-1946). **Queen Alexandra Mansions, Bidborough Street, WC1**
English painter; lived here, in flat 176, 1914-36. An official war artist in both world wars, he is best known for his slightly stylised, sensitive renderings of landscape, including Buckinghamshire scenes. His paintings include *The Menin Road* (1919) and *The Battle of Britain*, both at the Imperial War Museum, and *Totes Meer* ('Dead Sea'), 1940-1, at the Tate Gallery. *English Heritage*

NEAGLE, Dame Anna (1904-86). **63-4 Park Lane, W1**
Stage name of Marjorie Robertson, English actress; lived here 1950-64. After earlier appearances on stage, she made her film debut in 1930. Under the direction of her husband, Herbert Wilcox (q.v.), she went on to appear in a series of films including *Victoria the Great* (1937*), Odette* (1950), *The Lady with the Lamp* (1951) and several musicals, starring with Michael Wilding. The plaque is shared with Herbert Wilcox (q.v.). *Westminster City Council*

NECKER, Anne Louise Germaine (Madame de Staël) (1766-1817). **Argyll Street, W1 (rear of Dickens and Jones)**
French authoress; lived here 1813-14. She wrote several semi-autobiographical novels, and her *De L'Allemagne* was an account for the French of German life, critical of German literature. She was a notable 'salon' hostess but was banished from Paris by Napoleon for her outspokenness. After this she travelled extensively, visiting London on several occasions. Most of her later years were spent in Switzerland. *La Société d'Études Staëliennes*

NEHRU, Jawaharlal (1889-1964). **60 Elgin Crescent, W11**
First Indian prime minister; lived here in 1910 and 1912. Educated at Harrow and Cambridge, he resided here while he read for the bar. Returning to India, he joined the Indian Congress Committee (1918) and associated with Mahatma Gandhi (q.v.). From 1921 he spent many years in prison but became leader of the Indian National Congress and prime minister in 1947 when independence was achieved. *English Heritage*

NELSON, Horatio, Viscount Nelson (1758-1805). **147 New Bond Street, W1** *Royal Society of Arts;* **103 New Bond Street, W1** *London County Council*
English naval commander; lived at 147 in 1797 and at 103 in 1798. He entered the navy in 1770. After his marriage to Frances Nisbet he retired (1787) for five years. At the outbreak of war with France he returned to service and lost the sight of his right eye (1794), three years later losing his right arm. In 1798 he defeated the French fleet at the Battle of the Nile. He scored another victory at Copenhagen (1801) and was afterwards raised to the peerage. His affair with Emma, Lady Hamilton, in the latter part of his life is a famous romance. He was mortally wounded at his greatest victory, the Battle of Trafalgar, when he defeated the combined French and Spanish fleets. Brought home in a barrel of liquor, he was buried in St Paul's Cathedral.

NESBIT, Edith (1858-1924). **28 Elswick Road, Lewisham, SE13**
English writer of children's books and novels; lived here 1882-5. Her works include *Five Children and It* (1902), *The Railway Children* (1906) and *The Enchanted Castle* (1907). She was a member of the Fabian Society (q.v.). *Borough of Lewisham*

NEVILL, Lady Dorothy (1826-1913). **45 Charles Street, W1**
Writer and widow of Horatio Walpole, the third Duke of Orford; lived here 1873-1913. Her published writings include *A History of the Walpoles* (1906), *Leaves from the Notebooks of Lady Dorothy Nevill* (1907), *More Leaves* (1908) and *Under Five Reigns* (1910). *Westminster City Council*

NEW CROSS FIRE. Catford Road, SE6
A circular plaque commemorates the fourteen young people who died in the New Cross fire of 18th January 1981. Below it is a square plaque with a list of their names. *Private*

NEW GATE, site of. Newgate Street, EC1
The gate was built originally in the time of Henry I and rebuilt by Sir Richard Whittington (q.v.), destroyed in the Great Fire of London, rebuilt again in 1672 and finally demolished in 1777. *Corporation of the City of London*

NEWBERY, John (1713-67). **St Paul's Churchyard, EC4**
English bookseller, publisher and author; lived and worked on this site. He was a pioneer of children's publishing, his most notable

publications being *Goody Two-Shoes* and *Mother Goose*. The annual American award for the best children's book is named after him. *Pennsylvania Library Association*

NEWBOLT, Sir Henry John (1862-1938). **29 Campden Hill Road, W8**
English poet and naval historian; lived here from 1918. He is best known for works about the seafaring life, including *Admirals All* (1897), in which 'Drake's Drum' appears, *Songs of the Sea* (1904) and *Songs of the Fleet* (1910). *English Heritage*

NEWLANDS, John Alexander Reina (1838-98). **19 West Square, SE11**
Chemist; born and raised here. His discovery that every eighth atomic element was periodic led to their numbering and his subsequent recognition. He was awarded the Davy Medal in 1887 by the Royal Society. *Royal Society of Chemistry*

NEWMAN, Cardinal John Henry (1801-90). **Old Broad Street, EC2** *Private;* **Grey Court, Ham Street, Richmond** *Greater London Council;* **17 Southampton Place, WC1** *Duke of Bedford*
English theologian; born near the Old Broad Street site; lived during his youth at the other two addresses. He was ordained into the Church of England in 1824, became vicar of St Mary's, Oxford, in 1828, and by 1830 had rejected evangelicalism. He laid the foundations of the Tractarian movement in the Anglican church with his *Tracts for the Times*. His Tract 90 (1841) found the basic tenets of the Anglican church compatible with Roman Catholicism, and Newman was received into the Roman Catholic church in 1845. He was rector of Dublin University in 1854-8. His *Apologia pro Vita Sua* (1864) was one of his most important works; he was also the author of the much loved hymn 'Lead Kindly Light' and of the poem 'The Dream of Gerontius'; later set to music by Elgar (q.v.). He was made cardinal in 1879.

NEWTON, Sir Isaac (1642-1727). **87 Jermyn Street, SW1**
English scientist and mathematician; lived in a house on this site 1700-9.

The plaque to John Henry Newman in Southampton Place, NW1.

146

Educated at Trinity College, Cambridge, he was – traditionally – inspired by the sight of a falling apple in his discovery of gravity. He became not only a Fellow of the Royal Society (1672) but also a member of Parliament (1689 and 1701-2), Master of the Royal Mint (1699) and a knight (1705). He discovered that light is made up of many colours, developed the technique of differential calculus and discovered the binomial theorem. His position in the history of mathematics was unassailable until Einstein, and he was the first scientist to be buried in Westminster Abbey. *London County Council*

NICOLL FAMILY. Randall Court, Page Street, Mill Hill, NW7
Family that resided here from as early as 1321 until 1920. In the Black Survey, of 1321, one Stephen Nicoll was recorded as having a dwelling house with 15 acres and a second with 12 acres. Mention of the family in parish and local records continued until the twentieth century. In 1637 Randall Nicoll erected a red brick house in Page Street, which survived until 1920 and was occupied by generations of the family until its demolition. *Hendon Corporation*

NICOLSON, Harold George (1886-1968). **182 Ebury Street, SW1**
British author, biographer and diplomat; lived here. He was born in Iran and educated at Oxford. His diplomatic career began in 1909 and continued until his resignation from the service twenty years later. He was a member of Parliament 1935-45 and wrote several books, including biographies of George V, Tennyson (q.v.), Swinburne (q.v.) and Lord Curzon (q.v.). This plaque is shared with his wife, Vita Sackville-West (q.v.), whom he married in 1913. *English Heritage*

NIGHTINGALE, Florence (1820-1910). **90 Harley Street, W1** *Private;* **10 South Street, W1** *London County Council*
English nurse and nursing reformer; left her hospital on the Harley Street site to nurse in the Crimea 1854-6; lived and died in a house on the South Street site. Nursing in the Crimea led to her resolve to remove the insanitary conditions in the British Army (on which she became the authority) as well as to the improvement of nurse training. She founded the Nightingale School and Home for Nurses in London (1856) and was awarded the Order of Merit (1907).

The plaque at Harley Street, W1.

NIXON, David (1919-78). **Teddington Studios, Broom Road, Teddington**
English magician and comedian; frequently worked here. He began conjuring as a boy and made his first stage appearance in 1941. Nixon joined the panel of the television show *What's My Line?* and later had his own series. He also appeared regularly in pantomime. *Comic Heritage*

NOEL-BAKER, Baron Philip John (1889-1982). **16 South Eaton Place, SW1**
British politician; lived here. He distinguished himself at Cambridge and in 1912 was captain of the British Olympic team. He assisted in the drafting of the charter of both the League of Nations and the United Nations and was an MP from 1929, holding several ministerial posts. He published several books on

international problems and was awarded the Nobel peace prize in 1959 and created a life peer in 1977. A second plaque at this address comemorates Viscount Cecil of Chelwood (q.v.). *English Heritage*

NOLLEKENS, Joseph (1737-1823). **44 Mortimer Street, W1**
English sculptor; lived and died in a house on this site. He specialised in portrait busts. Among the figures he portrayed were George III, the Prince of Wales (later George IV), William Pitt the younger (q.v.), Fox (q.v.), Garrick (q.v.) and Goldsmith. *London County Council*

NORTHCLIFFE, First Viscount. See **HARMSWORTH, Alfred Charles William**

NORTHUMBERLAND HOUSE, site of. 1 St Martin-le-Grand, EC1
Dating back to 1352, the house was owned by Henry Percy, Earl of Northumberland, a descendant of William de Percy, who arrived with William the Conqueror. The second earl, known as Harry Hotspur, was killed at the battle of Shrewsbury in 1403. *Corporation of the City of London*

NOVELLO, Ivor (Ivor Novello Davies) (1893-1951). **11 Aldwych, WC2**
Welsh composer, dramatist and actor; lived and died in a flat in this building. He first appeared on stage in 1921 but is best remembered for his songs, including 'Keep the Home Fires Burning', which boosted popular morale during the First World War, and 'We'll Gather Lilacs'. His musical shows included *Glamorous Night* (1935), *The Dancing Years* (1939), *King's Rhapsody* (1949) and *Gay's the Word* (1951). *Greater London Council*

OATES, Captain Laurence Edward Grace (1880-1912). 309 Upper Richmond Road, SW15

English explorer; lived here 1885-91. He joined Robert Falcon Scott's (q.v.) Antarctic expedition and was one of the five to reach the South Pole. On the return journey, while suffering from severe frostbite, he walked out into a blizzard, sacrificing his own life in order not to delay his companions, who were in deadly peril. *Greater London Council*

OBRADOVICH, Dositey (1742-1811). 27 Clement's Lane, EC4

Serbian man of letters; lived in a house on this site in 1784. He was the first minister of education in Serbia and was directly involved in the Serbian struggle for independence (1804-13) and educational reforms. *Private*

> HERE LIVED IN 1784
> DOSITEY OBRADOVICH
> 1742~1811
> Eminent Serbian man of letters
> First Minister of Education
> in Serbia.

O'CASEY, Sean (1884-1964). 49 Overstrand Mansions, Prince of Wales Drive, SW11

Pen name of John Casey, Irish playwright; lived in a flat here. His humble origins in a poor area of Dublin are reflected in his early plays *Shadow of a Gunman* (1923) and *Juno and the Paycock* (1924). Later plays included *The Plough and the Stars* (1926), *The Silver Tassie* (1929), *Red Roses for Me* (1946) and *The Bishop's Bonfire* (1955). *English Heritage*

The house in Upper Richmond Road, SW15, where Captain Laurence Oates lived. The plaque commemorating him can be seen beside the left-hand downstairs window.

O'HIGGINS, Bernardo (1778-1842). **Clarence House, 2 The Vineyard, Richmond**
Chilean revolutionary leader; lived and studied here. He was an illegitimate son of an Irish viceroy. After leading the struggle (1810-17) against the Spanish occupation of Chile, he became head of the first independent Chilean government (1817-23). *English Heritage*

OLD LONDON BRIDGE, approach road to. St Magnus churchyard, Lower Thames Street, EC3
This plaque is erected in a churchyard through which the approach road to old London Bridge once passed . The first stone bridge was erected in 1176 on the site of earlier wooden constructions. Other bridges were constructed in the same position until the new bridge was built upstream in 1831. *Corporation of the City of London*

OLD SERJEANTS' INN, site of. 5 Chancery Lane, WC2
One of the three sites of Serjeants' Inn in the City. This site was used by the Inn 1442-59 and again 1732-1877. The plaque gives the overall dates of the Inn, 1415 to 1910. *Corporation of the City of London*

OLDFIELD, Ann (1683-1730). **60 Grosvenor Street, W1**
English actress; the first occupant of this house, where she lived 1725-30. Employed as a barmaid at the Mitre tavern (q.v.), she was 'discovered' by George Farquhar and given her first Drury Lane role by John Vanbrugh (q.v.). She excelled as a comedy actress, appearing in plays by Colley Cibber, William Congreve and Henry Fielding (q.v.) among others. Ann Oldfield was noted for the clarity of her speaking voice. *English Heritage*

An engraving of Old London Bridge by Gustave Doré.

OLIVER, Percy Lane (1878-1944). **5 Colyton Road, SE22**

Founder of the first voluntary blood donor service; lived and worked here. As a Red Cross worker, Oliver had the idea of creating a panel of donors, which he started from his own home. He moved to this larger house in 1928 in order to keep up with the increasing demand. *Greater London Council*

OLIVER, Thomas. 536-42 High Road, Leyton, E10

English politician; lived in the 'Great House' (q.v.) on this site 1750-1803. He was a champion of the reforms initiated by John Wilkes. He and his brother shared great wealth from plantations in Antigua. *Leyton Urban District Ratepayers' Association*

ONSLOW, Arthur (1691-1768). **20 Soho Square, W1**

Speaker of the House of Commons 1728-61; lived in a house on this site. The seventeenth-century house was occupied in the mid nineteenth century by the pickle firm Crosse & Blackwell, who demolished it in 1924 to make way for the present building. *London County Council*

ORFORD, Earl of. See **WALPOLE, Sir Robert**

ORPEN, Sir William Montague (1878-1931). **8 South Bolton Gardens, SW5**

Irish painter; lived here. He was famous in his day for his vivacious society portraits but is also known for his Irish genre subjects and his First World War paintings and sketches. He was a member of the Royal Academy from 1919. A plaque to Hugh Lane (q.v.) can be found at the same address. *Greater London Council*

ORTON, Joe (John Kingsley) (1933-67). **25 Noel Road, N1**

English playwright; lived here 1960-7. In his black comedies he deliberately set out to shock. His works include *Entertaining Mr Sloane* (1964), *Loot* (1966) and *What the Butler Saw* (published 1968). He was murdered by his lover, Kenneth Halliwell, who afterwards committed suicide. *Islington Borough Council*

ORWELL, George (1903-50). **3 Warwick Mansions, Pond Street, Hampstead, NW3** *Private;* **27 Canonbury Square, N1** *Borough of Islington;* **50 Lawford Road, NW5** *Greater London Council;* **77 Parliament Hill, Hampstead, NW3** *The Hampstead Plaque Fund;* **22 Portobello Road, W11** *Private*

This plaque to George Orwell can be found in Pond Street, Hampstead, NW3.

Pen name of Eric Arthur Blair, author; lived and worked in a bookshop on the Warwick Mansions site 1934-5; lived in Canonbury Square (1945); also lived at the other three addresses. Born in India of English parents, he was educated at Eton. He spent five years in the police force in Burma (1922-7) and also fought in the Spanish Civil War. His novel *Down and Out in Paris and London* (1933) recalled his hard times living in Paris and his struggle to make a living as a bookshop assistant in London. His novels, which reveal his socialist sympathies and his concerns about the destiny of the human society, include *The Road to Wigan Pier* (1937), *Animal Farm* (1945) and *1984* (written in 1948, published in 1949). Several of his stories have been filmed both for television and cinema. During the Second World War he worked as a radio and newspaper correspondent.

OUIDA (1839-1908). **11 Ravenscourt Square, W6**
Pen name of Maria Louisa de la Ramée, English novelist; lived here. Her father was a French teacher and 'Ouida' (her childish way of saying 'Louisa') was educated in Paris. Best-known among her extravagantly conceived novels was *Under Two Flags* (1867). She also wrote for children. Her last few years were spent in Italy. *London County Council*

OXFORD, Earl of. See **HARLEY, Robert**

OXFORD AND ASQUITH, First Earl of. See **ASQUITH, Herbert Henry**

P

PAGE, Walter Hines (1855-1918). **6 Grosvenor Square, W1**
American diplomat and journalist; lived here. He edited several American journals before becoming American ambassador to Great Britain (1913-18) . *English Speaking Union*

PAINE, Thomas (1737-1809). **Angel Square, Islington High Street, N1**
British-born revolutionary and writer; wrote *The Rights of Man* at the Angel. A friend of Benjamin Franklin (q.v.), he settled in America in 1774 and wrote in support of the revolutionary cause. A supporter of the French Revolution, he advocated a similar revolution in Britain, writing *The Rights of Man*, which led to his trial for treason. Fleeing to France, he was again arrested, having fallen into disfavour with Robespierre, but was released because of his American citizenship. Most renowned among his written works are *The Rights of Man* (1791-2) and *The Age of Reason* (1794-6). The plaque accompanies a sculpture by Kevin Jordan in honour of Paine. *BICC plc*

The plaque and sculpture honouring Thomas Paine.

PALGRAVE, Francis Turner (1824-97). **5 York Gate, Regent's Park, NW1**
English anthologist and poet; lived here 1862-75. Educated at Oxford, he eventually became professor of poetry there. Though he himself wrote poetry, he is best known as the editor of *The Golden Treasury of English Lyrics* (1861), probably the best-loved British poetry book. His other works include *Idylls and Songs* (1854), *Essays on Art* (1866) and *Landscape in Poetry* (1897). *Greater London Council*

PALMER, Samuel (1805-81). **6 Douro Place, W8** *Greater London Council;* **42 Surrey Square, SE17** *Private*
English landscape painter and etcher; born in Surrey Square; lived in Douro Place 1851-61. A friend of William Blake (q.v.) and John Linnell (q.v.), he formed a group called 'The Ancients' at Shoreham, Kent (1826-35). His works of this period include *A Hilly Scene* (1826) and *The*

The parish lock-up in Hampstead, NW3.

Magic Apple Tree (1830), pursuing a bucolic, mystical vision of the country-side. Palmer's later work, some of which was inspired by Italian scenes, is more conventional and less well-known.

PALMERSTON, Henry John Temple, Third Viscount (1784-1865). **4 Carlton Gardens, SW1** *London County Council;* **20 Queen Anne's Gate, SW1** *London County Council;* **94 Piccadilly, W1** *London County Council*
British statesman; born in Queen Anne's Gate; lived in a house on the Carlton Gardens site; lived in Piccadilly from 1855. He was educated at Edinburgh and Cambridge. As a Tory he served as Secretary of War, but in 1828 he joined the Whig party, becoming Foreign Secretary in 1830. He played a major role in European affairs, effected the independence of Belgium (1830-1) and annexed Hong Kong (1840-1) for Britain. He was prime minister in 1855-8 and 1859-65.

PANKHURST, (Estelle) Sylvia (1882-1960). **120 Cheyne Walk, SW10** *Greater London Council;* **45 Norman Grove, E3** *Historic Buildings of Bow*
British suffragette leader; lived in Cheyne Walk. The second plaque states that she 'set up the east London toy factory and babies' nursery in this house and the building in the rear garden 1914-34'. The factory, states the plaque, was financed by Norah Lyle-Smith (1874-1963). The daughter of Emmeline Pankhurst, founder of the suffragette movement, and the sister of Christabel, Sylvia was imprisoned nine times during the struggle for emancipation.

PARISH CAGE OR LOCK-UP, site of the. Junction of Brent Street and Bell Lane, NW4
Parish cages or lock-ups were in use as early as the thirteenth century and served as prisons to detain persons arrested by the parish constable. The earliest known record of this one is on a map by John Cooke dated 1796. It ceased use by 1882 and was sold for redevelopment the following year. *Hendon Corporation*

PARISH LOCK-UP. 11 Cannon Lane, Hampstead, NW3. See also previous above.
The plaque reads: 'About 1730 this lock-up was built into the garden wall of Cannon Hall, where local magistrates held court. Prisoners were kept in this dark single cell until more lasting arrangements could be made for them. Soon after the formation of the police force in 1829, business was transferred to the Watch House (q.v.) in Holly Walk. This lock-up is one of the very few left in London and is a listed building of historic interest'. *The Hampstead Plaque Fund*

PARK, Thomas (1759-1834) and **John James** (1795-1833). **18 Church Row, NW3** English historians (father and son); lived here. Thomas was known as the 'Poetical Antiquary'. John James wrote the first history of Hampstead and a treatise on the law of dower (1819). *Hampstead Antiquarian and Historical Society*

PARKINSON, James (1755-1824). **1 Hoxton Square, N1**
English physician and geologist; lived here. He was the first to describe appendicitis (1812) and to identify a ruptured appendix as a cause of death. He is remembered for his identification (1817) of *paralysis agitans*, which came to be called Parkinson's disease. *Private*

PARRY, Sir (Charles) Hubert (Hastings) (1848-1918). **17 Kensington Square, W8**
English composer; lived here 1887-1918. Educated at Eton and Oxford, he was at the forefront of the regeneration of the English musical tradition. Director of the Royal College of Music (1895) and professor of music at Oxford (1900), he wrote three oratorios, an opera and orchestral and instrumental music. His best-loved compositions include the church anthem 'I Was Glad' (1902), written for the coronation of Edward VII, and his setting of Blake's (q.v.) 'Jerusalem'. He was knighted in 1898 and made a baronet in 1903. *London County Council*

PASSMORE EDWARDS. See **EDWARDS, John Passmore**

PATEL, Sardar Vallabhbhai Javerbhai (1875-1950). **23 Aldridge Road Villas, W11**
Indian politician; lived here. He was a follower of Mahatma Gandhi (q.v.) and a leader of the Indian National Congress. After independence he held several posts in Nehru's (q.v.) government. *Greater London Council*

PATMORE, Coventry Kersey Dighton (1823-96). **14 Percy Street, W1**
English poet and essayist; lived here 1863-4. He was a librarian of the British Museum 1846-66 and a member of the Pre-Raphaelite circle. He married three times and had six children His best-known work, *The Angel in the House* (1854), is a poetic eulogy of the married state. *London County Council*

PAUL, Robert William (1869-1943). **49 Sydney Road, N10**
Inventor and pioneer film producer and director; lived here 1914-20. With Birt

Acres (q.v.) he produced a motion picture camera and started a studio near this site in 1895. He filmed the Oxford and Cambridge Boat Race the same year and the Derby in 1896. *British Film Institute*

PAVLOVA, Anna (1881-1931). **Ivy House, North End Road, NW11**
Russian ballerina; lived here 1912-31. Trained in St Petersburg, she created her most famous role, the 'Dying Swan', in 1907. After working with Diaghilev, she began a series of tours throughout Europe in 1909 and purchased Ivy Cottage in 1912. She was also a noted choreographer. *Hendon Corporation*

PEABODY, George (1795-1869). **80 Eaton Square, SW1**
American merchant, financier and philanthropist; died here. Born in Massachusetts in a town now named after him, he traded in Baltimore and began to amass a considerable fortune. He established himself in London in 1837. His philanthropic gestures included the endowment of two institutes, two museums and an education fund in the United States and the provision of social housing in London. He is buried in Peabody, Massachusetts. *Greater London Council*

PEACOCK INN. 11 Islington High Street, N1
The inn, which stood here 1564-1962, was a staging post and continued as a public house until its demolition. It was immortalised in Thomas Hughes's *Tom Brown's Schooldays* and in Dickens's story *Boots at the Cherry Tree Inn*. There is also a painting of 1823 by James Pollard entitled *North Country Mails at the Peacock, Islington. Islington Borough Council*

PEAKE, Mervyn Lawrence (1911-68). **1 Drayton Gardens, SW10** *English Heritage;* **Surrey Court, 55 Woodcote Road, Wallington** *Borough of Sutton*
English writer and artist; lived on the site of Surrey Court 1922-32 and 1952-62; lived in Drayton Gardens until 1968. Born in China, he attended the Royal Academy of Arts in London and became an illustrator, not only of his own works but also of such classics as *Treasure Island* and 'The Ancient Mariner'. His novels include *Titus Groan* (1946), *Gormenghast* (1950) and *Titus Alone* (1959). He also published two volumes of verse.

PEARCE, Stephen (1819-1904). **54 Queen Anne Street, W1**
Portrait and equestrian painter; lived here 1856-84. *Private*

PEARS, Sir Peter (1910-86). **45a St John's Wood High Street, NW8**
English tenor; lived and worked here with Benjamin Britten (q.v.), with whom he shares the plaque, 1943-6. He was an organ scholar at Hertford College, Oxford, and a student of the Royal College of Music. Pears was famed for his renderings of Britten's works, most notably in *Peter Grimes.* He and Britten were co-founders of the Aldeburgh Festival. *Westminster City Council*

PEARSON, John Loughborough (1817-97). **13 Mansfield Street, W1**
English architect; lived and died here. He was a forerunner of the Gothic revival of the mid nineteenth century. His most important designs include the church of St Augustine, Kilburn (1870-80), and Truro Cathedral (1879 onwards). The plaque is shared with Sir Edwin Landseer Lutyens (q.v.). *London County Council*

PEARSON, Karl (1857-1936). **7 Well Road, Hampstead, NW3**
English mathematician, statistician and scientist; lived here. He published works on eugenics, biometrics and mathematics and was a founder of modern statistical theory. *Greater London Council*

PECZENIK, Charles Edmund (1877-1967). **48 Grosvenor Square, W1**
Architect; lived here. A notable example of his work is the Kensington Close Hotel (1937). *Private*

PEEL, Sir Robert (1788-1850). **16 Upper Grosvenor Street, W1**
British statesman; lived here. He entered Parliament in 1809. As Home Secretary (1822-7), he was responsible for forming the police forces, which were

nick-named 'Bobbies' or 'Peelers' after him. Peel served as Conservative prime minister 1834-5 and 1841-6. The plaque also records his father, also Sir Robert Peel (1750-1830), who was a wealthy Lancashire cotton manufacturer, an MP from 1790, and created a baronet in 1800. *English Heritage*

PELHAM, Sir Henry (*c*.1695-1754). **Rear of 22 Arlington Street, SW1**
English statesman; lived here. A supporter of Walpole (q.v.), he held various offices under his leadership, prior to becoming prime minister (1753-4). *English Heritage*

PENN, William (1644-1718). **Watersmeet, High Street, Rickmansworth**
The plaque reads: 'Here William Penn, Quaker statesman and man of vision, founder

Sir Robert Peel.

of Pennsylvania and planner of Philadelphia, friend of the Indians, crusader for civil and religious liberty, designer of European peace, resided for five years after his marriage to Gulielma Maria Springett (1644-94). The stone above this tablet, from Pennsbury, Pennsylvania, the ancient home of William Penn on the Delaware river, was presented by the Pennsylvania Historical and Museum Commission, who are the custodians of the property.' *Pennsylvania Historical and Museum Commission*

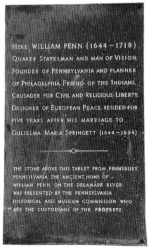

PEPYS, Samuel (1633-1703). **12 Buckingham Street, WC2** *London County Council;* **14 Buckingham Street, WC2** *London County Council;* **Seething Lane, Private Garden of PLA, EC3** *Corporation of the City of London;* **Salisbury Court, EC4** *Corporation of the City of London*
English diarist and Secretary of the Admiralty. There are four plaques, denoting that he: was born in a house on the Salisbury Court site; lived and worked in the Navy Office (destroyed by

The plaque at 12 Buckingham Street, WC2.

fire 1673) on the Seething Lane site; lived on the two Buckingham Street sites (number 12, 1679-88). He was educated in London and Cambridge. His diary, which was written between 1660 and 1669, chronicles his life – both public, as a member of the Admiralty, and private – and impressions of the Great Plague (1665), the Great Fire of London (1666) and other events of the time. Written in a form of shorthand, it was not deciphered until 1825.

PERCEVAL, Spencer (1762-1812). **59-60 Lincoln's Inn Fields, WC2**
British Conservative politician; lived here 1791-1808. Educated at Harrow and

Cambridge, he became a lawyer and then an MP (1796). Rising through the ranks, he was Chancellor of the Exchequer 1807-9 and prime minister 1809-12. He was shot and killed in the lobby of the House of Commons by a Liverpool merchant who blamed the government for his bankruptcy. His assassin was later hanged for the crime. *London County Council*

PERKIN, Sir William Henry (1838-1907). **Gosling House, Cable Street, E1**
English chemist; worked on this site. In 1856, while seeking a substitute for quinine, he discovered the first aniline dye, mauve. *Stepney Historical Trust*

PETER THE GREAT (1672-1725). **146 Deptford High Street, SE8**
Tsar of Russia; worshipped at Deptford Friends' Meeting House in 1697-8, which stood on this site until its demolition in 1907. During his tour of western Europe, he spent several months in Deptford. *Private*

PETRIE, Sir William Matthew Flinders, (1853-1942). **5 Cannon Place, NW3**
English archaeologist and Egyptologist; lived here 1919-35. He excavated the pyramids at Giza and other important historical sites in Egypt and Palestine. The professor of archaeology at University College London (1892-1933), he wrote numerous books. *London County Council*

PEVSNER, Sir Nikolaus Bernhard (1902-83). **2 Wildwood Terrace, NW3**
German-born architectural historian; lived here 1936-83. He fled to Britain in 1933 to escape the Nazis and became an authority on British architecture. He wrote several books, including *An Outline of European Architecture* (1942) and, most notably, the fifty-volume *The Buildings of England* (1951-74). *Heath and Old Hampstead Society*

PHELPS, Samuel (1804-78). **8 Canonbury Square, N1**
English actor and manager; lived here. An actor from 1826, he made his name

in the Shakespearean roles of Hamlet, Richard III and Shylock. As manager of Sadler's Wells, he produced thirty-four of Shakespeare's plays. *London County Council*

PHILLIPS, Morgan Walter (1902-63). **115 Rannoch Road, W6**
Welsh politician; lived here 1959-63. He was General Secretary of the Labour Party 1944-62 and held various positions on parliamentary and borough council socialist committees. He also published several political and economic pamphlets. *Borough of Hammersmith and Fulham*

PHILPOT, Glyn Warren (1884-1937). **Lansdowne House, 80 Lansdowne Road, W11.** See also **RICKETTS, Charles**
English artist; lived and worked here. He studied in Paris and the Lambeth School of Art, becoming a trustee of the Tate Gallery (1935-7). The plaque is shared with five other artists. *Greater London Council*

PICK, Frank (1878-1941). **15 Wildwood Road, NW11**
English administrator and designer; lived here. He was vice-chairman of the London Passenger Transport Board 1933-40 and a founder of the Design and Industries Association. The plaque describes him as a 'pioneer of good design for London Transport'. *Greater London Council*

PICTON, Cesar (1755-1836). **52 High Street, Kingston-upon-Thames**
Self-made man; lived here 1788-1807. An African, he was brought to England from Senegal to work as a servant boy. He went on to become a prosperous coal merchant and made this his residence as a gentleman. *Borough of Kingston*

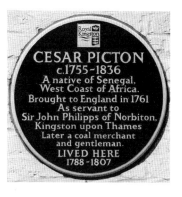

PINERO, Sir Arthur Wing (1885-1934). **115a Harley Street, W1**
English playwright; lived here 1909-34. He was the author of some fifty dramas and comedies, the best-known being *The Second Mrs Tanqueray* (1893). *Greater London Council*

PISSARRO, Camille (1830-1903). **National Westminster Bank, 77a Westow Hill, SE19** *Crystal Palace Foundation;* **Corner of Kew Green and Gloucester Road, Kew** *Private*
French Impressionist painter; stayed on the first site 1870-1 and at the second address in 1892. Born in the West Indies, he became a prolific artist who experimented with different styles, including pointillism. One of the most important and underrated of the Impressionists, he made several visits to England.

PISSARRO, Lucien (1863-1944). **27 Stamford Brook Road, Chiswick, W6**
French painter and engraver; lived here. The son of Camille Pissaro (q.v.), he adopted Seurat's pointillist technique. He settled in London in 1890 and founded the Eragny Press (1896). *Greater London Council*

PITT, William, 'the Elder', First Earl of Chatham (1708-78). **10 St James's Square, SW1** *London County Council;* **Chatham House, North End Avenue,**

NW3 *Private*
British Whig politician; lived in a house on the St James's Square site; lived in a house formerly on the site in North End Avenue, where Chatham House is named after him. He served as prime minister 1756-61 and 1766-8. He successfully led Britain in the war against France and spoke strongly in support of the American colonists, urging an amicable settlement.

PITT, William, 'the Younger' (1759-1806). **120 Baker Street, W1**
British statesman; lived here 1803-4. Son of the Earl of Chatham, he was educated at home and at Cambridge. He soon became a Tory MP and was Chancellor of the Exchequer aged twenty-three and Britain's youngest prime minister at the age of twenty-four (1783-1801). Pitt was prime minister again 1803-4. During his time in office he carried out many reforms and achieved unity with Ireland. He is buried in Westminster Abbey. *London County Council*

PITT-RIVERS, Augustus Henry Lane Fox (1827-1900). **4 Grosvenor Gardens, SW1**
English anthropologist and archaeologist; lived here. A soldier by training (he rose to become a lieutenant-general), he inherited estates in Wiltshire (1880) which were rich in Saxon and Roman artefacts, inspiring him to become an archaeologist. He revolutionised excavation methods and donated his collection to the museum bearing his name in Oxford. He was also the first Inspector of Ancient Monuments (from 1882). *Greater London Council*

PLAATJE, Solomon Tshekiso (1876-1932). **25 Carnarvon Road, E10**
Black South African community leader and writer; lived here. He was the founder of the African National Congress (1912). *Greater London Council*

PLACE, Francis (1771-1854). **21 Brompton Square, SW3**
English radical and reformer; lived here 1833-51. He contrived the repeal of the anti-union Combination Acts in 1824 and helped in the passing of the Reform Act in 1832. *London County Council*

PLAYFAIR, Sir Nigel Ross (1874-1934). **26 Pelham Crescent, SW7**
English actor-manager and producer; lived here. He became manager of the Lyric Theatre in 1919 and thereafter staged many successful productions. *London County Council*

POE, Edgar Allan (1809-49). **172 Stoke Newington Church Street, N16**
American poet and short-story writer; attended a school on this site. Between 1815 and 1820 his family lived in England, and for three years he went to the Manor House School here. Many of his stories centred on the macabre. Among his best-known works are *The Fall of the House of Usher* (1839) and *The Murders in the Rue Morgue* (1841). *Borough of Hackney*

EDGAR ALLAN POE
1809-1849
Writer and Poet
Was a pupil at the
Manor House School (1817-1820),
Which stood on this site.

POLIDORI, Dr John William (1795-1821). **38 Great Pulteney Street, W1**
British novelist of Italian descent; was born and died here. Polidori qualified as a medical practitioner at the age of nineteen. He was a friend of Lord Byron, Mary and Percy Shelley (q.v.) and Claire Clairmont, all of whom (including Polidori) agreed to write a story of terror. Polidori's *The Vampyre – A Tale* was the predecessor

The plaque to Dr John Polidori was unveiled by the Italian ambassador, Paolo Galli, on 15th July 1998. Members of the John Polidori Literary Society were dressed in costumes of the early nineteenth century.

to the Dracula legend and was contemporary with Mary Shelley's *Frankenstein. Westminster City Council*

POLLOCK'S TOY THEATRE SHOP. 1-22 McGregor Court, Hoxton Street, N1

Founded in 1851, it stood near this site until the premises were bombed during the Second World War. The shop's motto, according to the plaque, was 'Penny plain, twopence coloured'. *Borough of Hackney*

POMBAL, Sebastião José de Carvalho e Mello, Marquess of (1699-1782). 23-4 Golden Square, W1. See PORTUGUESE EMBASSY

Portuguese statesman; lived here while ambassador to Britain (1739-44). He was a reformer in his own country and was responsible for the rebuilding of Lisbon after the earthquake of 1775. *Greater London Council*

POPE, Alexander (1688-1744). Mawson Arms, 110 Chiswick Lane South, W4 *English Heritage;* Plough Court, 32 Lombard Street, EC3 *Corporation of the City of London*

English poet and satirist; born in a house on the Plough Court site; lived in Mawson's Buildings (the first address) 1716-19. Crippled from an early age and largely self-educated, he nevertheless became one of the greatest English poets, a master of metre. Many of his rhyming couplets have become idioms in the English language. His finest works include *An Essay on Criticism* (1711) and *The Rape of the Lock* (1712). In addition to translations of Homer's *Odyssey* and *Iliad*, he famously denounced a critic of his edition of Shakespeare in the embittered *The Dunciad* (1728).

Alexander Pope

PORTUGUESE EMBASSY. 23-4 Golden Square, W1

These two houses were the Portuguese embassy 1724-47. The Marquess of Pombal (q.v.), lived here. *Greater London Council*

POTTER, Beatrix (1866-1943). Corner of Old Brompton Road and The Boltons, SW3

English author and illustrator of children's books; lived in a house on this site 1866-1913.

Her first work, *The Tale of Peter Rabbit,* was published in 1900 and was followed by *The Tailor of Gloucester* in 1902. She lived in the Lake District for many years, and her house there, Hilltop, Sawrey, is now a museum owned by the National Trust, of which she was an early benefactress. Her coded diary was translated and published in 1966. *The Boltons Association, The Beatrix Potter Society and Frederick Warne & Company*

POULTERS' HALL (1630-66). **King Edward Street, EC1**
Moved here in 1630 from its original site at Leadenhall Market, the hall was destroyed by the Great Fire of London in 1666. *Corporation of the City of London*

PRE-RAPHAELITE BROTHERHOOD. 7 Gower Street, WC1
The Pre-Raphaelite Brotherhood was formed here in 1848 by a group of artists of whom the nucleus and leading exponents were Millais (q.v.), Holman Hunt (q.v.) and D. G. Rossetti (q.v.). They agreed to paint in a style similar to that of fifteenth-century artists with particular attention to detail and clarity of form. This new movement was given impetus by support from the critic John Ruskin (q.v.). *English Heritage*

PRIESTLEY, J. B. (John Boynton) (1894-1984).
3 The Grove, Highgate, N6
English novelist, playwright and essayist; lived here. Educated at Cambridge, he had written several books before *The Good Companions* (1929) made him popular. Other humorous books followed. His first stage play was *Dangerous Corner* (1932). Among his other dramas, *An Inspector Calls* (first performed in 1946) is perhaps best known. He was also renowned for his literary criticisms, travel writing and broadcasts. Unusually for English Heritage, the plaque is coloured brown. *English Heritage*

PRIESTLEY, Joseph (1733-1804). **113 Lower Clapton Road, E5**
English chemist and Presbyterian minister; lived in a house on this site 1792-4. Despite a full life as a minister, he applied himself to studying chemistry and did pioneering work on gases, identifying oxygen, ammonia and sulphur dioxide. His support for the French Revolution, however, made him unpopular in Britain, and his home in Birmingham was sacked by a mob in 1791. He afterwards lived here before emigrating to America. *Borough of Hackney*

PRITT, Denis Nowell, QC (1887-1972). **446 Uxbridge Road, W12**
Labour politician, lawyer and writer; lived here. He was called to the bar in 1909 and retired from practice in 1960. Pritt was Labour MP for North Hammersmith 1935-50 and published many books on political and legal subjects. He received many European honours. *Borough of Hammersmith and Fulham*

PRYDE, James (1866-1941). **Lansdowne House, 80 Lansdowne Road, W11.** See also **RICKETTS, Charles**
English artist; lived and worked here. He is best

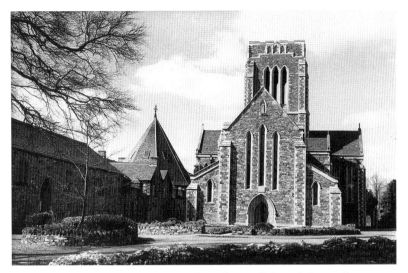

Augustus Welby Northmore Pugin was the architect of Mount St Bernard monastery in Leicestershire.

known for his posters, produced with Sir William N. P. Nicholson. The plaque is shared with five other artists.

PUGIN, Augustus Charles (1762-1832), and **Augustus Welby Northmore** (1812-52). **106 Great Russell Street, WC1**
Architects (father and son); lived here. Pugin the elder settled in London from his native France and set up an office, from which they designed Gothic-style buildings and furniture. The younger Pugin, who is the more famous, collaborated with Sir James Barry (q.v.) in the design of the Palace of Westminster and became the leader of the great nineteenth-century Gothic revival. His notable church designs include St Augustine, Ramsgate (1846-51), which he financed himself. He was also a prolific designer of stained glass, tiles and other fittings. *Duke of Bedford*

PURDEY, James (1828-1909). **57-8 Audley Street, W1**
English gunmaker; built these premises in 1880 to house his new showrooms and workshops. *Westminster City Council*

PURKOVIC, Miodrag A. (1907-76). **Serbian Community Centre, Lancaster Road, W11**
Serbian historian; lived here 1972-6. Dr Purkovic was the chairman of the Society of Serbian Writers and Artists Abroad. *Private*

PYTHON, Monty. Neals Yard, WC2
Fictional personage who, according to the blue plaque, 'lived here 1976-87'. The plaque in fact marks the studios where the comic television series *Monty Python's Flying Circus* was produced during that time. *Animation Lighting and Recording Studios*

R

RACKHAM, Arthur (1867-1939). **16 Chalcot Gardens, NW3**
English illustrator and artist; lived here 1903-20. His Art Nouveau-style draw-ings appeared in editions of *Peter Pan* (1906), *Hans Andersen's Fairy Tales* (1932) and other books. *Greater London Council*

RADCLIFFE, John (1650-1714). See under **BOW STREET**
English doctor. He was physician to William III and Mary and bequeathed the bulk of his estate to the Radcliffe Infirmary and Library, and to University College, Oxford.

RAFFLES, Sir (Thomas) Stamford (1781-1826). **Highwood House, Highwood Hill, Mill Hill, NW7**
British colonial administrator; lived here 1825-6. He served with the East India Company and participated in a campaign against Java in 1811, reforming its administration. He founded Singapore (1819) while governor of Sumatra (1818-23) and was also the founder and first president of London Zoo. *Hendon Corporation*

RAGLAN, Fitzroy James Henry Somerset, First Baron Raglan (1788-1855). **5 Stanhope Gate, Hyde Park, W1**
English general; lived here 1835-54. He served under Wellington in the Penin-sular War (1808-12) and lost his right arm at the Battle of Waterloo (1815). He won the battles of Alma and Inkerman in the Crimea but was responsible for the fateful order for the charge of the Light Brigade at the Battle of Balaclava. The Raglan sleeve is named after him. *London County Council*

RAMBERT, Dame Marie (1888-1982). **Kensington Temple, Ladbroke Road, W11** *Private;* **19 Campden Hill Gardens, W8** *English Heritage*
Stage name of Cyvia Rambam, Polish-born British ballet dancer and teacher; lived in Campden Hill Gardens; founded the Ballet Rambert at the first address. She danced with Diaghilev's Ballet Russe, later settling in London and marrying Ashley Dukes (q.v.) in 1918. Having opened her own dance studio, she became the foremost exponent of modern ballet technique. Her company became known as Ballet Rambert in 1935.

*The plaque in
Ladbroke Road, W11.*

RATCLIFF CROSS. See **WILLOUGHBY, Sir Hugh**

RATHBONE, Eleanor Florence (1872-1946). **Tufton Court, Tufton Street, SW1**
English social reformer; lived here. Of Quebec descent and Oxford-educated, she became a member of Liverpool City Council in 1909 and later MP for the

Combined English Universities. A pioneer of family allowances, she fought for women's rights at home and abroad (notably India) and opposed the government's appeasement of Hitler and unwillingness to intervene in the Spanish Civil War. *Greater London Council*

RAVILIOUS, Eric William (1903-42). **48 Upper Mall, Hammersmith, W6**
English artist and engraver; lived here 1931-5. He designed furniture and many patterns for Wedgwood pottery, including a mug for Edward VIII's coronation (which never took place). Renowned for his fine wood-engraved book illustration, he is known also for his watercolours and colour lithographs. As an official war artist, he lost his life on a flight near Iceland. *English Heritage*

RAY-JONES, Tony (Anthony) (1941-72). **102 Gloucester Place, W1**
English photographer; lived and worked here. He studied his art both in London and in the USA, where he later taught in San Francisco. Ray-Jones exhibited at photographic exhibitions but after a short illness died at an early age. *Westminster City Council*

RAYMOND, Ernest (1888-1974). **22 The Pryors, West Heath Drive, NW3**
English novelist; lived here. Raymond was ordained in 1914 but resigned his holy orders in 1923. He was the author of more than fifty books, including *We the Accused* (1935), for which he was awarded the gold medal of the Book Guild (1936). His autobiography, *The Story of My Days,* was published in 1968. *Hampstead Plaque Fund*

READING, First Marquess of. See **ISAACS, Rufus**

RED HOUSE. Red House Lane, Bexleyheath
Built during 1859 and 1860 by Philip Webb (q.v.), architect for the artist and polymath William Morris (q.v.), who lived here 1860-5. Morris filled the house with furnishings in the Arts and Crafts style of which he was the pioneer. *Greater London Council*

Below left: *The plaque commemorating Sir Humphry Repton in Romford.*
Below right: *This plaque in Hampstead, NW3, is to a well-known local woman, Maggie Richardson, who sold flowers at this spot for sixty years.*

REED, Sir Carol (1906-76). **213 King's Road, SW3**
English film director and producer; lived here 1948-76. His films include *Kipps* (1941), *The Way Ahead* (1944), *Odd Man Out* (1947), *The Fallen Idol* (1948), *The Third Man* (1949), *Our Man in Havana* (1959) and the Academy Award-winning *Oliver* (1968). *Private*

REES, Sir John Milsom (1866-1952). **18 Upper Wimpole Street, W1**
English surgeon; lived and practised here 1914-39. He was laryngologist to the Royal Household 1910-36, a consultant ear, nose and throat surgeon at several leading hospitals and received a knighthood in 1916. *Westminster City Council*

REITH, John Charles Walsham, First Baron Reith of Stonehaven (1889-1971). **6 Barton Street, SW1**
Scottish pioneer of broadcasting; lived here 1924-30. An engineer by training, he moved into telecommunications and became the first general manager of the BBC (1922-7) and later its Director-General (1927-38). MP for Southampton from 1940, he served as Minister of Works and Buildings (1940-2) and chairman of the Commonwealth Telecommunications Board (1946-50). *English Heritage*

RELPH, Harry (Little Tich) (1867-1928). **Blacksmiths' Arms, Cudham Lane, Cudham** *Borough of Bromley;* **93 Shirehall Park, Hendon, NW4** *Greater London Council*
Music-hall comedian; born in a house on the first site; lived and died at the second address. He earned his nickname as a chubby child, an allusion to the 'Tichborne Claimant', a fat man involved in a celebrated court case. Only 4 feet 6 inches (1.37 metres) tall, he usually appeared on stage in enormous long boots to perform his famous dance. Little Tich was the origin of the word 'titchy'.

The plaque in Cudham.

REPTON, Humphry (1752-1818). **182 Main Road, Gidea Park, Romford**
English landscape gardener; lived on this site. He worked for a period with the architect John Nash and was responsible for the landscaping of over two hundred gardens and parks. His gardens were less naturalistic than those of his predecessor 'Capability' Brown, containing more picturesque elements. (Photograph, page 165) *Private*

RESCHID PASHA, Mustapha (1800-58). **1 Bryanston Square, W1**
Turkish statesman and reformer; lived here as ambassador in 1839. *Greater London Council*

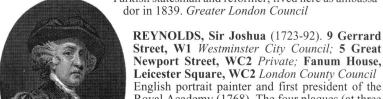

Sir Joshua Reynolds.

REYNOLDS, Sir Joshua (1723-92). **9 Gerrard Street, W1** *Westminster City Council;* **5 Great Newport Street, WC2** *Private;* **Fanum House, Leicester Square, WC2** *London County Council*
English portrait painter and first president of the Royal Academy (1768). The four plaques (at three addresses) denote that he lived in Great Newport Street 1753-61; founded The Club in 1764 with Dr Johnson in the Turk's Head Tavern, formerly in Gerrard Street; lived from 1761 until his death in a house on the third site. After studies in London, Rome and Venice, he became the leading portrait-

ist of his time. He and Dr Johnson (q.v.), with whom he shares the second plaque, belonged to a distinguished circle that included Garrick (q.v.), Burke (q.v.), Boswell (q.v.), Sheridan (q.v.) and Oliver Goldsmith. His best-known portraits include *Three Ladies Adorning a Term of Hymen* (1773-6) and Mrs Siddons as the *Tragic Muse* (1789).

REYNOLDS, St Richard (*c*.1492-1535). **Outbuilding, Syon House, Isleworth**
A monk of Syon Abbey; dwelt on this site. The abbey was founded by Henry V in 1422 on the site of the present Syon House. Reynolds, who was chaplain to the abbey, was hanged at Tyburn (q.v.) in 1535 for refusing to accept Henry VIII as head of the Church of England. In 1970 he was included among the forty English martyrs to be canonised. *Private*

RICHARDS, Frank (Charles Hamilton) (1875-1961). **Ealing Broadway Centre, W5**
British writer; born in a house on this site. Richards was the author of the 'Billy Bunter' stories. He wrote for the *Gem* and *Magnet* comic papers until the Second World War, after which his school stories appeared mainly in book and play form. The plaque is situated in the centre of a shopping mall. *Private*

RICHARDSON, Maggie (1901-74). **Corner of High Street and Willoughby Road, Hampstead, NW3**
A well-loved local character; sold flowers here for sixty years. The flower-ornamented plaque names the spot as Maggie's Corner and is dedicated to her 'fond memory'. (Photograph, page 165) *The Heath and Old Hampstead Society*

RICHMOND, George (1809-96). **20 York Street, W1**
English painter; lived here 1843-96. He met Samuel Palmer (q.v.) at the Royal Academy and became one of 'The Ancients' but was most successful as a portrait painter. Many famous people sat for him in York Street, including John Ruskin (q.v.), William Gladstone (q.v.), Cardinal Manning (q.v.) and the Duke of Wellington. *London County Council*

RICKETTS, Charles (1866-1931). **Lansdowne House, 80 Lansdowne Road, W11**
English artist and stage designer; lived and worked here. A friend of Charles Shannon (q.v.), he was an illustrator by training and also founded the Vale Press, for which he developed his own typefaces. The studios at Lansdowne House were frequented by other artists, and those recorded on the same plaque are Charles Shannon (q.v.), Glyn Philpot (q.v.), Vivian Forbes (q.v.), James Pryde (q.v.) and F. Cayley Robinson (q.v.). *Greater London Council*

RIPON, George Frederick Samuel Robinson, Marquess of (1827-1909). **9 Chelsea Embankment, SW3**
English Liberal statesman; lived here. His appointments included Under-Secretary for War (1859), Under-Secretary (later Viceroy) for India (1880-4), First Lord of the Admiralty (1886), Colonial Secretary (1892-5) and Lord Privy Seal (1905-8). *London County Council*

RIZAL, Dr Jose (1861-96). **37 Chalcot Crescent, NW1**
Filipino patriot and writer; lived here. He was exiled

from the Philippines after publication of a political novel. Rizal studied medicine in Spain and practised in Hong Kong. He was shot upon his return to the Philippines, having been accused of instigating an anti-Spanish revolt. *Greater London Council*

ROBERTS, Frederick Sleigh, First Earl (1832-1914). **47 Portland Place, W1**
British field marshal; lived here 1902-6. He won the Victoria Cross in 1858 following the siege of Delhi. Roberts defeated the Afghans in 1880 and was commander-in-chief, India, 1885-93. He became a field marshal and commander-in-chief in Ireland in 1895 and served in South Africa 1900-2. He became commander-in-chief of the British army and was created an earl in 1901. *London County Council*

ROBINSON, F. Cayley (1862-1927). **Lansdowne House, 80 Lansdowne Road, W1.** See also **RICKETTS, Charles**
British artist, lived and worked here. The plaque is shared with five other artists.

Earl Roberts.

ROBINSON, George. See RIPON, Marquess of

ROBINSON, James (1813-62). **14 Gower Street, WC1**
British physician; lived and worked here. He was a pioneer of anaesthesia and dentistry. *English Heritage*

ROBINSON, W. (William) Heath (1872-1944). **75 Moss Lane, Pinner**
English cartoonist and illustrator; lived here 1913-18. He became famous for his comic drawings of ridiculous contraptions to do simple tasks. *Greater London Council*

ROE, Sir Edwin Alliot Verdon (1877-1958). **Railway Arches, Walthamstow Marshes, E17**
English aircraft manufacturer; assembled his AVRO No.1 triplane here. He was the first Englishman to design, build and fly his own aircraft. In July 1909 he

made the first all-British powered flight from Walthamstow Marshes. The plaque is situated on the railway arches by the towpath of the river Lea. *Greater London Council*

The railway arches on Walthamstow Marshes with the plaque to Sir Edwin Roe.

The plaque to Sir Samuel Romilly in Gray's Inn Square, WC1.

ROGERS, Dr Joseph (1821-89). **33 Dean Street, W1**
British health care reformer; lived here. *English Heritage*

ROHMER, Sax (1886-1959). **51 Herne Hill, SE24**
Pen name of Arthur Henry Ward, British writer; lived here. He was the author of the *Fu Manchu* novels. Some of his stories were later filmed, with the actor Christopher Lee playing Fu Manchu. *Greater London Council*

ROMILLY, Sir Samuel (1757-1818). **6 Gray's Inn Square, WC1** *Private;* **21 Russell Square, WC1** *Greater London Council*
English lawyer; occupied chambers at Gray's Inn Square 1778-91; lived in Russell Square. He entered Gray's Inn at the age of twenty-one, becoming Solicitor-General in 1806. He was a member of Parliament and pursued many law reforms.

ROMNEY, George (1734-1802). **Holly Bush Hill, NW3**
English portrait painter; lived here 1796-9. He was renowned with Reynolds (q.v.) and Gainsborough (q.v.), as one of the most eminent artists of his day. Emma, Lady Hamilton, sat for him on more than one occasion. *London County Council*

The building in Holly Bush Hill, NW3, where George Romney lived.

RONALDS, Sir Francis (1788-1873). **26 Upper Mall, Hammersmith, W6**
English inventor, set up the first electric telegraph (8 miles long) here in 1816. His invention was turned down when offered to the Admiralty. He also invented a system of photographic registration. *Private*

ROSE, Miss. 133 Old Church Street, Chelsea, SW3
The blue enamel plaque has a Latin inscription, which translates: 'Miss Rose who held sway in this house and holds sway, now and forever, in our hearts.' The plaque was erected in 1966, and it has been suggested that Miss Rose was a cat. *Private*

ROSEBANK. The Ridgeway, Mill Hill, NW7
This plaque records that this was a Quaker meeting house, founded in 1678. By 1719 attendance had dropped so much that meetings ceased. The building was afterwards turned into a dwelling house. (Photograph, page 170) *Hendon Corporation*

169

Rosebank in Mill Hill, NW7.

ROSEBERY, Archibald Philip Primrose, Fifth Earl of (1847-1929). **20 Charles Street, W1**
British Liberal statesman; born here. He was the first chairman of the London County Council (1889-90 and 1892) and Secretary for Foreign Affairs in the Gladstone (q.v.) administration, becoming prime minister 1894-5. A keen breeder of racehorses, he won the Derby three times. *London County Council*

ROSENBERG, Isaac (1890-1918). **Whitechapel Library, 77 High Street, E1**
English poet and artist; studied here. He trained at the Slade School of Art but is best remembered for his poetry written during the First World War. After twenty months serving at the front he died during the Somme offensive. *English Heritage*

ROSS, Sir James Clark (1800-62). **2 Eliot Place, Blackheath, SE23**
English polar explorer; lived here. He discovered the magnetic North Pole in 1831 and led an expedition to the South Pole 1839-43. The Ross Sea, Ross Island and Ross Dependency are all named after him. *London County Council*

ROSS, Sir Ronald (1857-1932). **18 Cavendish Square, W1**
British physician; lived here. He served in the Indian Medical Service 1895-98. With Sir Patrick Manson (q.v.), he discovered the malaria parasite and deduced its transmission by mosquitoes. He won the Nobel prize for physiology or medicine in 1902 and directed the Ross Institute for tropical diseases from 1926. *Greater London Council*

ROSSETTI, Christina Georgina (1830-94). **30 Torrington Square, WC1**
English poet; lived and died here. She was the sister of Dante Gabriel Rossetti (q.v.). Her religious devotion is evident in many of her poems, as is her sense of alienation, which increased during her life. Her best-known work is probably *Goblin Market and Other Poems*, published in 1862. She also wrote the carol 'In the Bleak Midwinter'. Despite poor health she continued to write up to the time of her death. *Greater London Council*

ROSSETTI, Dante Gabriel (1828-82). **110 Hallam Street, W1** *London*

The plaque to Dante Gabriel Rossetti at 17 Red Lion Square, WC1.

County Council; **16 Cheyne Walk, SW3** *London County Council;* **17 Red Lion Square, WC1** *London County Council*
British painter and poet; born in a house on the Hallam Street site; lived in Cheyne Walk (so too did Swinburne (q.v.), with whom he shares the plaque); lived in Red Lion Square, where he became the mentor of Morris (q.v.) and Burne-Jones (q.v.), with whom he shares the plaque. Of Italian descent, he was the brother of Christina Rossetti (q.v.). With Holman Hunt (q.v.) and Millais (q.v.) he formed the Pre-Raphaelite Brotherhood in 1848. His *Girlhood of Mary Virgin* (1849) was the first official Pre-Raphaelite painting. Several of his poems were interred with his wife Elizabeth Siddall, who had modelled for him and Millais but died prematurely in 1860. He later recovered and published the poems.

ROSSI, John Charles Felix (1762-1839). **116 Lisson Grove, NW11**
English sculptor; lived here. He studied at the Royal Academy and in Rome, was elected a member of the Royal Academy in 1802 and became sculptor to the Prince Regent and William IV. Much of his work can be seen in St Paul's Cathedral. This plaque is shared with Benjamin Haydon (q.v.). *London County Council*

ROWLAND, E. C. H. (1883-1955). **Times 2 Shopping Mall Entrance, High Street, Sutton**
Music-hall artist; general manager of Surrey County (Gaumont) Cinema, which opened here 1921. He is best remembered for his First World War songs, the most famous being 'Mademoiselle from Armentières'. After the war he retired from the stage to become manager of the cinema. (Photograph, page 172) *Borough of Sutton*

ROWLANDSON, Thomas (1757-1827). **16 John Adam Street, Adelphi, WC2**
English caricaturist and painter; lived in a house on this site. Having inherited a considerable sum at an early age, he squandered it gambling and drinking. In his mid twenties he turned from portrait to caricature painting and illustrated novels by, among others, Goldsmith, Smollett and Sterne. He published three series of drawings with the title *Tour of Dr Syntax in Search of the Picturesque* (1812, 1820 and 1821). *London County Council*

ROY, Ram Mohun (1772-1833). **49 Bedford Square, WC1**
Indian scholar and reformer; lived here. He studied Buddhism in Tibet and worked as a revenue collector for some years before receiving an inheritance. Roy, who turned to writing books on religion, had the title 'Rajah' bestowed on him in 1830. *Greater London Council*

ROY, Major-General William (1726-90). **10 Argyll Street, W1**
Scottish military surveyor, antiquarian and founder of the Ordnance Survey; lived here. He received a medal in 1784 from the Royal Society for his work. His *Military Antiquities of the Romans* was published in 1793. *Greater London Council*

ROYAL COLLEGE OF PHYSICIANS, site of. Warwick Lane, EC4
Founded in the early sixteenth century, the college moved to Warwick Lane in 1674, after the Great Fire of London. It remained here until 1825, when it was relocated in Pall Mall. *Corporation of the City of London*

ROYAL MARYLEBONE THEATRE, 71 Church Street, NW8
Site of the Royal Marylebone Theatre 1837-68 and the Royal West London Theatre 1896-1913. Charlie Chaplin (q.v.) appeared here in 1904. *Westminster City Council.*

ROYAL SOCIETY FOR THE ENCOURAGEMENT OF ARTS, MANUFACTURES AND COMMERCE. 8 John Adam Street, WC2

Better known as the Royal Society of Arts. These premises were built 1772-4 by the architects Robert and James Adam (q.v.). *Private*

RUSKIN, John (1819-1900). **26 Herne Hill, SE24**
English author and art critic; lived in a house on this site. He published five volumes of *Modern Painters* (1843-60) and advanced the appreciation of the work of J. M. W. Turner (q.v.) and also the Pre-Raphaelite Brotherhood. From 1860 he also turned his attention to social and economic problems. He was Slade Professor of Art at Oxford 1869-79 and an accomplished watercolourist in his own right. Ruskin College, Oxford, was founded in his name (1899). The plaque is situated on a plinth in the garden of the modern house now standing on the site. *London County Council*

RUSSELL, Admiral Edward (1653-1727). **43 King Street, WC2**
British admiral; lived and died here. A supporter of William III of Orange, he played an important part in the French war of 1689-97 as commander of the British and Dutch fleet in its victory at La Hogue (1692). Russell was First Lord of the Admiralty three times in the period 1694-1717. *Duke of Bedford*

RUSSELL, John, First Earl Russell (1792-1878). **37 Chesham Place, SW1**
British statesman; lived here. Son of the Sixth Duke of Bedford, he was prime minister 1846-52, Foreign Secretary under Palmerston (q.v.) 1859-65 and prime minister again 1865-6. He was created an earl in 1861. *London County Council*

RUSSELL, John Scott (1808-82). **Westferry Road, E14.** See **GREAT EASTERN**
British civil engineer who built the *Great Eastern* (1858) to the design of Isambard Kingdom Brunel (q.v.). *London County Council*

RUTHERFORD, Mark. See **WHITE, William Hale**

The plaque to E. C. H. Rowland at the entrance to the shopping mall in High Street, Sutton.

SACKVILLE, Charles, Sixth Earl of Dorset (1638-1706). See **BOW STREET**

English courtier, poet and favourite of Charles II. In later years he was a patron of the poet Dryden (q.v.).

SACKVILLE-WEST, Vita (Victoria Mary) (1892-1962). **182 Ebury Street, SW1**

English writer and gardener; lived here with her husband Harold Nicolson (q.v.). Born at Knole House, Kent, the daughter of the third Baron Sackville, she married Harold Nicolson (q.v.) in 1913. Members of the Bloomsbury Group, they lived an unconventional lifestyle. Her finest work is probably the poem *The Land* (1926), but she is better known as the model for Virginia Woolf's (q.v.) *Orlando*. Her estate at Sissinghurst, Kent, is a lasting memorial to her love of gardening. (Photograph, page 143) *English Heritage*

ST ANTHONY'S HOSPITAL, site of. **53 Threadneedle Street, EC2**

The hospital was started by brothers from France who received the building from Henry III in 1242. It was developed in the fourteenth and fifteenth centuries to include a chapel and grammar school. By the mid sixteenth century the school had declined and the chapel became the French Protestants' church. This was rebuilt after the Great Fire of 1666 and finally demolished in 1840. *Corporation of the City of London*

ST BARTHOLOMEW, site of. **62-3 Threadneedle Street, EC2**

Church. Burnt down in 1666 during the Great Fire of London, it was rebuilt by Sir Christopher Wren (q.v.) and finally demolished in 1841. *Corporation of the City of London*

ST BENET GRACECHURCH, site of. **60 Gracechurch Street, EC3**

Church. First mentioned 1181, it was repaired 1630-3 and destroyed shortly afterwards in the Great Fire. Having been rebuilt to Sir Christopher Wren's (q.v.) design, it was used until declining congregations forced a union with All Hallows, Lombard Street, in 1844. The church was finally closed and demolished in 1876. *Corporation of the City of London*

ST BENET SHEREHOG, site of. **Pancras Lane, EC4**

Church. Built in the early twelfth century, it was destroyed in the 1666 fire. A sherehog is a ram that has been castrated after its first shearing, and the church was in the centre of the wool district of London. In addition to the rectangular blue plaque, similar wording can be found etched into the stonework on the adjacent wall. *Corporation of the City of London*

ST GABRIEL FENCHURCH, site of.
Plantation House, Fenchurch Street, EC1
Church. First recorded in 1315, it was destroyed by the Great Fire of London in 1666 and never rebuilt. *Corporation of the City of London*

ST JOHN STREET TURNPIKE, site of.
Tunbridge House, St John Street, EC1
Stood here *c*.1746-1830. *Borough of Islington*

ST JOHN THE BAPTIST, HOLYWELL, Priory of, and THE THEATRE, site of. 86-8 Curtain Road, EC2
The plaque reads: 'The site of this building forms part of what was once the precinct of the priory of St John the Baptist, Holywell. Within a few yards stood from 1577 to 1598 the first London building specially devoted to the performance of plays and known as 'The Theatre'. A second plaque at the same address also records the fact that William Shakespeare acted at The Theatre, which was built by James Burbage, and that plays by Shakespeare were performed here. *London County Council* and *Borough of Hackney.*

ST JOHN THE EVANGELIST, site of. Watling Street, EC4
Church. Dedicated in the mid thirteenth century, it was repaired and improved 1626, but was destroyed by the Great Fire forty years later. Situated in Friday Street off Watling Street, it served the smallest parish in the City of London. *Corporation of the City of London*

ST JOHN ZACHARY, site of. Public Gardens, Gresham Street, EC2
Church. Originally St John the Baptist, it was given to a man named Zacharie in 1180 by the canons of St Paul's. It was rebuilt several times until destroyed by the Great Fire, when the parish was united with St Anne and St Agnes, Gresham Street. *Corporation of the City of London*

ST LEONARD, site of. 35 Foster Lane, EC2
Church. Destroyed in the Great Fire of 1666. *Corporation of the City of London*

ST LEONARD EASTCHEAP, site of. Eastcheap, EC3
Church. First mentioned in 1214, it was also known as St Leonard's Milkchurch. In 1618 it was enlarged and repaired after the steeple had been burnt down. It only survived a few more years, as it was destroyed in the Great Fire of 1666 and not replaced. *Corporation of the City of London*

ST MARGARET'S CHURCH AND THE BOROUGH COMPTER, site of. 34 Borough High Street, SE1
At the dissolution of the monasteries (1540) this thirteenth-century church was combined with St Mary Magdalene Overy and renamed St Saviour's. The original building was partly used as a courthouse and partly as the borough

prison (or compter, as it was known). *Borough of Southwark*

ST MARTIN, site of. Empire House, St Martin-le-Grand, EC1
Collegiate church. It was originally a monastery and college founded by two brothers in the

eleventh century, the foundation being confirmed by charter in 1068. The church was rebuilt in 1360 and was the largest and safest sanctuary in England. Prisoners on their way to execution often escaped to enter it. Counterfeit jewellery was made here for many years, despite efforts to stop the practice, and in the sixteenth century it was famous for lacemaking. It was demolished in 1548. *Corporation of the City of London.*

ST MARTIN ORGAR CHURCH, site of. Martin Lane, EC4
Church. It was first mentioned in the twelfth century when it was granted by the deacon Ordgar to the canons of St Paul's. It was badly damaged in the Great Fire of London but partly restored and used by French Protestants until finally being demolished in 1820. *Corporation of the City of London*

ST MARTIN OUTWICH, site of. 39 Threadneedle Street, EC2
Church. Founded in 1403, it escaped the Great Fire of London, only to be burnt down a century later in 1765 by a fire that swept through Cornhill. It was rebuilt in 1796 but served a declining congregation and was finally demolished in 1874. *Corporation of the City of London*

ST MARY BOTHAW, site of. Cannon Street Station, EC4
Church. Its old name was St Mary Boatehaw by the Erber, *haw* being another word for yard; it must therefore have been close to a boatyard. It was destroyed in the Great Fire of 1666. *Corporation of the City of London*

ST MARY COLE CHURCH, site of. 82 Poultry, EC2
This medieval church was built by a man named Cole and was the church where St Thomas à Becket (q.v.) was baptised. It was destroyed in the Great Fire of 1666 and not rebuilt. *Corporation of the City of London*

ST MARY WOOLCHURCH HAW, site of. Walbrook, EC4
Church. First mentioned in the eleventh century, it received its name from the fact that wool was weighed in the churchyard (*haw* meaning yard). It was not severely damaged in the Great Fire, but it was later demolished. The Mansion House now stands on the site. *Corporation of the City of London*

ST MICHAEL BASSISHAW, site of. Basinghall Street, EC2
Church. This was a small red-brick church designed by Sir Christopher Wren (q.v.) in 1676. The parish was united with St Lawrence Jewry when the church was demolished in 1900. *Corporation of the City of London*

ST MILDRED'S CHURCH, site of. St Mildred's Court, Poultry, EC2
It was first recorded in 1175, burnt down in the Great Fire of 1666 and rebuilt by

Wren (q.v.) in 1670-6. It was demolished in 1872 under an Act of Parliament. *Corporation of the City of London*

ST PANCRAS CHURCH, site of. Pancras Lane, EC4
The church belonged to the monastery of Christchurch, Canterbury, and is first mentioned in 1257. The rector from 1593 to 1607 was the poet Abraham Fleming, who was the first translator of Virgil. The church was destroyed in the Great Fire of 1666. *Corporation of the City of London*

ST PAUL'S SCHOOL, site of. New Change, EC4
The school stood near this spot from 1512 until 1884. It was founded by Dean Colet. *Corporation of the City of London*

ST THOMAS'S HOSPITAL, site of. Post Office, Borough High Street, SE1
Founded in 1225, it was rebuilt in 1552 and survived here until 1865. St Thomas's Hospital is now located at Lambeth Palace Road. *Borough of Southwark*

ST THOMAS THE APOSTLE CHURCH, site of. 28 Queen Street, EC4
First mentioned in 1170 and rebuilt by the lord mayor, John Barnes, in 1371, it was destroyed in 1666 in the Great Fire. The parish was united with that of St Mary Aldermary in 1670. *Corporation of the City of London*

SALISBURY, Francis Owen (Frank) (1874-1962). 23 West Heath Road, NW3
English artist; lived here. He was a portrait and figure painter, depicted historical and ceremonial subjects and also worked in stained glass. Among the famous persons who sat for him were various members of the royal family, Archbishops of Canterbury, British prime ministers, American presidents and other heads of state. His magnificent paintings of ceremonial scenes brought him admiration and worldwide awards. *Hampstead Plaque Fund*

SALISBURY, Robert (Arthur Talbot) Gascoyne Cecil, Third Marquess of (1830-1903). 21 Fitzroy Square, W1
British Tory statesman; lived here. Educated at Eton and Oxford, he had a long and eventful political career, which included opposition to Gladstone's 1865 Reform Bill. He was Foreign Secretary 1878-80 and prime minister 1885-6, 1886-92 and 1895-1902. *London County Council*

SALISBURY COURT PLAYHOUSE, site of. 8 Salisbury Square, EC4

Built in 1629 as a private theatre, it was used for twenty years until the interior was destroyed by Parliamentary soldiers. At the Restoration it reopened but was burnt down in the Great Fire of 1666. *Corporation of the City of London*

SALVATION ARMY. 23 New Road, E1
The plaque reads: 'The first indoor meeting of the mission which became the Salvation Army was held here on 3rd September 1865'. See also Booth, William. *Tower Hamlets Environment Trust*

SALVIN, Anthony (1799-1881). **11 Hanover Terrace, Regent's Park, NW1**
English architect; lived here. A pupil of John Nash, he became an authority on the restoration and improvement of castles, notably the Tower of London, Windsor, Caernarvon and Warwick. He also specialised in the design of large private houses, the most outstanding example of his work being Harlaxton Manor in Lincolnshire (1835-43). *English Heritage*

SAMBOURNE, Edward Linley (1844-1910). **18 Stafford Terrace, W8**
English cartoonist and illustrator; lived here. He worked for *Punch* magazine from 1867 to 1910. He also illustrated several books including Charles Kingsley's (q.v.) *The Water Babies.* Now called Linley Sambourne House, his home is a museum of his life and work. *Private*

SAN MARTÍN, José de (1778-1850). **23 Park Road, NW1**
Argentinian statesman and soldier; stayed here in 1824. He led an army liberating Argentina and, with Bernardo O'Higgins (q.v.), Chile and Peru, earning his nickname 'the Liberator'. He became the Argentine national hero. His residence here lasted less than three months. *London County Council*

SANTLEY, Sir Charles (1834-1922). **13 Blenheim Road, NW8**
English baritone opera singer; lived and died here. Although his great love was Italian opera, he became more widely known through concerts and oratorios. *London County Council*

SARACEN'S HEAD INN, site of. Snow Hill, EC1
A well-known tavern, described in the sixteenth century as having thirty beds and stabling for forty horses. It was mentioned by Dickens in *Nicholas Nickleby* but was demolished in 1868. *Corporation of the City of London*

SARGENT, Sir (Harold) Malcolm Watts (1895-1967). **Albert Hall Mansions, Kensington Gore, SW7**
English conductor; lived and died in a flat here. An organist by training, he conducted the Royal Choral Society from 1928, Liverpool Philharmonic Orchestra 1942-8 and the BBC Symphony Orchestra 1950-7. Popular for his skill in choral work and his general exuberance, he was also conductor of the Henry Wood Promenade Concerts at the Royal Albert Hall. *English Heritage*

SARGENT, John Singer (1856-1925). **31 Tite Street, SW3**
American artist; lived and worked here for twenty-four years and died here.

Born in Florence, he had a cosmopolitan life, settling in London in 1885 and becoming a fashionable portrait painter. His subjects included Ellen Terry (q.v.) and Robert Louis Stevenson (q.v.). He made many visits to the USA, where he painted some notable murals and was an official war artist during the First World War. *Private*

SARTORIUS, John F. (*c*.1755-*c*.1830). **155 Old Church Street, SW3**
British painter of sporting themes; lived here 1807-12.

His favoured topics were horse races and fox hunts. He exhibited at the Royal Academy from 1802. *London County Council*

SASSOON, Siegfried Lorraine (1886-1967). **23 Campden Hill Square, W8**
English writer; lived here 1925-32. His experiences of the First World War led him to the view that war is a moral outrage, which he expressed in his early works *Counterattack* (1918) and *War Poems* (1919). His best-known work, *Memoirs of a Fox Hunting Man* (1928), is among several of his books that were autobiographical. *English Heritage*

SAUNDERS, Sir Edwin, FRCS (1814-1901). **89 Wimbledon Parkside, SW19**
Royal dentist; lived and died here. He was dentist to Queen Victoria and King Edward VII and was also a lecturer at St Thomas's Hospital and president of the Orthodontist Society. *English Heritage*

SAVAGE, James. See **ESSEX STREET**

SAVARKAR, Vinayak Damodar (1883-1966). **65 Cromwell Avenue, Highgate, N6**
Indian patriot and philosopher; lived here. He came to England in 1906 and four years later was implicated in the murder of an Indian and shipped back to India. During the journey he escaped but was recaptured in France. Upon arrival in India he was tried and sentenced to fifty years' imprisonment. While in gaol he wrote two political books and was actively involved in the politics of his country. Upon release in 1937 he became leader of the Indian Communist party. *Greater London Council*

SAVOY THEATRE. The Strand, WC2
Built in 1881 by Richard D'Oyly Carte (q.v.). The plaque states: 'This was the first public building in the world to be lit throughout by electricity.' *Westminster City Council*

SCAWEN-BLUNT, Wilfrid (1840-1922). **15 Buckingham Gate, SW1**
English diplomat, poet and traveller; lived here. His travels took him to Europe, the Near East and Egypt. He married Lord Byron's granddaughter after having an affair with Catherine Walters (q.v.). The plaque cites him as the founder of Crabbet Park Arabian Stud. *Greater London Council*

SCHREINER, Olive (1855-1920). **16 Portsea Place, W2**
South African writer and feminist; lived here. Her best-known novel, *The Story of an African Farm* (1883), was published under the pseudonym Ralph Iron. She lived in England 1881-9 but spent only a few months in this house. *London County Council*

SCHWITTERS, Kurt (1887-1948). **39 Westmoreland Road, Barnes, SW13**
German artist; lived here. He resided in Norway from 1937 and England from 1940. His abstract works were often in the form of collages, made up from scraps of paper, bus tickets, buttons and so forth. His later three-dimensional constructions were mostly destroyed. *Greater London Council*

Admiral's Walk, Hampstead, NW3: the left-hand plaque commemorates John Galsworthy, the right-hand one Sir George Gilbert Scott.

SCOTLAND YARD, site of. Ministry of Agriculture, Whitehall Place, SW1
First headquarters of the Metropolitan Police 1829-90. *Greater London Council*

SCOTT, Sir George Gilbert (1811-78). **Admiral's House, Admiral's Walk, Hampstead, NW3**
English architect; lived here. A leading exponent of the Victorian Gothic revival, he was responsible for the design or restoration of many public buildings, including the Albert Memorial, St Pancras Station and Glasgow University. Numerous churches throughout Britain were adapted or restored by him. He is buried in Westminster Abbey. *London County Council*

SCOTT, Sir Giles Gilbert (1880-1960). **Chester House, Clarendon Place, W2**
English architect; designed this house and lived here from 1926 until his death. The grandson of Sir George Gilbert Scott (q.v.), he designed the Liverpool Anglican Cathedral (1904), Cambridge University Library (1931-4), the new Bodleian Library at Oxford (1936-46), Waterloo Bridge (1939-45) and the red telephone kiosk. He also supervised the rebuilding of the House of Commons after the Second World War. *English Heritage*

SCOTT, John. See ELDON, First Earl of.

SCOTT, Captain Robert Falcon (1868-1912). **56 Oakley Street, SW3**
English Antarctic explorer; lived here 1905-8 (although much of this time was spent at sea). He led two expeditions, one in 1900-4 and the tragic one of 1910-12. Having reached the South Pole one month later than the Norwegian expedition led by Amundsen, Scott, accompanied by Edward Wilson (q.v.),

Laurence Oates (q.v.), Bowers and Evans, perished in a blizzard on the return journey. *London County Council*

SEFERIS, George (1900-71). **7 Sloane Avenue, SW3**
Assumed name of Georgios Seferiades, Greek poet and diplomat; lived here. He was ambassador to the Lebanon 1953-7 and to Great Britain 1957-62, when he lived at this address. He was awarded the Nobel prize for literature in 1963. *Private*

SELLERS, Peter (1925-80). **10 Muswell Hill Road, N6**
English actor and comedian; lived here 1936-40 as a boy. He first received public recognition with Spike Milligan in *The Goon Show* on radio (1951-9). Sellers appeared in many films from 1951 until his death, including the 'Pink Panther' films as the bumbling Inspector Clouseau. *The Dead Comics Society*

SHACKLETON, Sir Ernest Henry (1874-1922). **12 Westwood Hill, SE26**
Irish Antarctic explorer; lived here during childhood. He accompanied Captain Scott (q.v.) on his first expedition (1900-4) and in all made four expeditions to Antarctica. He located the magnetic South Pole 1907-9. *London County Council*

SHAKESPEARE, William (1564-1616). **86-8 Curtain Road, EC2.** See also **BELL** and **GLOBE PLAYHOUSE, site of.**
England's greatest dramatist and playwright; acted at the Theatre (q.v.) on this site. Born in Stratford-upon-Avon, where he attended the grammar school, he married a local woman, Anne Hathaway. Eight years later he was writing and performing plays in London, both at the Theatre and at his own playhouse, the Globe (q.v.). Among the most admired of his thirty-eight plays are the tragedies *Hamlet* and *Macbeth*, the comedies *Much Ado about Nothing* and *A Midsummer Night's Dream* and the history plays *Richard III* and *Henry V*. He was also Britain's greatest writer of sonnets. *Borough of Hackney*

SHANNON, Charles (1863-1937). **Lansdowne House, 80 Lansdowne Road W11.** See also **RICKETTS, Charles.**
British artist and lithographer; lived and worked here. His works include *An Idyll*, *The Sapphire Bay*, *Tibullus in the House of Delia*, *The Sleeping Nymph*, and *The Infant Bacchus*. The plaque is shared with five other artists. *Greater London Council*

SHARP, Cecil James (1859-1924). **4 Maresfield Gardens, NW3**
Collector of English folk songs and dances; lived here. He was principal of the Hampstead Conservatory 1896-1905 and founder of the English Folk Dance and Song Society (1911), the headquarters of which are named after him. *Greater London Council*

SHAW, George Bernard (1856-1950). **29 Fitzroy Square, W1.** See also **ADELPHI TERRACE**.
Irish author, dramatist and critic; lived here 1887-98. An early member of the Fabian Society (q.v.), he wrote more than fifty plays. Among his many works are *Arms and the Man* (1894), *The Devil's Disciple* (1897), *Caesar and Cleopatra* (1901), *Man and Superman* (1905), *Pygmalion* (1913) and *Saint Joan* (1924). He lived in this house before moving to Hertfordshire. The plaque quotes: 'From the coffers of his genius he enriched the world.' *St Pancras Borough Council, later adopted by Greater London Council*

GEORGE BERNARD SHAW
LIVED IN THIS HOUSE
FROM 1887 TO 1898

FROM THE COFFERS OF HIS GENIUS
HE ENRICHED THE WORLD"

SHAW, Richard Norman (1831-1912). **Grim's Dyke, Old Redding, Harrow Weald**
British architect; designed this house. With W. E. Nesfield he

led the trend away from the Gothic back to traditional materials and a simpler architecture that matured into what became popularly known as 'Queen Anne' style. His designs include that of Cragside, Northumberland. The two plaques at this address are shared with Frederick Goodall (q.v.) and W. S. Gilbert (q.v.). *Greater London Council and Borough of Harrow*

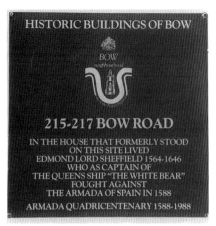

SHEFFIELD, Lord Edmond (1564-1646). **215-17 Bow Road, E3**
English naval officer; lived in a house on this site. As captain of the ship *The White Bear* he fought against the Spanish Armada in 1588. *Historic Buildings of Bow*

SHELLEY, Mary, née Godwin (1797-1851). **24 Chester Square, SW1**
English novelist and poet; lived and died here. The daughter of Mary Wollstonecraft (q.v.) and William Godwin, she became the second wife of

Percy Bysshe Shelley (q.v.). Her most famous novel is *Frankenstein* (1818). She also wrote *Valperga* (1823), *The Last Man* (1826) and *Faulkner* (1837). *Private*

SHELLEY, Percy Bysshe (1792-1822). **Applegarth House, Nelson Square, SE1** *Borough of Southwark;* **15 Poland Street, W1** *Greater London Council*
English poet and dramatist; lived in a house near the Southwark site; lived in Poland Street. Educated at Eton and Oxford, he was rejected by his wealthy father after marrying an unsuitable girl. He wrote numerous poems, including 'Alastor' (1815), 'The Revolt of Islam' (1818), 'Ode to the West Wind' (1819) and 'Adonais' (1821). His life was a stormy one; he left his first wife (who later committed suicide) for Mary Godwin, whom he married (q.v.); he amassed large debts and finally was drowned while sailing near Italy. His ashes were buried in Rome.

SHEPARD, Ernest Howard (1879-1976). **10 Kent Terrace, NW1**
English cartoonist and book illustrator; lived here. His most notable works were the illustrations for A. A. Milne's (q.v.) *Winnie the Pooh* (1926) and Kenneth Grahame's *The Wind in the Willows* (1931). *English Heritage*

SHEPHEARD, Sir Victor George (1893-1989). **Manor Place, Manor Park, Chislehurst**
British naval architect; lived here. From an apprenticeship in 1907 at HM Dockyard, Devonport, he graduated in 1915 and joined the Grand Fleet as a constructor lieutenant. He served at the Battle of Jutland and after the First World War returned to Whitehall, where he worked on cruiser and warship design. Shepheard was professor of naval architecture at Greenwich 1934-9 and

during the Second World War was at the Naval Constructions Department in Bath, becoming director in 1952. He was created CB in 1950 and KCB in 1954. *Borough of Bromley*

SHEPHERD, Thomas Hosmer (1793-1864). **26 Batchelor Street, N1**
English engraver; lived here 1820-42. He illustrated *A Picturesque Tour on the Regent's Canal* (1825) and made 159 engravings for *Metropolitan Improvements* (1826). His other great work was *Mighty London* during the 1850s. *Greater London Council*

SHERATON, Thomas (1751-1806). **163 Wardour Street, W1**
English furniture designer; lived here. Influenced by Hepplewhite and Chippendale (q.v.), he was noted for his neoclassical style furniture and inlaid work. He wrote several books on cabinet making. *London County Council*

SHERIDAN, Richard Brinsley (1751-1816). **10 Hertford Street, W1** *London County Council;* **14 Savile Row, W1** *Royal Society of Arts*
Irish-born dramatist and politician; lived in Hertford Street 1795-1802; lived and died in Savile Row. His plays include *The Rivals* (1775), *The School for Scandal* (1777) and *The Critic* (1779). He purchased Garrick's (q.v.) share of the Drury Lane Theatre, becoming its manager. Entering Parliament in 1780, he became a strong supporter of Fox (q.v.). His last years, spent in Savile Row, were marred by the burning down of his Drury Lane Theatre and his subsequent financial ruin, together with poor health. He is buried in Westminster Abbey.

SHINWELL, Manny (Emmanuel), **Baron** (1884-1986). **Brune House, Toynbee Street, E1**

English socialist politician; born in a house on this site. He was a member of Parliament from 1931 and became Minister of Fuel and Power (1946), Secretary of State for War (1947), Minister of Defence (1950-1) and Parliamentary Labour Party chairman (1964-7). In his later years he was known as 'the Father of the House' and was awarded a life peerage in 1970. *Borough of Tower Hamlets*

SHORT, Sir Frank (1857-1945). **56 Brook Green, W6**
English engraver and painter; lived here 1893-1944. He was head of the engraving school at the Royal College of Art, president of the Royal Society of Painters and Etchers (1910-39) and treasurer of the Royal Academy (1919-32). *London County Council*

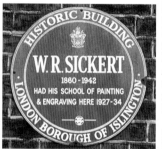

SIBELIUS, Jean (1865-1957). **15 Gloucester Walk, W8**
Finnish composer; lived here in 1909. His ardent nationalism was reflected in his work. His compositions include *En Saga* (1892) and *Finlandia* (1899), a violin concerto and seven symphonies. From 1940 he became a virtual recluse, and no further compositions were published. *English Heritage*

SICKERT, Walter Richard (1860-1942). **1 Highbury Place, N5** *Borough of Islington;* **6**

Mornington Crescent, NW1 *Greater London Council*
English artist; had his school of painting and engraving in Highbury Place 1927-34; lived and worked in Mornington Crescent. Born in Munich of a Danish father, he befriended Whistler (q.v.) when studying at the Slade School of Art, and Degas when studying in Paris. Although spending much of his time abroad, he lived at several addresses in Islington and in 1927 he set up a studio at Highbury Place. His earlier circle became known as the 'Camden Town Group' and his painting *Ennui* (1911) is a good example from that period.

SILVER STUDIO (1880-1963). **84 Brook Green Road, W6**
Arthur Silver (1853-96) and his sons Rex Silver (1879-1965) and Harry Silver (1881-1971), designers, lived here. Their designs, mainly for furnishing fabrics and wallpapers, were produced here 1880-1963 and included Art Nouveau, chintz and period designs. *Greater London Council*

SIMMS, Frederick Richard (1863-1944). **Railway Arch, Putney Bridge Station, SW6**
Motor-car entrepreneur; had his first workshop (1893) beneath this arch. The plaque calls him the 'father of the British motor industry'. Having made the acquaintance of Gottlieb Daimler, Simms obtained the British rights to Daimler engines. Here he made the first British motor cars and motor launches from 1893. Two years later he sold the company and the Daimler factory opened in Coventry; by this time the speed limit had been increased to 12 mph (19 km/h). Simms also helped to establish the forerunner of the RAC and the Society of Motor Manufacturers and Traders. *Society of Motor Manufacturers and Traders*

SIMON, Sir John (1816-1904). **40 Kensington Square, W8**
Pioneer of public health; lived here 1868-1904. A surgeon at St Thomas's Hospital, he was responsible for many sanitary reforms. He became first Medical Officer of Health for London (1848) and, later, Chief Medical Officer to the Privy Council. *London County Council*

SITWELL, Dame Edith (1887-1964). **Greenhill, Hampstead High Street, NW3**
English poet; lived here. She first came to notice with 'Facade' (1923) and over the next forty years produced a steady stream of poems, often reflecting her indignation over the cruelty of man and the evil in society. *English Heritage*

SITWELL, Sir Osbert (1892-1969). **2 Carlyle Square, SW3**
English author and poet; lived here 1919-63. The brother of Edith (q.v.) and Sacheverell Sitwell, he became a literary acquaintance of T. S. Eliot (q.v.) and Percy Wyndham Lewis (q.v.). He wrote novels, verse, travel books, criticism and biographies. *Park Lane Group*

SKITTLES. See **WALTERS, Catherine**

SLOANE, Sir Hans (1660-1753). **4 Bloomsbury Place, WC1**
Irish physician and naturalist; lived here 1695-1742. He

settled in London after studies there and in France. Sloane spent a year as physician to the governor of Jamaica, where he began his large collection of plants. He later became secretary to the Royal Society (1693-1713) and George II's royal physician. The founder of Chelsea Physic Garden (1721), he bequeathed his library of 50,000 books and many manuscripts to become the basis of the British Museum. *London County Council*

SMILES, Samuel (1812-1904). 11 Granville Park, SE13
Scottish physician and writer; lived here. He gave up medicine to become editor of the *Leeds Times* and was also appointed secretary of the Leeds & Thirsk Railway (1845-54) and of the South Eastern Railway (1854-66). He wrote a biography of George Stephenson and, most notably, *Self Help* (1859). His other works included *Lives of the Engineers* (1862). *London County Council*

SMIRKE, Sir Robert (1781-1867). 81 Charlotte Street, W1
English architect; lived here 1833-42. His most notable designs are the Covent Garden Theatre (1809), the British Museum (1823-47), the General Post Office (1824-9) and the College of Physicians (1825). *Greater London Council*

SMITH, F. E. (Frederick Edwin), First Earl of Birkenhead (1872-1930). 32 Grosvenor Gardens, SW1
English lawyer, Conservative politician and brilliant orator; lived here. Educated at Oxford, he was called to the bar in 1899. He entered Parliament in 1906 and was a supporter of Edward Carson's resistance to Irish home rule (1914). He moved to Grosvenor Gardens a year later when he became Attorney-General. He was Lord Chancellor 1919-22 and Secretary of State for India 1924-8. *Private*

SMITH, John Christopher (1712-95). 6 Carlisle Street, W1
English composer; lived and died here. A friend of Handel (q.v.), he acted as his secretary when the great composer's eyesight was failing. He wrote several operas while living here and presented Handel's scores and harpsichord to George III. The plaque mistakenly gives his dates as 1712-63. *Private*

SMITH, Stevie (1902-71). 1 Avondale Road, N13
Pen name of Florence Margaret Smith, British poet and novelist; moved here with her family at the age of three and lived here most of her life. Among her novels are *Novel on Yellow Paper* (1936), *Over the Frontier* (1938) and *The Holiday* (1949). Her poetry collections include *A Good Time Was Had by All* (1937) and *Selected Poems* (1962). One of her best-known individual poems is 'Not Waving But Drowning' (1957). *Borough of Enfield*

SMITH, Sydney (1771-1845). 14 Doughty Street, WC1
English author, clergyman and wit; lived here for three years from 1803. Educated at Winchester and Oxford, he was ordained in 1794. One of the founders of *The Edinburgh Review* (1802), he lived in London for six years, preaching and lecturing on moral philosophy. After several other clerical appointments he was made

a canon of St Paul's. His numerous articles and other writings examined such subjects as Catholic emancipation, the electoral system and conditions in prisons. *London County Council*

SMITH, William (1756-1835). **16 Queen Anne's Gate, SW1**
Pioneer of religious liberty; lived here. A follower of Fox (q.v.), he became an MP and represented several constituencies (1784-1830); Smith opposed the war with France. *Greater London Council*

SMITH, William Henry (1825-91). **12 Hyde Park Street, W2**
English bookseller and politician; lived here. The son of the founder of a bookseller's and newsagent's business, he took over on his father's death and expanded the chain. He entered Parliament in 1868, becoming First Lord of the Admiralty (1877-80) and Secretary of State for War (1885). He was also First Lord of the Treasury and Leader of the House of Commons (1886-91). *London County Council*

SMOLLETT, Tobias George (1721-71). **16 Lawrence Street, SW3**
Scottish novelist; lived here in part of the house 1750-62. He had been a seafarer and a surgeon before becoming a serious writer. His noted novels are *Roderick Random* (1748), *Peregrine Pickle* (1751) and *Humphrey Clinker* (1771). He also wrote a three-volume *History of England.* He died in Italy. The plaque is shared with Chelsea China (q.v.). *London County Council*

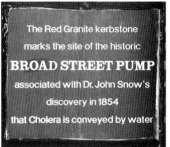

SNOW, Dr John (1813-58). **53 Frith Street, W1**
Pioneer anaesthetist and epidemiologist; lived in a house on this site. When cholera broke out in Britain in 1831-2 he became convinced that the epidemic was spread by infected water. During further outbreaks he conducted an experiment that confirmed this. At the John Snow public house, Broadwick Street, the site of Broad Street pump (which led to his discovery) is marked with a plaque. He used ether and chloroform as anaesthetics and devised special equipment for administering gas. Queen Victoria was one of the beneficiaries during the birth of Prince Leopold. *Association of Anaesthetists of Great Britain and Ireland*

SOKOLOW, Dr Nahum (1861-1936). **43 Compayne Gardens, NW6**
Statesman and author; lived and worked here 1921-36. He was president of the World Zionist Organisation. *Private*

SOMERSET, Lord Fitzroy. See **RAGLAN, Fitzroy**

SOPWITH, Sir Thomas Octave Murdoch (1888-1989). **46 Green Street, W1**
British aviator, aircraft designer and yachtsman; lived here 1934-40. He founded the Sopwith Aviation Company in 1912 and from 1935 was chairman, later president, of the Hawker Siddeley Group. *English Heritage*

SOUTHGATE LOCAL GOVERNMENT. 40 The Green, Southgate, N14
In 1881 this house became the first seat of local government in Southgate. *Borough of Enfield*

Charles Haddon Spurgeon.

SOUTHGATE VILLAGE HALL, site of. 151 High Street, Southgate, N14
Erected for the benefit of the parish of Southgate in 1882, the village hall was later demolished. *Borough of Enfield*

SPURGEON, Charles Haddon (1834-92). **99 Nightingale Lane, SW12**
English Baptist preacher; lived here. The Metropolitan Tabernacle was erected for him, and he preached there for thirty years to congregations of up to six thousand people. He published many works, including fifty volumes of sermons. *London County Council*

STANDARD IN CORNHILL, site of. Corner of Cornhill and Gracechurch Street, EC3
It supplied water from the Thames to the area by lead pipes until about 1603. It was afterwards used as a measurement point but was removed in 1674. *Corporation of the City of London*

STANFIELD, Clarkson (1793-1867). **Stanfield House, Hampstead High Street, NW3** *Hampstead Plaque Fund;* **14 Buckingham Street, WC2** *London County Council*
English artist; lived in Hampstead 1847-65, and at Buckingham Street. He trained as an heraldic painter but, after spending ten years at sea, he became a painter of seascapes and landscapes. He exhibited at the Royal Academy. The second plaque is shared with Pepys (q.v.).

STANFORD, Sir Charles Villiers (1852-1924). **56 Horton Street, W8**
Irish-born composer and teacher; lived here 1894-1916. He was professor at the Royal College of Music (1882) and Cambridge professor of music (1887). Stanford was a key figure in the nineteenth-century revival of the English choral tradition and wrote many fine canticle settings and anthems. He also taught many other notable composers and wrote symphonies, oratorios and operas. *London County Council*

STANHOPE, Charles, Third Earl Stanhope (1753-1816). **20 Mansfield Street, W1**
London-born inventor and politician; lived here. He married the sister of William Pitt the Younger (q.v.), with whom he disagreed in Parliament. Stanhope invented a microscopic lens that bears his name, printing systems and calculating machines and also experimented with electricity. *London County Council*

STANLEY, Edward Geoffrey Smith. See DERBY, Fourteenth Earl of

STANLEY, Sir Henry Morton (1841-1904). **2 Richmond Terrace, Whitehall, SW1**
Assumed name of John Rowlands, Welsh-born explorer and journalist; lived and died here. He travelled to the USA at the age of eighteen and also made four journeys to Africa with the backing of leading newspapers. In 1871 he set out to find the explorer David Livingstone (q.v.) and met him at Ujiji. He

A portrait of Henry Morton Stanley by Robert Gibb, painted in 1885.

explored Lake Tanganyika and the course of the Congo river and was MP for Lambeth 1895-1900. *Greater London Council*

STANLEY, William Ford Robinson (1829-1909). **12 South Norwood Hill, SE25**
Inventor, manufacturer and philanthropist; founded and designed the technical school and halls here. He was a scientific instrument maker and had a drawing-instrument business. His inventions included an inexpensive stereoscope and surveying and mathematical instruments. He was also an accomplished artist, musician and photographer. *English Heritage*

STEER, Philip Wilson (1860-1942). **109 Cheyne Walk, SW10**
English artist; lived and died here. He studied in Paris and was much influenced by the Impressionist movement. Steer was a friend of Sickert (q.v.) and a founder of the New English Art Club. Examples of his work can be found in the Tate Gallery. *Greater London Council*

STEPHEN, Sir Leslie (1832-1904). **22 Hyde Park Gate, SW7**
English scholar and critic; lived here. Brought up in the Clapham Sect (q.v.), he later became an agnostic (1870), publishing his reasons for this step. He was a founder of the *Pall Mall Magazine*, editor of the *Cornhill Magazine* (1871-2) and the first editor of *The Dictionary of National Biography* (1882-91). Stephen had several other works published, including biographies, and was the father of Virginia Woolf (q.v.). *London County Council*

STEPHENS, Henry C. (1841-1918). **Avenue House, East End Road, N3**
British entrepreneur and philanthropist; lived here and bequeathed the house to the people of Finchley. The son of Dr Henry Stephens (1796-1864), inventor of Stephens' ink, he controlled and expanded the family business. He was a great local benefactor. *The Finchley Society*

STEPHENSON, Robert (1803-59). **35 Gloucester Square, W2**
English engineer; lived at a house on this site and died there. The son of George Stephenson, designer of the 'Rocket' railway locomotive, he built the London–Birmingham railway, constructed the high-level bridge at Newcastle-upon-Tyne, the

Robert Stephenson assisted his father, George, in the design and construction of the 'Rocket', winner of the Rainhill Trials for steam locomotives in 1829.

THE 'ROCKET' OF M! ROB! STEPHENSON OF NEWCASTLE.

Conway and Menai bridges and several others. *London County Council*

STEVENS, Alfred (1817-75). **9 Eton Villas, Hampstead, NW3**
English painter, designer and sculptor; lived here. He worked in many media, including bronze, porcelain and silver. Among his numerous works are the Wellington monument in St Paul's and the lions at the British Museum. *London County Council*

STEVENSON, Robert Louis (Balfour) (1850-94). **Abernethy House, Mount Vernon, Hampstead, NW3**
Scottish novelist, essayist and poet; lived here 1873-9. Although qualified as a lawyer, he never practised. His novels include *Treasure Island* (1883), *Kidnapped* (1886), *Dr Jekyll and Mr Hyde* (1886), *The Black Arrow* (1888), *The Master of Ballantrae* (1889) and *Catriona* (1893). He spent the last five years of his life in Samoa. *Hampstead Plaque Fund*

STEWART, Donald Ogden (1894-1980). **103 Frognal, Hampstead, NW3**
American playwright and screenwriter; lived here. He won an Academy Award in 1940 for his screenplay adaptation of *The Philadelphia Story* and was successful with many films, including *The Barratts of Wimpole Street* (1934), *That Certain Feeling* (1941), *Life with Father* (1947) and *Cass Timberlaine* (1947). He retired to England in the 1950s. The plaque is shared with James Ramsay MacDonald (q.v.). *Hampstead Plaque Fund*

STILL, Sir George Frederic (1868-1941). **28 Queen Anne Street, W1**
Paediatrician; lived here. *English Heritage*

STOCKS MARKET, site of. Mansion House, EC4
Stood near this spot 1282-1737. It was a meat and fish market until the Great Fire of London (1666). When rebuilt it was used for fruit and vegetables until relocated in 1737. *Corporation of the City of London*

STOKER, Bram (Abraham) (1847-1912). **18 St Leonard's Terrace, SW3**
Irish-born novelist; lived here. He assisted Henry Irving (q.v.) in the running of the Lyceum Theatre (1878-1905). Stoker is famous for his novel *Dracula* (1897) and also wrote several other books. *Greater London Council*

STOKOWSKI, Leopold Anthony (1882-1977). **63 Marylebone High Street, W1**
American conductor of Polish origins. Born in London, he attended this school and the Royal College of Music and went on to become conductor of the Philadelphia Symphony Orchestra (1912-36), the New York Philharmonic (1946-50) and the Houston Symphony Orchestra (1955-60). He also founded the American Symphony Orchestra (1962). *Leopold Stokowski Society*

STONE, Marcus (1840-1921). **8 Melbury Road, W14**
Painter and illustrator; lived here 1877-1921. A specialist in 'history paintings', he also illustrated many of the books of Dickens (q.v.). and Trollope (q.v.) and worked for the *Cornhill Magazine*. His fine art was exhibited at the Royal Academy in sixty-three consecutive exhibitions. *English Heritage*

STONES END. Borough High Street, SE1
The plaque reads: 'Here was "Stones End" where Town Street met the old turnpike road. One of the parliamentary forts, erected to defend London during the civil war, stood here.' The site is now occupied by a police station. *Borough of Southwark*

HISTORIC SOUTHWARK

HERE WAS "STONES END" WHERE "TOWN STREET" MET THE OLD TURNPIKE ROAD. ONE OF THE PARLIAMENTARY FORTS, ERECTED TO DEFEND LONDON, DURING THE CIVIL WAR STOOD HERE

STOPES, Dr Marie Charlotte Carmichael (1880-1958). **14 Well Walk, Hampstead, NW3** *Hampstead Plaque Fund;* **61 Marlborough Road, N19** *Borough of Islington;* **108 Whitfield Street, W1** *Private*
English pioneer of birth control. She lived in Hampstead with her first husband R. R. Gates. Her second marriage to H. V. Roe (1878-1949), aircraft manufacturing brother of A.V. Roe (q.v.), was successful, and together they opened the first family planning clinic at Marlborough Road in 1921. This moved to Whitfield Street in 1925. Her book *Married Love* caused a sensation when published in 1916 because of its frank handling of the subject of sex. Altogether she wrote seventy books.

The plaque in Hampstead, NW3.

STOTHARD, Thomas (1755-1834). **28 Newman Street, W1**
English painter and engraver; lived and died here. He exhibited at the Royal Academy and is well known for engravings as diverse as *Canterbury Pilgrims* and *Flitch of Bacon.* He was also a designer of architectural fittings, monuments and jewellery. *London County Council*

STRACHEY, (Giles) Lytton (1880-1932). **51 Gordon Square, WC1**
English biographer and critic; lived here briefly. He was a member of the Bloomsbury Group (q.v.). His works include *Landmarks in French Literature* (1912), *Eminent Victorians* (1918) and *Queen Victoria* (1921). *Greater London Council*

STRANG, William (1859-1921). **20 Hamilton Terrace, NW8**
English painter and etcher; lived here 1900-21. Among the works he illustrated were *The Ancient Mariner* (1896), Kipling's short stories (1900) and *Don Quixote* (1902). His output of etching plates totalled over seven hundred. Another plaque at this address records the occupancy of Sir George MacFarren (q.v.). *London County Council*

STREET, George Edmund (1824-81). **14 Cavendish Place, W1**
English architect; lived here. Having been an assistant to Sir George Gilbert Scott (q.v.), he started his own practice in 1849, which he

George Edmund Street.

moved from Oxford to London in 1855. He designed many neo-Gothic buildings, including the London Law Courts and a number of churches. Influenced by the views of Ruskin (q.v.) he was himself influential upon Webb (q.v.) and Morris (q.v.), who trained in his Oxford practice. *Greater London Council*

STRYPE STREET, 10 Leydon Street, E1
Formerly Strype's Yard. The plaque states that it 'derives its name from the fact that the house of John Strype (died 1648) silk merchant, was situated there'. His son, John Strype (1643-1737), a historian and biographer, was born here. Strype junior's works include a biography of Thomas Cranmer, Archbishop of Canterbury. *London County Council*

STUART, Prince Charles Edward (1720-88). See ESSEX STREET
Known as 'Bonnie Prince Charlie' or 'The Young Pretender'; pretender to the British throne.

STUART, John McDouall (1815-66). 9 Campden Hill Square, W8
Scottish-born explorer; lived and died here. He made seven expeditions in Australia and in 1860 became the first man to cross the continent from south to north. *London County Council*

STURDEE, Thankfull (1852-1934). 16 Bolden Street, Deptford, SE8
Photographer and local historian; lived here 1900-3. He was known as 'the father of Fleet Street photographers'. Sturdee is remembered mainly for *Reminiscences of Old Deptford* (1895) and many photographs of the area. *Borough of Lewisham*

SUESS, Eduard (1831-1914). 4 Duncan Terrace, N1
Austrian geologist and statesman; was born here and lived here for his first three years, his family moving to Prague in 1834. He was a professor of geology in Vienna (1857-1901) and served as a municipal councillor. Suess was responsible for regularising the course of the Danube and providing Vienna with clean drinking water. His theories led to the modern concepts about continental drift. *Geological Society of London*

SUFFOLK, Duke of (died 1545). Brandon House, Borough High Street, SE1 *Borough of Southwark;* 160 Borough High Street, SE1 *Borough of Southwark*
Site of Suffolk Palace. Charles Brandon, who was the first Duke of Suffolk, was a brother-in-law of Henry VIII. The plaques refer to his uncle Thomas Brandon (spelled Branden on the plaque), who died c.1509.

The plaque on Brandon House, SE1.

SULLONIACAE, site of. Brockley Hill, Stanmore
Roman pottery, situated next to the old Roman road Watling Street *c*.65-160 AD. Relics have been found throughout Great Britain that can be traced back to this site. *Borough of Hendon*

SUNDAY TIMES. 4 Salisbury Court, EC4
The first number of the *Sunday Times* was edited at this address by Henry White, 20th October 1822. *Private*

SUN YAT SEN (1866-1925). **4 Warwick Court, WC1**
Chinese revolutionary leader and provisional president (1912); lived in a house on this site while in exile. As founder of the united China, he is accepted by both nationalist and communist regimes as the father of the Chinese republic. *Private*

SURREY IRON RAILWAY. Wall of Ram Brewery, Ram Street, SW18
The plaque reads: 'The Surrey Iron Railway was the first public railway in England, probably the first in the world. The railway ran along this road on its route from Croydon to the mouth of the river Wandle, a distance of nearly nine miles. Goods wagons were pulled by horses along a track of cast-iron plates laid on stone sleepers, some of which are set in the wall below. The gauge was 4' 2". It opened

in 1803, following the passing of the Surrey Iron Railway Act of 1801, and closed in 1846, the victim of the success of newer railways powered by steam.' *Wandsworth Society*

SUTHERLAND, Graham Vivian (1903-80). **Four Winds, Upland Road, Sutton**
English artist; lived here 1922-4. Early in his career he produced paintings and etchings of rural scenes and exhibited at the Royal Academy 1923-30. During the Second World War he was an official war artist. His most notable portraits included depictions of W. Somerset Maugham (q.v.) and Sir Winston Churchill (q.v.), the latter being disliked by Lady Churchill and destroyed upon her instructions. His most famous work is his large tapestry for the new Coventry Cathedral. *Borough of Sutton*

SVEVO, Italo (1861-1928). **67 Charlton Church Lane, SE7**
Italian-born novelist; lived here. Italo Svevo was the pen name of Ettore Schmitz. His early novels were unsuccessful, but under the patronage of James

Joyce (q.v.) he achieved recognition for his work. His novels include *As a Man Grows Older* (1898) and *Confessions of Zeno* (1923). *English Heritage*

SWINBURNE, Algernon Charles (1837-1909). **16 Cheyne Walk, SW3** *London County Council;* **11 Putney Hill, SW15** *London County Council*
English poet and critic; lived at both addresses. In poor health for many years, he was friendly with some of the Pre-Raphaelites and lived for a time with Dante Gabriel Rossetti (q.v.) in Cheyne Walk, sharing the plaque there with him. From 1879 until his death he lived in Putney with his friend Theodore Watts-Dunton (q.v.), who is also commemorated on the Putney plaque. Swinburne published several volumes of poems, plays and essays.

SYMONS, George James (1838-1900). **62 Camden Square, NW1**
English meteorologist; lived here 1868-1900. A pioneer in the scientific study of rainfall, he was the founder of the British Rainfall Organisation, by which means he increased the number of reporting stations in Britain from 168 to over 3500. He was twice president of the Royal Meteorological Society. *Private*

SYNAGOGUE, site of the first. 25 Thistlethwaite Road, N5
The first synagogue in the present-day London Borough of Hackney, built 1779-80, stood to the rear of this building in the grounds of Clapton House. *Borough of Hackney*

SZABO, Violette (1921-45). **18 Burnley Road, Stockwell, SW9**
French-born secret agent and heroine; lived here. Brought up in Brixton, she married a French soldier, who was killed in 1941. Working for the French Resistance, she was captured and executed by the Nazis. She was posthumously awarded the George Cross (1946) and the Croix de Guerre (1947). A film of her experiences entitled *Carve Her Name with Pride* was made in 1958. *Greater London Council*

TAGLIONI, Marie (1804-84). **14 Connaught Square, W2**

Italian ballerina; lived here 1875-6. The quintessential romantic ballerina, with an almost faultless technique, she excelled in the title role of *La Sylphide*. There seems to be some dispute as to her date of birth as the plaque gives it as 1809 while most sources record her as being five years older. *London County Council*

TAGORE, Rabindranath (1861-1941). **3 Villa on the Heath, Vale of Health, NW3**

Indian poet and philosopher; stayed here in 1912. He received the Nobel prize for literature in 1913 and was knighted 1915 but resigned his knighthood four years later as a protest against British policy in the Punjab. His works include *Binodini* (1902), *The Crescent Moon* (1913), *Chitra* (1914) and *The Religion of Man* (1931). *London County Council*

TALLEYRAND, Prince (Prince Charles Maurice de Talleyrand-Périgord) (1754-1838). **21 Hanover Square, W1**

French statesman; lived here 1830-4. Educated for the church, he became bishop of Autun in 1788, but later president of the French Assembly (1790). He was excommunicated by the Pope for suggesting the confiscation of the church's property and was exiled (to London and the United States). He returned to Paris after the fall of Robespierre and became foreign minister under different administrations and represented France at the Congress of Vienna (1814). *Greater London Council*

The plaque to Marie Taglioni in Connaught Square, W2.

TALLIS, John (1816-76). **233 New Cross Road, SE14**
Publisher of *London Street Views*; lived here from 1870 until his death. He over-reached himself with his publishing business and became bankrupt in 1861. *Greater London Council*

TANDY, Jessica (1909-94). **58a Geldeston Road, E5**
Stage and film actress; born at this address. She is best remembered for her role in *Driving Miss Daisy,* a film in which she starred late in life. *Borough of Hackney*

The plaque commemorating Harry Tate in Camden Road, Sutton.

TATE, Harry (1872-1940). **27 Camden Road, Sutton** *Borough of Sutton;* **72 Longley Road, SW17** *Greater London Council*
Stage name of Ronald MacDonald Hutchinson, Scottish-born music-hall comedian; lived 1920-31 in Camden House, which stood near the first site; also lived on the site of the second address. He appeared in silent films and was one of the first entertainers to broadcast.

TAUBER, Richard (1891-1948). **Park West, Kendal Street, W2**
German-born British tenor; lived in a flat here 1947-8. He gained popularity in light opera, particularly in Franz Lehar's works, and was regularly heard on radio and seen in films. *English Heritage*

TAWNEY, Richard Henry (1880-1962). **21 Mecklenburgh Square, WC1**
English historian; lived here for the last ten years of his life. Born in Calcutta, he was educated at Rugby and Oxford, becoming a Fellow of Balliol College. He was president of the Workers Educational Association 1928-44 and professor of economic history at London University 1931-49. He wrote a number of studies in English economic history. A second plaque here commemorates Sir Syed Ahmed Khan (q.v.). *Greater London Council*

TAYLOR, James Hudson (1832-1905). **6 Pyrland Road, N5**
English missionary; made his headquarters here 1872-95. He was trained as a physician but moved into missionary work, founding the China Inland Mission in 1865. *Private*

TELEVISION. Alexandra Palace, Wood Green, N22. See also **BAIRD, John Logie.**
The plaque records: 'The world's first regular high-definition television service was inaugurated here by the BBC, 2nd November 1936.' *Greater London Council*

TEMPEST, Dame Marie (1864-1942). **24 Park Crescent, W1**
Stage name of Mary Susan Etherington, English actress; lived here 1899-1902. She excelled in the drawing-room comedies of Noel Coward (q.v.) and W. Somerset Maugham (q.v.). *Greater London Council*

194

TEMPLE, Henry John. See **PALMERSTON, Third Viscount**

TENNYSON, Alfred, First Baron Tennyson (1809-92). **9 Upper Belgrave Street, SW1** *English Heritage;* **15 Montpelier Row, Twickenham** *Private*
English poet; lived in Upper Belgrave Street in 1880 and 1881; also lived in Montpelier Row. Born and educated in Lincolnshire, he later went to Trinity College, Cambridge. His most famous works include 'The Lady of Shalott', 'The Lotus Eaters', 'Ulysses' and 'The Charge of the Light Brigade'. His poem 'In Memoriam' (1850) was written after the death of his friend A. H. Hallam. Although living mainly in Sussex and the Isle of Wight, he resided for a time in London. He was Poet Laureate 1850-92.

TERRISS, William (1847-97). **Adelphi Theatre, Maiden Lane, WC2**
English actor; murdered here. While principal actor at the Adelphi Theatre he was stabbed through the heart at the stage door by a jealous out-of-work rival. A fund set up after his death financed the Terriss Memorial Lifeboat House at Eastbourne, where the RNLI Lifeboat Museum now stands. *Westminster City Council*

Dame Ellen Terry.

TERRY, Dame Ellen (1847-1928). **22 Barkston Gardens, SW5** *London County Council;* **215 King's Road, SW3** *Private*
English actress; lived in Barkston Gardens from 1888 and in King's Road 1904-20. The leading Shakespearian actress of her time in London and America, she performed between 1878 and 1902 with Henry Irving (q.v.) at the Lyceum Theatre. Married three times, she had two children from her association with the architect E. W. Godwin. She carried on extended correspondence with the playwright George Bernard Shaw (q.v.) and is depicted in several well-known paintings.

THACKERAY, William Makepeace (1811-63). **18 Albion Street, W2** *Private;* **16 Young Street, W8** *London County Council;* **36 Onslow Square, SW7** *London County Council;* **2 Palace Green, W8** *Royal Society of Arts*
English novelist; lived at all four addresses (1854-62 in Onslow Square). Born in India of English parents, he earned his living from journalism, having previously studied art in Paris. He contributed to *The Cornhill Magazine* and *Punch.* His novels include *Vanity Fair* (1847), *Pendennis* (1848), *Henry Esmond* (1852) and *The Virginians* (1857-9). Thackeray's final home in Palace Green is now an embassy.

THEATRE, The. See **ST JOHN THE BAPTIST, HOLYWELL**

THOMAS, Dylan Marlais (1914-53). **54 Delancey Street, NW1**
Welsh poet; lived here. Having worked as a reporter in south Wales, he came to

London to further his career. His first published work was *Eighteen Poems* in 1934. Other works followed, his most memorable being *Under Milk Wood*, published after his early death from alcoholism. *Greater London Council*

THOMAS, Edward (Philip) (1878-1917). **61 Shelgate Road, SW11**
English poet and novelist; lived here. Most of his poetry was written while he was on active service in the First World War and published after his death at the front. *London County Council*

THOMAS, Terry (1911-90). **11 Queensgate Mews, SW7**
Stage name of Thomas Terry Hoar Stevens, actor; lived here 1949-81. Born in the London suburb of Finchley, he came to be noted for his parts as a cad and is remembered for his famous grin which displayed the gap between his two front teeth. He appeared in several radio and television shows and starred in many films, notably *Those Magnificent Men in their Flying Machines* (1965) and *It's a Mad, Mad, Mad, Mad World* (1965). *Comic Heritage*

THORNDIKE, Dame Sybil (1882-1976). **6 Carlyle Square, SW3**
Dramatic actress; lived here with her husband Sir Lewis Casson and family 1921-32. She first appeared on stage in 1904 and toured in Shakespearian repertory, afterwards appearing at the Old Vic. She played the title role in George Bernard Shaw's *St Joan* (1924) and between 1921 and 1963 appeared in eighteen films. Dame Sybil was awarded her DBE in 1931. *English Heritage*

THORNE, Will (William) (1857-1946). **1 Lawrence Road, West Ham, E13**
Socialist politican; lived here. A founder member of the National Union of General and Municipal Workers in 1889, he was general secretary until 1934. He became an MP and was a member of the parliamentary committee of the Trades Union Congress 1894-1934. Thorne was also a borough councillor, mayor (1917) and freeman of the borough of West Ham. *Greater London Council*

THORNYCROFT, Sir (William) Hamo (1850-1925). **2a Melbury Road, W14**
London-born sculptor; lived here. Among his better-known works are the statues of General Gordon on the Victoria Embankment (1885) and Cromwell at Westminster (1899). His grandfather and both his parents were also sculptors. *London County Council*

THORPE, John (1715-92). **123 Bexley High Street, Bexley**
English historian and antiquary; lived here 1750-89. On his father's death in 1750 he undertook to edit and publish the latter's leisure-time research work into the history of Rochester. This completed in 1769, he continued the research and wrote further historical books for publication. During his residence in this property he extended and improved it. *Borough of Bexley*

THURLOE, John (1616-68). **Wall of Lincoln's Inn, Chancery Lane, WC2**
English politician and lawyer; lived here (in Old Square) at various times until his death. A bencher at Lincoln's Inn from 1647, he became Oliver Cromwell's Secretary of State five years later and also supported Richard Cromwell. Although accused of high treason after the Restoration, he was released and continued to practise as a lawyer. *Cromwell Association*

TILAK, Lokamanya (1856-1920). **10 Howley Place, W2**
Indian newspaper owner, lawyer, philosopher and patriot; lived here 1918-19. He was active in the extreme elements of the Indian quest for self-government and was imprisoned on more than one occasion for his part in the political unrest at the turn of the century. He stayed in this house on coming to London in 1918 to take part in a law suit. *English Heritage*

TOLLGATE, Archway, site of. 1 Pauntley Street, N19
Stood near here 1813-64. Local roads were in such poor condition that bodies such as the Islington Turnpike Trust and the Highgate and Hampstead Trust levied tolls to provide funds for their improvement. *Borough of Islington*

TOLLGATE, Castle, site of. Castle Public House, Child's Hill, NW2
Stood near here 1826-71. An Act was passed in 1826 for 'making a turnpike road from St John's Chapel [opposite Lord's Cricket Ground] to the north-east end of Ballards Lane, abutting upon the North Road in the parish of Finchley, with a branch there from in the county of Middlesex'. The tolls were abolished in 1851 and the gate twenty years later. *Hendon Corporation*

TOMPION, Thomas (1638-1713). **69 Fleet Street, EC4**
English clockmaker; lived on this site. Known as 'the father of English watchmaking', he made one of the first English watches equipped with a balance spring and also patented the cylinder escapement in 1695. He became a Fellow of the Royal Society and is buried in Westminster Abbey. The plaque is shared with another clockmaker, George Graham (q.v.). *Private*

TOPHAM, Frank (1838-1924). **4 Arkwright Road, NW3.**
Artist; lived and worked here in the 1870s. From 1863 he was a constant exhibitor at the Royal Academy, and many of his paintings can be seen in London and provincial art galleries. The plaque is almost completely obscured by a clinging vine. *Hampstead Plaque Fund*

TOSTI, Sir Francesco Paolo (1846-1916). **12 Mandeville Place, W1**
Italian-born naturalised British composer; lived in a house on this site 1886-1916. He wrote many popular songs including 'Good-bye' and 'Mattinata', was singing master to the royal family and was knighted in 1908. *Westminster City Council*

TOWLE, Arthur. See **LUCAN, Arthur**

TOWNLEY, Charles (1737-1805). **14 Queen Anne's Gate, SW1**
Antiquary and collector; lived here. His collection consisted mainly of marble and terracotta reliefs. After his death it was purchased by the British Museum. *Greater London Council*

TREE, Sir Herbert Beerbohm (1853-1917). **31 Rosary Gardens, SW7** *London County Council;* **76 Sloane Street, SW1** *Private;* **Mansion Gardens, West Heath Road, NW3** *Hampstead Plaque Fund* British actor and theatre manager; lived at the first address and on the sites of the other two. The half-brother of Sir Max Beerbohm (q.v.), he was a fine Shakespearian and character actor. He built and managed His Majesty's Theatre and was a founder of the Royal Academy of Dramatic Art (RADA). The Mansion Gardens plaque is shared with John Constable (q.v.).

The plaque in Sloane Street, SW1.

TREVITHICK, Richard (1771-1833). **University College London, Gower Street, WC1** English engineer and inventor; ran his first passenger steam locomotive near here in 1808. He built several high-pressure steam engines and, in 1808, the first locomotive to draw passengers on rails. *Trevithick Centenary Memorial Committee*

TROLLOPE, Anthony (1815-82). **Grandon, Hadley Green, Barnet** *Borough of Barnet;* **39 Montagu Square, W1** *London County Council* English novelist; lived in Hadley Green (1836-8) with his mother, Fanny Trollope (q.v.), and also in Montagu Square. A prolific writer, he at first worked for the Post Office in Britain and Ireland, where he instigated the first pillar-boxes. He is best known for his series of books about the fictitious cathedral city of Barchester, the first being *The Warden* (published in 1855). His forty-seven novels also include the Palliser series. His *Autobiography* gives amusing insights into his attitude towards the art of writing. Most of his work was written in the early hours of the morning, before breakfast. The Hadley Green plaque is shared with his mother.

TROLLOPE, Fanny (Frances) (1780-1863). **Grandon, Hadley Green, Barnet** English novelist; lived here 1836-8 with her son, Anthony Trollope (q.v.). Having been widowed in 1835, she travelled extensively and earned a living by writing over one hundred novels. Her most successful were *The Vicar of Wrexhill* (1837), *The Widow Barnaby* (1839) and *The Widow Married* (1840). She eventually settled in Florence, where she died. The plaque is shared with her son. *Borough of Barnet*

Anthony Trollope.

The home of the architect Ernest George Trowbridge in Edgware. He designed the house himself.

TROWBRIDGE, Ernest George (1884-1942). **19 Heather Walk, Edgware**
English architect, surveyor and estate agent; designed and lived in this house. The plaque, which calls him 'architect extraordinaire', leaves the W out of his name. After designing a house for the 1920 Ideal Home Exhibition, he received many commissions. His designs of private homes were in unusual styles and bordered on the world of fantasy. Working mainly in north-west London, he was responsible for many houses, flats and housing developments, several having timber frames, thatched roofs, towers or battlements. *Private*

TUDOR HALL. Wood Street, Barnet
Housed the Free Grammar School of Queen Elizabeth I, who granted its charter in 1573. *Borough of Barnet*

TURING, Alan (1912-54). **2 Warrington Crescent, W9**
British code-breaker and computer scientist; born here. He was the chief scientific figure at Bletchley Park, where he played an important part in breaking the German codes during the Second World War. He was also responsible for the world's first detailed computer hardware and software design in 1945. (Photograph, page 200) *English Heritage*

Tudor Hall in Barnet.

The English Heritage plaque commemorating Alan Turing was unveiled by his biographer, Dr Andrew Hodges, on 23rd June 1998.

TURK'S HEAD TAVERN, site of. 9 Gerrard Street, W1

It was here in 1764 that Dr Samuel Johnson (q.v.) and Sir Joshua Reynolds (q.v.) founded The Club. *Westminster City Council*

TURNER, Joseph Mallord William (1775-1851). 21 Maiden Lane, WC2
Westminster City Council; **119 Cheyne Walk, SW3** *Turner House Committee;* **23 Queen Anne Street, W1** *Portman Estate Trustees;* **40 Sandycombe Road, Twickenham** *Greater London Council*

This plaque to J. M. W. Turner is in Queen Anne Street, W1.

English landscape painter; born at Maiden Lane; lived and worked at Cheyne Walk; lived at Queen Anne Street; lived in Twickenham. He joined the Royal Academy as a student aged fourteen. His early paintings were topographical scenes in watercolour, but from 1796 he took to oils. In 1802 his style of seascapes and ships began to develop. Later visits to Italy produced some of his best artistic works, including pictures of Venice and *The Fighting Téméraire* (1838). He bequeathed over three hundred of his paintings and twenty thousand watercolours and drawings to the nation. The Cheyne Walk and Queen Anne Street plaques are both attractively modelled, the latter bearing a portrait of the artist. A fifth plaque, accessible only to local residents, is situated on a tree in Campden Hill Square Gardens.

TURNERS' HALL, site of (1736-66). 22 College Hill, EC4

Stood here 1736-66. Turners made cups, platters, furniture and similar items using a lathe. The original livery hall stood in Philpot Lane from 1591 until destroyed in the Great Fire of 1666. It was rebuilt in 1670 and in 1736 transferred to this site. It remained here until 1766, when it was sold and not replaced. *Corporation of the City of London*

200

TWAIN, Mark (1835-1910). **23 Tedworth Square, SW3**

Pen name of Samuel Langhorne Clemens, American writer and wit; lived here 1896-7. After working as a journalist, a printer, a Mississippi river-boat pilot and a gold miner he turned to writing. An overseas journey contributed to his *The Innocents Abroad* (1869), and other books followed. His great masterpieces were *The Adventures of Tom Sawyer* (1876) and *The Adventures of Huckleberry Finn* (1884), both of which became established children's classics and have been filmed. Other well-known novels include *A Tramp Abroad* (1880) and *A Connecticut Yankee in King Arthur's Court* (1889). *London County Council*

TWEED, John (1863-1933). **108 Cheyne Walk, SW10**
British sculptor; lived here. Among his notable works are the statues of Lord Kitchener at Horse Guards Parade, Sir George White in Portland Place, Lord Beresford in St Paul's Cathedral and Joseph Chamberlain in Westminster Abbey. *Greater London Council*

TYBURN MARTYRS. Tyburn Shrine, Bayswater Road, W2
This shrine contains many relics of the Catholic martyrs who perished on the Tyburn gibbet. The nuns who maintain the church will be pleased to conduct visitors around upon request. The plaque can be readily seen, in contrast to the LCC 'Tyburn Tree' plaque, which is at ground level. *Westminster City Council*

TYBURN TREE, site of. Traffic island at junction of Edgware and Bayswater Roads, W2
Gallows, named after the river Tyburn which flowed nearby, stood here from the thirteenth century until moved to Newgate in 1783. Public hangings were regularly held at this spot, and the unfortunate victims were driven in open carts along Tyburn Lane, now called Park Lane, to their execution. *London County Council.*

U

UNDERHILL, Evelyn (1875-1941). 50 Campden Hill Square, W8
English Christian philosopher and teacher; lived here 1907-39. She was a lecturer on the philosophy of religion at Oxford University from 1921 and wrote many books, volumes of verse and novels. Her most notable work was *Mysticism* (1911). *English Heritage*

UNITED STATES EMBASSY. See ADAMS, Henry Brooks

UNWIN, Sir Raymond (1863-1940). Old Wyldes, North End, Hampstead Way, NW3
Architect and town planner; lived here 1906-40. He followed the path of Sir Ebenezer Howard (q.v.) and put into practice the development of the new towns of Letchworth, Hampstead Garden Suburb and Wythenshawe. A second plaque at this address commemorates John Linnell (q.v.) and William Blake (q.v.). *Private*

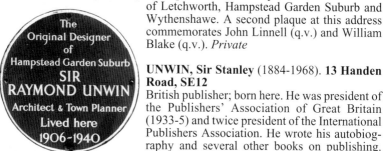

UNWIN, Sir Stanley (1884-1968). 13 Handen Road, SE12
British publisher; born here. He was president of the Publishers' Association of Great Britain (1933-5) and twice president of the International Publishers Association. He wrote his autobiography and several other books on publishing. *Greater London Council*

VANBRUGH, Sir John (1664-1726). Vanbrugh Castle, Maze Hill, Greenwich, SE10

English architect and dramatist; designed this house and lived here c.1719-26. He was the designer of Blenheim Palace, Oxfordshire, and Castle Howard, Yorkshire. He also wrote the comic dramas *The Relapse* (1696), *The Provok'd Wife* (1697) and *The Confederacy* (1705). During the war with France he was imprisoned in the Bastille as a suspected spy (1690-2). *Private*

VAN BUREN, Martin (1782-1862). 7 Stratford Place, W1

Eighth president of the USA (1837-41); lived here. Before becoming president he was Secretary of State 1829-31, ambassador to Great Britain 1831-3 and vice-president 1833-7. *Greater London Council*

VANE, Sir Harry (Henry) (1612-62). Vane House, Rosslyn Hill, NW3

English statesman; lived here. Educated at Westminster School and Oxford, he sailed to New England in 1635, later becoming governor of

Vanbrugh Castle, Greenwich, SE10, the home of Sir John Vanbrugh, who designed the house himself. The plaque commemorating him can be seen to the right of the gate.

Massachusetts. Returning after two years, he entered Parliament and, between 1643 and 1653, was the civilian head of the Parliamentary government. After the Restoration he was accused of high treason and beheaded. The outer wall is the only part of the original house remaining. *Royal Society of Arts*

VAN GOGH, Vincent (1853-90). **87 Hackford Road, SW9** *Greater London Council;* **160 Twickenham Road, Isleworth** *Private*
Dutch-born post-Impressionist painter; lived at both addresses. Working for a

The plaque in Isleworth.

firm of international art dealers, he was sent to London, where he lodged in Hackford Road for about a year (1873-4). Returning again in 1876, he stayed in Twickenham Road. He also frequently visited his sister, who worked as a school teacher in Welwyn, Hertfordshire, and there are plaques in the village recording the fact that, owing to his impoverished state, he had walked from London to see her. He always remained poor and, though continuing to paint, suffered from a mental illness and eventually died by his own hand.

VARDON, Harry (1870-1937). **35 Totteridge Lane, N20**
British golfer; lived here 1903-37. Born in Jersey, he won the British Open golf championship six times between 1896 and 1914, the US Open in 1900 and the German Open in 1911. His overlapping grip continues to be called the 'Vardon grip'. *Borough of Barnet*

VAUGHAN WILLIAMS, Ralph (1872-1958). **10 Hanover Terrace, NW1**
English composer; lived in this Nash terrace for the last five years of his life. He studied at Cambridge, at the Royal College of Music in London, in Berlin under Bruch and in Paris under Ravel. Influenced by Gustav Holst (q.v.), he became a leader in the English folk-song revival. His works include *Sea Symphony* (1910), *London Symphony* (1914), *Pastoral Symphony* (1922) and music for the film *Scott of the Antarctic*. He also wrote many other works including sacred music. *Greater London Council*

VE AND VJ DAYS. Corner of King's Road and Park Road, Kingston-upon-Thames
The plaque reads: 'On the 22nd January 1945 at 2.35 pm the last V2 long-range rocket to hit Kingston fell near this spot, resulting in the deaths of eight persons and causing injury to 117 more. A total of 33 homes were destroyed and over 2000 more were damaged, making it the most severe and widespread incident of World War II in the Royal Borough. This memorial was erected by the Kingston Town and Royal Park Neighbourhood Committee to commemorate the 50th Anniversary of VE Day and VJ Day, 1995.' *Borough of Kingston*

VE DAY COMMEMORATION. City Hall, 64 Victoria Street, SW1
The plaque reads: 'In recognition of Westminster's councillors and officers and

the civil and emergency services for their actions during World War II (1939-1945). This plaque was unveiled by the lord mayor of Westminster City Council, councillor Angela Hooper, CBE, for the 50th anniversary of VE Day, 8th May 1995.' *Westminster City Council*

VENTRIS, Michael George Francis (1922-56). **19 North End, Hampstead, NW3**
English architect and linguist; lived here. He deciphered the Minoan script found on stone tablets at Knossos and Pylos, known as Linear B, proving it to be an early form of the Greek language. He died in a road accident before his work was published. *English Heritage*

VICKY. See **WEISZ, Victor**

VJ DAY COMMEMORATION. Council House, Marylebone Road, NW1
The plaque reads: 'In recognition of the steadfast endurance of the people of Westminster during World War II (1939-45). This plaque was unveiled by the lord mayor of Westminster City Council, councillor Alan Bradley, for the 50th anniversary of VJ Day, 16th August 1995.' *Westminster City Council*

VOLTAIRE, François Marie Arouet de (1694-1778). **10 Maiden Lane, WC2**
French writer and philosopher; lodged in a house on this site 1727-8. He was twice imprisoned in the Bastille for his outspoken writings. Among his best-known works are *Philosophical Letters on the English* (1733), *The Age of Louis XIV* (1751), *Candide* (1759) and *Irène* (1778). *Westminster City Council*

VON HÜGEL, Baron Friedrich (1852-1925). **4 Holford Road, NW3**
Austrian-born British theologian; lived here 1882-1903. He was the founder of the London Society for the Study of Religion (1905). His writings include *The Mystical Elements in Religion* (1908), *Eternal Life* (1912) and *The Reality of God* (1931). *Greater London Council*

VOYSEY, Charles Francis Annesley (1857-1941). **6c Carlton Hill, NW8**
English architect and designer; lived here. His architecture and designs of wallpaper, furniture and textiles in the Arts and Crafts style were influenced by William Morris (q.v.). In his designs for country houses he made a feature of the buttresses, gables, chimney stacks and long sloping roofs. *English Heritage*

WAINRIGHT, Lincoln Stanhope (1847-1929). **Clergy House, Wapping Lane, E1**
Vicar of St Peter's, London Docks, for fifty-five years; lived here 1884-1929. He worked tirelessly for his parishioners in London's East End. On his fiftieth

jubilee the Bishop of London stated that Wainright had not taken a holiday for forty-seven years and while presenting him with a cheque for £1000 said he hoped that he would spend some of it on himself. *London County Council*

WAKEFIELD, Charles Cheers, Viscount Wakefield of Hythe (1859-1941). **41 Trinity Square, EC3**
English philanthropist; with his wife, 'gave this house for good to church and people' in 1937. After working for an oil broker in Liverpool he came to London and, in 1899, founded his own firm dealing in lubricating oils, using the brand name 'Castrol'. His philanthropic gestures were widespread and included the restoration of Tower Hill and the Guildhall Library. He was lord mayor of London 1915-6 and was made a Freeman of the City of London in 1935. The plaque bears his portrait in bas-relief. *Private*

WAKEFIELD, Edward Gibbon (1796-1862). **1-5 Adam Street, WC2**
London-born colonial statesman. He wrote a paper on his theory of colonisation while in prison for abduction (1826-9). His influence extended to Canadian and Australian associations and in 1837 he formed the New Zealand Association. The plaque states that

'from offices on this site the New Zealand company on 5th May 1839 despatched the survey ship *Tory* to begin the colonisation of New Zealand on the Wakefield plan'. Wakefield founded the Anglican colony at Canterbury, New Zealand, and emigrated there in 1853. *New Zealand Historic Places Trust*

WAKLEY, Thomas (1795-1862). **35 Bedford Square, WC1**
English surgeon; lived here. He was the founder editor of the medical journal *The Lancet* (1823). Later he became MP for Finsbury (1835-52), and the coroner for West Middlesex (1839-62). He died in Madeira. Another plaque at this address commemorates Thomas Hodgkin (q.v.). *London County Council*

WALEY, Arthur (1889-1966). **50 Southwood Lane, Highgate, N6**
Poet, translator and orientalist; lived and died here. He translated Chinese and Japanese classical books, though he never visited the Far East. *English Heritage*

WALKER, Sir Emery (1851-1933). **7 Hammersmith Terrace, W6**
Typographer and antiquary; lived here 1903-33. Having worked for a typographic etching company in his youth, he founded his own firm in 1886. With Cobden-Sanderson (q.v.) he founded the Doves Press in 1900. He was also an early member of the Labour Party, being secretary of the Hammersmith branch. *London County Council*

WALL, Thomas (1846-1930). **25 Worcester Road, Sutton** *Borough of Sutton;* **12 Worcester Road, Sutton** *Borough of Sutton*
British entrepreneur and benefactor; lived at 25 Worcester Road 1899. A manufacturer of ice-cream, pork pies and sausages, he built the family business into a national one and was a great local benefactor. The first plaque records that 25 Worcester Road was built in 1885 and has also been a registrar's office (from 1953) and the publishing house for a 'talking newspaper', 1994. The second plaque records that Wall founded an adult education school.

The plaque to Thomas Wall at 25 Worcester Road, Sutton.

WALLACE, Alfred Russel (1823-1913). **44 St Peter's Road, Croydon**
Welsh-born naturalist; lived here. He travelled extensively in South America and south-east Asia collecting specimens. His work on natural selection gave weight to Darwin's theory of evolution and he published many works between 1853 and 1910. *Greater London Council*

WALLACE, Edgar (1875-1932). **6 Tressillian Crescent, SE4** *London County Council;* **Junction of Fleet Street and Ludgate Circus, EC4** *Private*
English novelist and journalist; lived in Tressillian Crescent. He worked for a time as a journalist with the *Daily Mail* and wrote over 170 novels and plays. In later life he wrote scripts for Hollywood films. His novels include *Four Just Men* (1905), *Sanders of the River* (1911) and *The Ringer* (1926). The second plaque bears his portrait in bas-relief and states: 'he knew wealth and poverty... of his talents he gave lavishly... but to Fleet Street he gave his heart.'

WALLACE, Sir William (*c.*1272-1305). **Outer wall of St Bartholomew's Hospital, EC1**
Scottish patriot; executed near this spot. He defeated the English at Stirling Bridge in 1297 but was himself defeated a year later by Edward I's army. He continued a guerrilla war against the English and was finally captured and taken to London in 1305. Near the site of this ornate granite plaque he was hanged,

drawn and quartered. His life story was the subject of the 1996 film *Braveheart*. *Private*

WALLIS, Sir Barnes (Neville) (1887-1979). **241 New Cross Road, SE14**
British aeronautical engineer and inventor; lived here 1892-1909. He designed the R100 airship, the Wellington bomber, the bouncing bombs which destroyed the Mohne and Eder dams in 1943, and the first 'swing-wing' aircraft. He also assisted in the development of the supersonic airliner Concorde. *Borough of Lewisham*

WALPOLE, Sir Robert (1676-1745) and **Horace** (1717-97). **5 Arlington Street, SW1**

Father and son, the former being a statesman and prime minister, the latter a connoisseur and man of letters; lived here. Educated at Eton and Cambridge, Sir Robert served as first prime minister from 1721 to 1742, was created Earl of Orford and was given 10 Downing Street, which became the home of all later prime ministers. Horace also went to Eton and Cambridge, where he met Thomas Gray (q.v.). He became the fourth Earl of Orford and, despite spending twenty-six years in Parliament, is remembered chiefly for his writings, which included over four thousand letters. He converted his home at Strawberry Hill into a neo-Gothic castle. *Greater London Council*

Sir Robert Walpole.

WALTER, John (1739-1812). **113 Clapham Common North Side, SW4**
English printer and founder of *The Times* newspaper; lived here. He worked as a coal-merchant (1755-81) and afterwards as a Lloyds (q.v.) underwriter, which led him to bankruptcy. In 1784 he acquired a printing office and started a scandal sheet, *The Daily Universal Register*. This was renamed *The Times* in 1788. *Greater London Council*

WALTERS, Catherine (1839-1920). **15 South Street, W1**
Known as 'Skittles', and described as 'the last Victorian courtesan'; lived here 1872-1920. She was brought to London from the slums of Liverpool by a businessman who established her in Fulham. She soon became mistress to the heir of the Duke of Devonshire, who settled an annuity on her that enabled her to live in style for the rest of her life. Her tea parties in South Street attracted some of the most eminent men of her day. *Private*

WALTON, Sir William Turner (1902-83). **10 Holly Place, Holly Walk, NW3**
English composer; lived here. As a boy he was a chorister at Christchurch, Oxford. His many works included *Facade* (1923), *Belshazzar's Feast* (1931),

the coronation marches of 1937 and 1953, and the music for the films of *Henry V, Hamlet* and *Richard III. Hampstead Plaque Fund*

WANDSWORTH, Sidney **James Stern, First Baron** (1844-1912). **Nightingale House, Nightingale Lane, SW12**

British politician; lived here. He was a member of Parliament 1891-5, until elevated to the peerage, and the head of the London firm Stern Brothers. He owned considerable property in London and donated his house to be used as a Home for Aged Poor of the Jewish Faith, in memory of his parents. *Private*

WARE, Edwin M. (1888-1971). **13 High Street, Pinner**
Pinner historian and parish clerk for thirty-two years; lived here 1912-15. *Private*

WARLOCK, Peter (1894-1930). **30 Tite Street, SW3**
Pseudonym of Philip Arnold Heseltine; composer and writer; lived here. His works were in the Elizabethan manner and were also influenced by Delius, of whom he wrote a biography under his own name (1923). *Greater London Council*

WARRISS, Ben (1909-93). **Brimsworth House, Staines Road, Twickenham**
Comedian and actor. He partnered his cousin Jimmy Jewel (q.v.) for many years in the music hall and on radio and television as the 'straight man' of the duo. Together they starred in such shows as *Up the Pole* (1947-52), *The Jewel and Warriss Show* (1957), *Turn It Up* and (on television) *Startime*. Like his partner, he turned to serious acting late in life. This plaque, with that of Hylda Baker (q.v.), is at the rear of the building and cannot be seen from the road. *Comic Heritage*

This plaque to William Wallace is on the outer wall of St Bartholomew's Hospital in SE3, near the spot where he was executed.

WARTIME DISASTER, site of the worst civilian. Bethnal Green Station, E1
The plaque reads: 'Site of the worst civilian disaster of the Second World War. In memory of 173 men, women and children who lost their lives on the evening of Wednesday 3rd March 1943 descending these steps to Bethnal Green underground air-raid shelter. Not forgotten.' (Photograph, page 224) *Borough of Tower Hamlets*

WATCH HOUSE. 9 Holly Place, Holly Walk, NW3
The plaque states: 'In the 1830s the newly formed Hampstead Police Force set out on its patrol and nightly watch from this house.' *Hampstead Plaque Fund*

WATERHOUSE, Alfred (1830-1905). **61 New Cavendish Street, W1**
English architect; lived here. He began his career in Manchester, where he later designed the town hall (1869-77). Among his other notable works are the Natural History Museum, South Kensington; University College Hospital; Balliol College, Oxford; Caius and Pembroke colleges, Cambridge; and Liverpool University College. *English Heritage*

WATSON, Joshua (1771-1855). **117 Lower Clapton Road, E5**
Philanthropist, educationalist, lay churchman and wine merchant; lived here. An active member of many church institutions and associations, he was also the first treasurer of the National Society 1811-42. *Borough of Hackney*

WATTS-DUNTON, Walter Theodore (1832-1914). **11 Putney Hill, SW15**
English poet and critic; lived here. He was a friend of Dante Gabriel Rossetti (q.v.), William Morris (q.v.), Alfred, Lord Tennyson (q.v.) and most particularly A. C. Swinburne (q.v.), whom he looked after for thirty years at this address and who shares the plaque. Most of Watts-Dunton's notable works were published in the *Athenaeum* (1876-98). A selection of these was printed in 1916 under the title *Old Familiar Faces*. He also wrote a verse tale of gypsy life, *The Coming of Love* (1897), and a once popular novel, *Alwyn* (1898). *London County Council*

WAUGH, Reverend Benjamin (1839-1908). **Christ Church, Friern Barnet Road, N11** *Borough of Barnet;* **33 The Green, Southgate, N14** *Private;* **26 Croom's Hill, SE10** *Greater London Council*
Congregational minister 1865-87; founder minister of Christ Church, Barnet 1883-7; lived at the other two addresses. He founded the National Society for the

Prevention of Cruelty to Children (NSPCC) in 1884, becoming its director 1889-1905 and its consulting director from 1905.

WAUGH, Evelyn Arthur St John (1903-66). **145 North End Road, NW11**
English novelist; lived here. His first writings, about the Pre-Raphaelite Brotherhood and Dante Gabriel Rossetti (q.v.),

The plaque in Southgate, N14.

were followed by the novel *Decline and Fall* (1928). For the next few years he travelled extensively and contributed to newspapers. In 1938 *Scoop* appeared; several more books followed, including *Brideshead Revisited* in 1945. Other works included *Men at Arms* (1952), *Officers and Gentlemen* (1955) and *Unconditional Surrender* (1961). His diaries were published in 1976, and several of his novels have been filmed for both cinema and television. *English Heritage*

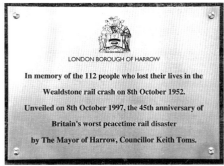

LONDON BOROUGH OF HARROW

In memory of the 112 people who lost their lives in the Wealdstone rail crash on 8th October 1952.

Unveiled on 8th October 1997, the 45th anniversary of Britain's worst peacetime rail disaster by The Mayor of Harrow, Councillor Keith Toms.

WEALDSTONE RAIL DISASTER. Civic Centre Library, Milton Road, Wealdstone, Harrow

The plaque reads: 'In memory of the 112 people who lost their lives in the Wealdstone rail crash on 8th October 1952. Unveiled on 8th October 1997, the 45th anniversary of Britain's worst peacetime rail disaster...' *Borough of Harrow*

WEBB, Philip (1831-1915). 91-101 Worship Street, EC2

English architect; designed these buildings as workshops and dwellings 1862. With R. Norman Shaw (q.v.) and C. F. A. Voysey (q.v.) he was one of the leading figures in the revival of domestic English architecture. He designed The Red House (q.v.) for William Morris (q.v.) and is mentioned on that plaque. Together they were co-founders of the Society for the Protection of Ancient Buildings (1877). (Photograph, page 224) *Borough of Hackney*

WEBB, Sidney James, Lord Passfield (1859-1947) and (Martha) Beatrice (1858-1943). 44 Cranbourn Street, WC2 *Westminster City Council;* 10 Netherhall Gardens, NW3 *Greater London Council*

Social scientists and political reformers (husband and wife), Sidney was born in a house on the Cranbourn Street site, and he and Beatrice lived at Netherhall Gardens when first married in 1892. They were instrumental in the establishment of the London School of Economics (1895), where Sidney was a professor 1912-27. He was a member of Parliament, President of the Board of Trade (1924) and was created Baron Passfield in 1929. They were both active members of the Fabian Society (q.v.) and founded the *New Statesman* journal in 1913.

WEBER, Carl Maria (Friedrich Ernst) von (1786-1826). 103 Great Portland Street, W1

German composer, conductor and pianist; died here. He wrote the operas *Der Freischutz* (1821), *Euryanthe* (1823) and the popular 'Invitation to the Dance' (1819), as well as many other compositions. He died in this house two months after his *Oberon* was first performed at Covent Garden. *Incorporated Society of Musicians*

VICTOR WEISZ "VICKY" 1913-1966 Cartoonist lived in a flat in this building

WEISZ, Victor (Vicky) (1913-66). Welbeck Mansions, New Cavendish Street, W1

German-born cartoonist; lived in a flat in this building. He emigrated to Britain in 1935 to escape Nazi persecution. Vicky, as he signed his cartoons, became one of the leading political cartoonists of his time and worked for several national newspapers. *English Heritage*

WEIZMANN, Chaim (1874-1952). **67 Addison Road, W14**
Russian-born Jewish chemist, Zionist and first president of the state of Israel; lived here. Educated in Germany, he taught in Switzerland and Britain, becoming a naturalised British subject. During the First World War, he discovered a process for manufacturing acetone. He conducted the negotiations leading to the Balfour Declaration (1917) and became head of the Hebrew University in Jerusalem. He became first president of Israel in 1948. *Greater London Council*

WELLCOME, Sir Henry (1853-1936). **6 Gloucester Gate, NW1**
Pharmacist, philanthropist and archaeologist; lived here. The founder of the Wellcome Trust and Foundation, he was also a member and founder of many other associations in the fields of medicine and archaeology, both in Britain and overseas. *English Heritage*

WELLS, H. G. (Herbert George) (1866-1946). **25 Langley Park Road, Sutton** *Borough of Sutton;* **Allders Store, High Street, Bromley** *Private;* **13 Hanover Terrace, NW1** *Greater London Council*
English novelist and short-story writer; born in Bromley; lived in Sutton 1893-4 (and Worcester Park); lived and died at 13 Hanover Terrace. One of the foremost science-fiction writers, he wrote over a hundred novels including *The Time Machine* (1895), *The Invisible Man* (1897), *The War of the Worlds* (1898), *The First Men in the Moon* (1901), *Kipps* (1905), *The History of Mr Polly* (1910) and *The Shape of Things to Come* (1933).

The plaque in Bromley High Street.

WESLEY, Charles (1707-88). **24 West Street, WC2** *Private;* **1 Wheatley Street, W1** *London County Council;* **13 Little Britain, EC1** *Corporation of the City of London*
English hymnwriter and evangelist; was converted to evangelism in the house of John Bray, formerly on the Little Britain site; preached in West Street chapel; lived and died in a house on the Wheatley Street site. The brother of John Wesley (q.v.), he wrote around six thousand hymns. He shares the plaque at West Street with his brother, and that at Wheatley Street with his two musician sons, Charles (1757-1834) and Samuel (1766-1837), who also lived there.

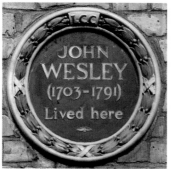

WESLEY, John (1703-91). **Wall at Aldersgate Street, EC1** *Drew Theological Seminary, USA;* **24 West Street, WC2** *Private;* **47 City Road, EC1** *London County Council*
English priest, evangelist and founder of Methodism; was converted to evangelism in Aldersgate Street (1738); preached in West Street chapel; lived in City Road. The Aldersgate Street plaque records that here he 'felt his heart strangely warmed' [and]

The plaque at 47 City Road, EC1.

this experience of grace was the beginning of Methodism. With his brother Charles Wesley (q.v.), he formed a circle of friends at Oxford University who were nicknamed 'Methodists' because of their religious observances. After his experience in Aldersgate Street, he preached to the people, going around the country on horseback and gathering a vast following. He visited America in 1735 and founded the *Methodist Magazine* in 1778. The plaque at West Street is shared with his brother.

WESTFIELD COLLEGE. 6 Maresfield Road, Hampstead, NW3
The plaque reads: 'In these two houses on 2nd October 1882 Westfield College opened its doors for the higher education of women. It is now a college of the University of London with over 1000 students.' *Hampstead Plaque Fund*

WESTMACOTT, Sir Richard (1775-1856). 14 South Audley Street, W1
English neo-classical sculptor; lived and died here. He studied under Canova in Rome and was professor of sculpture at the Royal Academy 1827-54. Apart from many fine church monuments, including some in St Paul's Cathedral and Westminster Abbey, he is noted for his group of figures on the pediment of the British Museum and the *Achilles* statue in Hyde Park. *London County Council*

The plaque to the sculptor Richard Westmacott can be seen on this building in W1.

WHALL, Christopher Whitworth (1849-1924). **19 Ravenscourt Road, W6**
Stained-glass artist; lived here. He studied at the Royal Academy and in Italy and was influenced by Leighton (q.v.) and Ruskin (q.v.). His first important commission was the east window of the Lady Chapel at St Mary's, Stamford, Lincolnshire. Other important works can be seen in Gloucester Cathedral. *Greater London Council*

WHEATSTONE, Sir Charles (1802-75). **19 Park Crescent, W1**
English physicist and inventor; lived here. He patented a railway telegraph in 1837 and devised the 'Wheatstone bridge', an electrical device for measuring resistance. He also invented the concertina, the harmonica and a microphone. *Greater London Council*

WHEELER, Sir Charles (1892-1974). **49 Old Church Street, SW3**
English sculptor; lived here. A member of the Royal Academy from 1940, he was president 1956-66. His sculptures, both in bronze and stone, can be found in many galleries and on South Africa House and other buildings. *Private*

WHEELER, Sir Mortimer (1890-1976). **27 Whitcomb Street, WC2**
English archaeologist; lived here. His important excavation work included Verulamium and Maiden Castle in Britain and ancient city sites in India. A keeper of the London Museum (1926-44), he was also well known for his broadcasts, television appearances and books on archaeology. *English Heritage*

WHISTLER, James Abbott McNeil (1834-1903).
96 Cheyne Walk, SW10
American painter and etcher; lived here. He left the USA in 1855 for Paris but settled in London four years later. Criticism of his work by John Ruskin (q.v.) led to a libel case in which he was awarded one farthing in damages. His most famous painting is *Arrangement in Grey and Black: Portrait of the Painter's Mother* (1871). This and *Old Battersea Bridge* (*c*.1872) were both painted while he lived at this address. *London County Council*

James Whistler.

WHITBREAD, Samuel (1720-96). **Whitbread's Brewery, Chiswell Street, EC1**
Founder of the Whitbread brewery. The plaque commemorates the visit of King George III and Queen Charlotte to the brewery on 24th May 1787. *Private*

WHITE, Antonia (1899-1980). **22 Perham Road, W14**
Pen name of Eirene Botting, English novelist and translator; lived here 1899-1921. Educated at a convent, she had three marriages and suffered intermittent bouts of mental illness. Her works include *Frost in May* (1933), *The Lost Traveller* (1950), *The Sugar House* (1952) and many translations of French books. *Borough of Hammersmith and Fulham*

WHITE, William Hale (1831-1913). **19 Park Hill, Carshalton**
English journalist and writer who gave himself the fictional name 'Mark Rutherford'; lived here. He was a civil servant from 1854, having been expelled from ministry training. Through journalistic correspondence he associated with Philip Webb (q.v.) and John Ruskin (q.v.). His main works were *The Autobiography of Mark Rutherford* (1881), *Mark Rutherford's Deliverance* (1885) and *The Revolution in Tanner's Lane* (1887). *Greater London Council*

WHITE HART INN, site of. White Hart Yard, Borough High Street, SE1
Immortalised by Shakespeare (q.v.) in *Henry VI* and by Charles Dickens (q.v.) in *The Pickwick Papers*. It was destroyed by fire in 1767, rebuilt and finally demolished in 1889. *Borough of Southwark*

WHITTAKER, Joseph (1820-95). **White Lodge, Silver Street, Enfield**
English publisher and founder of *Whittaker's Almanac*; lived and died here. *English Heritage*

WHITTINGTON, Richard (Dick) (*c.*1358-1423). **Church at College Hill, EC4** *Corporation of the City of London;* **19 College Hill, EC4** *Corporation of the City of London*
Mayor of London 1397, 1398, 1406 and 1419; lived in a house on the second site; founded, and was buried in, the original church on the first site. He travelled to London from his home at Pauntley in Gloucestershire, and the story

was embellished, the legend of his cat being first recorded in the early seventeenth century. He became a member of the Mercers' Company (from 1392) and an alderman and sheriff. He was also a member of Parliament (from 1416) and a generous benefactor to the City of London.

Dick Whittington at Highgate by Gustave Doré.

WIGRAM, Sir Robert (1744-1830). **Walthamstow House, Shernhall Street, E17**
English politician and trader merchant; lived here from 1782 until his death. He entered Parliament in 1802 and was created a baronet in 1805. His company ran a fleet of East Indiamen, one of which was named *Walthamstow. Borough of Walthamstow*

WILBERFORCE, William (1759-1833). **111 Broomwood Road, SW11** *London County Council;* **Holy Trinity Church, Clapham Common, SW4** *Greater London Council;* **Site of Hendon Park, Barnet Road, Arkley** *Hendon Corporation;* **44 Cadogan Place, SW1** *London County Council;* **St Paul's Church, The Ridgeway, Mill Hill** *Borough of Barnet*
English philanthropist and reformer; commemorated by five plaques, the significance of which is explained below. Born in Hull, he was educated at Cambridge and entered Parliament in 1780. He is famed for his role in the abolition

On the site behind this house stood until 1904 Broomwood House (formerly Broomfield) where WILLIAM WILBERFORCE resided during the // CAMPAIGN against // SLAVERY which he .c successfully conducted in Parliament ././././.

The plaque in Broomwood Road, SW11.

of slavery in the British Empire (1833). He was for a long time a member of the 'Clapham Sect' (q.v.) of evangelists, who prayed at Holy Trinity Church. From 1797 to 1807, during his campaign against slavery, he lived at Broomwood (formerly Broomfield) House (destroyed 1904). Upon his retirement he lived at Hendon Park, Mill Hill (1826-31), neighbouring Sir Stamford Raffles (q.v.). He built St Paul's Church but did not live to see its completion, his final days from 1831 being spent at the house of his cousin in Cadogan Place.

WILCOX, Herbert (1890-1977). **63-4 Park Lane, W1**
English film producer and director; lived here 1950-64. He was the husband of Dame Anna Neagle (q.v.), who shares this plaque, and who starred in many of his films. Among his many films are *Bitter Sweet, The Scarlet Pimpernel, Brewster's Millions, Nell Gwyn, Sixty Glorious Years, The Courtneys of Curzon Street, Spring in Park Lane*, and *Odette*. He received the National Film Award four times. *Westminster City Council*

WILDE, Oscar (Fingall O'Flahertie Wills) (1854-1900). **34 Tite Street, SW3** *London County Council;* **Rear of Theatre Royal, Haymarket, SW1** *Westminster City Council*
Irish playwright, poet and wit; lived in Tite Street; had two of his plays first

THE FIRST PERFORMANCES OF 'A WOMAN OF NO IMPORTANCE' 19TH APRIL 1893 AND 'AN IDEAL HUSBAND' 3RD JANUARY 1895 BY OSCAR WILDE WERE PRESENTED AT THIS THEATRE THIS PLAQUE WAS UNVEILED BY SIR JOHN GIELGUD ON 3RD JANUARY 1995

performed at the Theatre Royal. His works include the novel *The Picture of Dorian Gray* (1890) and the plays *Lady Windermere's Fan* (1892), *A Woman of No Importance* (1893), *An Ideal Husband* (1895) and *The Importance of Being Earnest* (1895), his most popular work. He wrote the poem 'The Ballad of Reading Gaol' while in prison for homosexual practices. He died in poverty in Paris and was buried there.

This plaque to Wilde is on the rear of the Theatre Royal in Haymarket, SW1.

WILHELMINA, Queen (1880-1962). **77 Chester Square, SW1**
Queen of the Netherlands; had her secretariat in this house during the Second World War, 1940-5. *Private*

WILKS, Reverend William (1843-1923). **47 Shirley Church Road, Croydon**
Priest and horticulturalist; lived here 1879-1912. While vicar of Shirley in Yorkshire he propagated the Shirley poppy. *Borough of Croydon*

WILLAN, Dr Robert (1757-1812). **10 Bloomsbury Square, WC1**
Dermatologist; lived here 1800-12. He was physician to the public dispensary in London and was the first to classify diseases of the skin in a concise manner. *London County Council*

WILLETT, William (1856-1915). **82 Camden Park Road, Chislehurst**
English builder; lived here. He was the initiator of British Summer Time, which was not adopted until a year after his death. *Borough of Bromley*

WILLIAMS, Sir George (1821-1905). **13 Russell Square, WC1** *Private; Juxon House, St Paul's Churchyard, EC4 Private*
English social reformer and draper; lived at Russell Square 1879-1905. He was the founder of the Young Men's Christian Association (YMCA) on the site in St Paul's Churchyard in 1884.

WILLIAMS, John (1796-1839). **316 High Road, Tottenham, N15**
English missionary; born in a house near this site. He sailed to the South Sea Islands in 1817, where he worked successfully, returning to England 1834. Visiting the islands again four years later, he went on to the New Hebrides but was killed by cannibals on the island of Erromanga. *Private*

WILLIAMS, Kenneth (1926-88). **Marlborough House, Osnaburgh Street, NW1**
London-born comedian and actor; lived here 1972-88. He made his stage debut in *Peter Pan* in 1952 and appeared in several stage revues in the 1950s. He was well known for his camp character parts in the 'Carry On' series of films and also appeared in several radio shows, including *Round the Horne* and *Just a Minute*. *The Dead Comics Society*

WILLIAMSON, Henry (1895-1977). **21 Eastern Road, Ladywell, SE4**
English novelist; lived here 1902-20 but spent most of his later life in Devon. His best-known book is

Tarka the Otter (1927). Other works include *The Peregrine's Saga* (1923), *The Old Stag* (1926) and the series *A Chronicle of Ancient Sunlight* (1951-69). *Henry Williamson Society*

WILLIS, 'Father' Henry (1821-1901). **9 Rochester Terrace, NW1**
British organ builder; lived here. He began building organs in 1845 and the one he made for the Great Exhibition of 1851 was later used in Winchester Cathedral. Other organs were built for St George's Hall, Liverpool, the Royal Albert Hall and St Paul's Cathedral. *Greater London Council*

WILLIS, Lord Ted (1918-92). **5 Shepherd's Green, Chislehurst**
English playwright and author; lived here 1959-92. He is best known as the creator of the *Dixon of Dock Green* television series starring Jack Warner as the police constable (1953-75). In 1983 Willis won an award for forty years service to screen and television scriptwriting. A socialist from youth, he sat in the House of Lords for nearly thirty years and spoke out in support of the entertainment industry. He was also a president of the Writers' Guild and a fellow of the Royal Television Society. *Borough of Bromley*

WILLOUGHBY, Sir Hugh (died *c.*1554). **King Edward Memorial Park, Shadwell, E1**
English naval explorer. The illustrated plaque records that in the sixteenth century he and other navigators, including Stephen Borough (1525-85), William Borough (1536-99) and Sir Martin Frobisher (*c.*1535-94), set sail from this reach of the Thames, near Ratcliff Cross, to explore the northern seas. Unfortunately Willoughby's ship parted company from the others in a storm and he and

The house in Aldford Street, W1, where the American statesman John Winant lived.

The house in St George's Square, SW1, where Walter Wingfield lived.

sixty-two shipmates perished from scurvy. His ship was later discovered by Russian fishermen, and his journal of the voyage was published in 1903. (Photograph, page 224) *London County Council*

WILSON, Edward Adrian (1872-1912). **Battersea Vicarage, St Mary's House, 42 Vicarage Crescent, SW11**
Antarctic explorer, physician and naturalist; lived here. He first went to the Antarctic with Scott (q.v.) in the *Discovery,* 1900-4, and was one of the five in Scott's expedition of 1912 who died on the return journey from the South Pole. *London County Council*

WINANT, John Gilbert (1889-1947). **7 Aldford Street, W1**
American statesman and US ambassador to Britain in the Second World War; lived here 1941-6. The house was loaned to him by his great friend Sir Winston Churchill (q.v.). *Greater London Council*

WINGFIELD, Major Walter Clopton (1833-1912). **33 St George's Square, SW1**
Inventor of the modern game of lawn tennis; lived here. He was a member of HM Bodyguard of Gentlemen-at-Arms. He came from one of the oldest families in England, who were resident at Wingfield Castle, Suffolk, before the time of William the Conqueror. *Greater London Council*

WINTERS, Bernie (Bernard) (1932-91). **Teddington Studios, Broom Road, Teddington**
London-born actor and comedian; worked here. He was the 'funny man' in the stage partnership with his brother Mike, and together they appeared in several radio and television shows. When their partnership dissolved he made his debut as an actor with his portrayal of Bud Flanagan (q.v.) in the television play *Bud 'n' Ches* and the stage production *Underneath the Arches.* He later did a solo comedy act with his eleven-stone St Bernard dog. *Comic Heritage*

WODEHOUSE, P. G. (Pelham Grenville) (1881-1975). **17 Dunraven Street, W1**
English novelist; lived here. He wrote over a hundred novels, creating the legendary characters Bertie Wooster, Jeeves, Lord Emsworth,

McCartney House in Greenwich Park was once the home of General James Wolfe.

Psmith and others. He caused discontent by making some broadcasts for the Germans during the Second World War and thereafter lived in America becoming a US citizen in 1955. *English Heritage*

WOLFE, General James (1727-59). **McCartney House, Greenwich Park, SE10**
English general; lived here. He served gallantly at Dettingen, Falkirk and Culloden and was allotted the task of regaining Quebec, having already played an important part in the siege of the French stronghold of Louisburg (1758). His troops were victorious, but Wolfe lost his life in his hour of triumph. His family bought McCartney House in 1751, but, owing to his military commitments, he spent little time here. *London County Council*

WOLLSTONECRAFT, Mary (1759-97). **209-15 Blackfriars Road, SE1** *Borough of Southwark;* **Oakshott Court, Werrington Street, NW1** *Borough of Camden;* **373 Mare Street, E8** *Borough of Hackney*

English feminist and writer; lived or stayed in houses on all three sites. She was a teacher before becoming a publisher's assistant and making the acquaintance of several well-known figures, including the revolutionary Thomas Paine (q.v.) and William Godwin, with whom she lived (they later married). She wrote *A Vindication of the Rights of Woman* (1792), which advocated equal educational rights for women, and other feminist works. She was the mother of Mary Shelley (q.v.).

The plaque in Blackfriars Road, SE1.

WOLSELEY, Garnet Joseph, First Viscount (1833-1913). **Ranger's House, Chesterfield Walk, Blackheath, SE10**
British field marshal; lived here 1888-91. Born in County Dublin, of English parentage, he entered the army in 1852 and lost the use of an eye in the Crimea; he also served in India during the Mutiny and in the Chinese War of 1860. He was the commander during the Ashanti War of 1873-4, a member of the In-

dian Council (1876), and high commissioner for Cyprus (1878). He was made a general in 1882, when he was commander-in-chief of the Egyptian expedition, and a field-marshal and the commander-in-chief of the entire British army 1890-5. A second plaque at this address commemorates the Earls of Chesterfield (q.v.). *London County Council*

WOOD, Lieutenant Charles Campbell. Hammersmith Bridge, W6
A member of the Royal Air Force from Bloemfontein, South Africa, he dived from this spot into the Thames at midnight on 17th December 1919 and saved a woman's life but died from the injuries he received. The bronze plaque is on the west handrail in the centre of the bridge. *Private*

WOOD, Sir Henry Joseph (1869-1944). **4 Elsworthy Road, NW3**
English conductor; lived here 1905-37. He was the founder with Robert Newman of the Promenade concerts, which he conducted annually from 1895. He was knighted in 1911. *Greater London Council*

WOOLF, Leonard Sidney (1880-1969) and **Virginia (née Stephen)** (1882-1941). **29 Fitzroy Square, W1** *Greater London Council;* **Hogarth House, Paradise Road, Richmond** *Greater London Council;* **50 Gordon Square, WC1** *Camden Borough Council*
English writers and publishers; founded the Bloomsbury Group (q.v.) in Gordon Square; Virginia lived in Fitzroy Square; they both lived in Hogarth House 1915-24 and founded the

Hogarth House in Richmond.

Hogarth Press there. Married in 1912, they were the nucleus of the Bloomsbury Group and founded the Hogarth Press in 1917. Leonard originally worked for the Ceylon Civil Service (1904-11) and this is reflected in his early novels. A member of the Fabian Society (q.v.) from 1916, he published several works. Virginia, who was a daughter of Sir Leslie Stephen (q.v.) and the sister of Vanessa Bell, is regarded as one of the great modern innovators of the English novel. Her works include *To the Lighthouse* (1927), *Orlando* (1928) and *The Waves* (1931). After leaving Hogarth House they returned to Bloomsbury. A sufferer from mental illness, Virginia eventually took her own life.

WOOLLEY, Sir (Charles) Leonard (1880-1960). **Bridge on Southwold Road, E5**
Archaeologist; born in a house on this site. He undertook excavations in the Middle East and is best remembered for his discoveries, including many lavish works of art, at Ur of the Chaldees in Iraq (formerly Sumeria). He published several accounts of his work. *Borough of Hackney*

WOOLNER, Thomas (1826-92). **29 Welbeck Street, W1**
English poet and sculptor; lived here from 1860 until his death. He became a member of the Pre-Raphaelite Brotherhood. A collection of his poems was published as *My Beautiful Lady* (1863), but his most notable works were his statues and portrait busts of many famous contemporaries, including Darwin (q.v.), Tennyson (q.v.) and Cardinal Newman (q.v.). This plaque bears his own portrait in relief. *Private*

WOOLWORTH'S V2 INCIDENT. 277-81 New Cross Road, SE14
The plaque commemorates Britain's worst V2 rocket attack on 25th November 1944, when 168 people were killed at this spot. *Deptford History Group*

WORDE, Wynkyn de. See **DE WORDE, Wynkyn**

WORTH, Harry (1917-89). **Teddington Studios, Broom Road, Teddington**
English comedy actor; worked here. Born Harry Burlon Illingsworth, the youngest of eleven children, he began as a ventriloquist, working mainly in working men's clubs and pantomimes in the North of England. He first appeared on the London stage at the Windmill Theatre in 1947. After touring England and South Africa he finally made his name in television, to which his bumbling style of comedy was best suited. His weekly show ran for 104 episodes in the 1960s. *Comic Heritage*

WREN, Sir Christopher (1632-1723). **49 Bankside, Cardinal's Wharf, SE1** *Private;* **Old Court House, Hampton Court Green, Hampton** *English Heritage*
English architect; lived at both addresses. Originally a professor of astronomy at Oxford, he gained recognition as an architect after the Great Fire of London in 1666, when he re-designed St Paul's Cathedral (while living on Cardinal's Wharf) and fifty other London churches. He was also the architect of the Sheldonian Theatre, Oxford, the Royal Exchange and many other buildings. His plans for an overall design for London were not adopted. The plaque at Bankside also records the earlier visit of Queen Catherine of Aragon (q.v.). (Photograph, page 224)

Sir Christopher Wren

WYATT, Thomas Henry (1807-80). **77 Great Russell Street, WC1**
English architect; lived and died here. A member of a family of architects, he built up a large practice designing country houses as well as churches and hospitals. One of his most interesting designs is that of the church of Saints Mary and Nicholas in Wilton, Wiltshire (1840-6). *Greater London Council*

Left: *The plaque to the architect Philip Webb in Worship Street, EC2.*

Below: *This plaque at the entrance to Bethnal Green Underground Station commemorates the worst civilian disaster of the Second World War. See under 'Wartime disaster'.*

Left: *In memory of Sir Hugh Willoughby and other seamen who set sail to the northern seas in the latter half of the sixteenth century. This plaque can be found in the King Edward Memorial Park, Shadwell, E1.*

Right: *The architect Sir Christopher Wren lived at Cardinal's Wharf, SE1, where this plaque can be seen.*

39 Brook Street, W1, the home of Sir Jeffry Wyatville.

WYATVILLE, Sir Jeffry (1766-1840). **39 Brook Street, W1**
English architect; lived and died here. His most notable work was the remodelling of Windsor Castle, commissioned by King George IV in 1824. He specialised in neo-Gothic and neo-Tudor mansions and superintended the alterations and interior refurbishment of Chatsworth House, Derbyshire. *Greater London Council*

WYCHERLEY, William (*c*.1640-1716). See **BOW STREET**
English playwright. His works include *Love in a Wood* (1671), *The Gentleman Dancing-Master* (1672) and *The Country Wife* (1675). Money problems plagued him throughout his life, and he spent some years in Fleet debtors' prison as a result.

WYNDHAM, Sir Charles (1837-1919). **20 York Terrace East, NW1**
English actor-manager; lived and died here. Trained as a doctor, he turned to

acting, making his London stage debut in 1866. He opened Wyndham's Theatre in 1899 and the New Theatre, St Martin's Lane, in 1903, having been knighted in 1902. *Greater London Council*

YEARSLEY, Dr James (1805-69). **32 Sackville Street, W1**
English physician; founded the Metropolitan Ear Institute here in 1838. *Westminster City Council*

YEATS, Jack Butler (1871-1957). **3 Blenheim Road, W4**
Irish artist; lived here. He was the son of John Butler Yeats (q.v.) and the brother of W. B. Yeats (q.v.). His early works were small-scale illustrations and cartoons, but after 1918 he turned to oil painting and writing. His vividly coloured expressionistic works came to be seen as an emblem of Irish national-ism and are to be found in many Irish galleries. The plaque is shared with his father and brother. *Bedford Park Society*

YEATS, John Butler (1839-1922). **3 Blenheim Road, W4**
Irish-born artist; lived here. He was educated in Dublin and stud-ied at the Royal Academy and Slade schools of art. He exhib-ited at the Royal Academy and had some of his letters and es-says published. He was the fa-ther of W. B. Yeats (q.v.) and Jack Butler Yeats (q.v.), with whom he shares the plaque. *Bedford Park Society*

YEATS, W. B. (William But-ler) (1865-1939). **3 Blenheim Road, W4** *Bedford Park Soci-ety;* **23 Fitzroy Road, NW1** *Lon-don County Council;* **5 Woburn Walk, WC1** *St Pancras Borough Council*
Irish poet and dramatist; lived at all three addresses. He was the son of John Butler Yeats (q.v.) and the brother of Jack Butler Yeats (q.v.). His early work was lyrical and romantic in content, and he later revealed his interest in Irish mythology, legend and mysticism. He was an Irish senator 1922-8 and was awarded the Nobel prize for literature in 1923.

YMCA, Juxon House, St Paul's Churchyard, EC4
The plaque reads: 'Here in 1844 George Williams (1821-1905) (q.v.) with

The plaque to William Butler Yeats in Woburn Walk, WC1.

eleven other young men employed in the City of London who shared his zeal and vision, founded the Young Men's Christian Association, in a drapery house on this site in which he worked and lived. From its beginning in this place, inspired of God, the association grew to encompass the world.' *Private*

YOUNG, Thomas (1773-1829). **48 Welbeck Street, W1**
British physicist, physician and linguist; lived here. He expounded a theory of light and was instrumental in deciphering the hieroglyphic inscription on the Rosetta Stone. *London County Council*

YOVANOVITCH (JOVANOVIC), Slobodan (1869-1958). **48-52 Cromwell Road, SW7**
Serbian scholar and statesman; lived here 1945-58. He was for nearly fifty years a leader of the Serbian intelligentsia. He lived here while prime minister of the Yugoslav government in exile. Besides his pre-Second World War historical and other works, his books written in exile were published posthumously 1961-2. *Private*

ZANGWILL, Israel (1864-1926). 288 Old Ford Road, Bethnal Green, E2

London-born writer, philanthropist and Zionist; lived here. He wrote plays, essays and poems but is best known for his novels on Jewish themes. His works include *Children of the Ghetto* (1892), *Ghetto Tragedies* (1894) and the play *The Melting Pot* (1908). *London County Council*

ZEPPELIN RAID. 61 Farringdon Road, EC1

The plaque reads: 'These premises were totally destroyed by a zeppelin raid during the World War on September 8th 1915. Rebuilt 1917.' *Private*

The house in Strand-on-the-Green, Chiswick, where the painter Johann Zoffany lived.

ZOFFANY, Johann (1733-1810). **65 Strand-on-the-Green, Chiswick, W4**
British German-born painter; lived here 1790-1810. Under the patronage of
George III he painted many portraits of notable contemporaries and was a
founder member of the Royal Academy. He had previously worked in Florence
(1772-9) and India (1783-90). *Greater London Council*

ZOLA, Émile Edouard Charles Antoine (1840-1902). **Queen's Hotel, 122
Church Road, SE19**
French novelist; lived here. He was the leading exponent of naturalism in
literature. His pamphlet *J'accuse,* supporting Dreyfus, the soldier wrongly
accused of spying, resulted in his being prosecuted by the authorities. He fled to
London, where he stayed at this address for about a year. Having been pardoned, he returned to France and was hailed as a public hero. *English Heritage*

ZYGIELBOJM, Szmul 'Artur' (1895-1943). **Porchester Square, W2**
Polish–Jewish wartime leader; lived nearby 1942-3. As a Polish trade union
official and councillor in the 1930s he was outspoken against Nazi tyranny. He
joined the government in exile in England (1940) and lobbied politicians and
the press in his efforts to save European Jewry. Despairing at the world's
apparent indifference to the Nazi extermination of the Jews, he eventually
committed suicide, as this plaque near his final home records. *Westminster City
Council*

Index by profession or category

230

Baird
Baring
Baxter
Bentley car
Blumlein
Brown, F.M.
Brunel
Caslon
Cayley
Chippendale
Cole, H.
Creed
Crompton, R.E.B.
Cruft
De Worde
Earnshaw
Garth
General Letter Office
Graham, G.
Great Eastern
Hall
Hansom
Harrison
Hoare
Hughes, D.E.
Johnson, D.
Knight, J.P.
Lewis, J.
Lovelace
Marconi
Maxim
Morris, W.
Morse
Muirhead
Paul
Perkin
Picton
Purdey
Ronalds
Sheraton
Simms
Stanhope
Stanley, W.F.R.
Stephens
Suffolk
Surrey Iron Railway
Tompion
Trevithick
Turing
Wakefield, C.C.
Wall
Wallis
Wheatstone
Whitbread
Willett
Willis, H.

Journalism and
Publishing
Arnold
Brockway
Daily Courant
De Worde
Edwards
Fry, C.B.

Godwin
Haden-Guest
Harmsworth
Holtby
Hunt, J.L.
Huxley, L.
Knox
Lloyd, E.
Mayhew
Mee
Morgan
Morris, W.
Newbery
Page
Pissarro, L.
Smiles
Stephen, L.
Sunday Times
Tallis
Tilak
Unwin, S.
Wallace, E.
Walter
White, W.H.
Whittaker
Woolf, L. and V.

Law
Bridgeman
Brougham
Denman, G.
Denman, T.
Eldon
Fielding, J.
Haldane
Hallam
Isaacs
Jinnah
Krishna Menon
Pritt
Romilly
Smith, F.E.
Thurloe
Tilak

Literature (see also
Journalism, Novelists
and **Poets**)
Ashbee
Barbould
Beerbohm
Beeton
Belloc
Bloomsbury Group
Borrow
Boswell
Brailsford
Brittain
Burney
Carlyle
Chateaubriand
Chesterton
Churchill, W.S.
Cole, H.
Cruden

Davies, T.
De La Mare
De Quincey
Dickinson
D'Israeli, I.
Dobson, H.A.
Dukes
Du Maurier, George
Edwards
Ellis, H.H.
Fabian Society
Fiennes
Froude
Gilpin
Gosse
Haden-Guest
Hall, N.
Hazlitt
Heine
Herbert
Herzen
Hilton
Hudson
Hunter, R.
Irving, W.
Jacobs, W.W.
Jefferies
Jerome
Johnson, S.
Johnston
Jones
Kingsley, M.H.
Knox
Kropotkin
Lamb
Lang
Lawrence, T.E.
Lecky
Lewis, P.W.
Loudon
Lovelace
Mallon
Malone
Maurice
Mayhew
Mee
Meynell
Milne
Mitford
Moore, T.
Morgan
Morrell
Morris, W.
Murray
Murry
Nevill
Newbery
Nicolson
Noel-Baker
Obradovitch
Paine
Palgrave
Patmore
Peake
Pepys

Pevsner
Plaatje
Pope
Potter
Pritt
Roy, R.M.
Ruskin
Sassoon
Schreiner
Sitwell, O.
Smiles
Smith, Sydney
Sokolow
Stephen
Stevenson
Strachey
Swinburne
Underhill
Voltaire
Von Hugel
Walpole, H.
Warlock
Wollstonecraft
Yeats, W.B.
Zangwill

Medicine
Anaesthetic, first
Anderson
Bastian
Bethlehem Hospital
Billig
Blackwell
Bright, R.
Cavell
Cedar Lawn
Christ's Hospital
Clover
Copeman
Dale
Dick-Read
Drysdale
Ellis
Fleischmann
Fleming, A.
Freud
Gillies
Gray, H.
Guy
Haden-Guest
Hall, K.C.
Hodgkin
Hunter, J.
Hunter, W.
Hutchinson
Huxley, T.H.
Jackson
Jones
Klein
Linacre
Lister
MacKenzie, J.
MacKenzie, M.
Macmillan
Manson

Marsden
Moody
Nightingale
Oliver, P.L.
Parkinson
Radcliffe
Rees
Rizal
Robinson, J.
Rogers
Ross, R.
Saunders
Simon
Sloane
Smiles
Snow
Still
Stopes
Taylor
Wakley
Wellcome
Willan
Yearsley
Young

Musicians, Composers, Conductors and Singers (see also **Dancers**)
Arne
Balfe
Barbirolli
Bartók
Bax
Beard
Beecham
Benedict
Bennett, W.S.
Berlioz
Bliss
Bolan
Boult
Brain
Bridge
Britten
Britton
Bruckner
Butt
Chopin
Clementi
Coates
Coleridge-Taylor
Collins, J.
Colyer
Connell
Cory
Dawson
Du Pré
Elgar
Evans, G
Ferrier
Fields
Goossens family
Gounod
Grainger

Grove
Hall, H.
Handel
Hendrix
Hess
Holst
Ireland
Ives
Lambert
Lind
Liszt
MacColl
MacFarren
Matthay
Mayer
Medtner
Meek
Melba
Mozart
Novello
Parry
Pears
Santley
Sargent, M.W.
Sharp
Sibelius
Smith, J.C.
Stanford
Stokowski
Tauber
Tosti
Vaughan-Williams
Walton
Warlock
Weber
Willis
Wood, H.J.

Music-Hall Artists and Comedy Actors
Baker
Chaplin
Chevalier
Coborn
Collins, J.
Collins music hall
Cooper, T.
Elen
Fields
Flanagan
Grimaldi
Grossmith, Jnr
Grossmith, Snr
Hancock
Handl, I.
Handley
Haynes
Hill, B.
Hope, B.
Howerd
Jacques
James, S.
Jewel
Lauder
Le Mesurier

Leno
Leybourne
Lloyd
Lowe
Lucan
Morecambe
Nixon
Relph
Rowland
Sellers
Tate
Thomas, T.
Warriss
Williams
Winters
Worth

Novelists
Austen
Bagnold
Ballantyne
Barker
Barrie
Beerbohm
Bennett, A.
Benson
Besant, W.
Blyton
Borrow
Burnett
Burney
Charles
Chesterton
Christie
Collins, W.W.
Compton-Burnett
Conrad
Crompton, R.
Defoe
De Morgan
Dickens
Doolittle
Douglas
Doyle
Eliot, G.
Fielding, H.
Fleming, I.L.
Ford
Forester
Forster
Galsworthy
Gaskell
Gissing
Gosse
Grahame
Graves
Haggard
Hall, M.R.
Hardy
Harte
Hawthorne
Henty
Herbert
Herzen
Hilton

Holtby
Hope, A.
Huxley, A.L.
James, H.
Jerome
Joyce
Kingsley, C.
Kipling
Lawrence, D.H.
Lewis, P.W.
Macaulay, R.
MacDonald, G.
Mansfield
Marryat
Maugham
Mayhew
Meredith
Milne
Mitford
Moore, G.A.
Morgan
Necker
Nesbit
Newbery
Orwell
Ouida
Peake
Poe
Polidori
Priestley, J.B.
Raymond
Richards
Rohmer
Sackville-West
Schreiner
Shelley, M.
Sitwell, O.
Smith, Stevie
Smollett
Stevenson
Stoker
Svevo
Thackeray
Thomas, E.
Trollope, A.
Trollope, F.
Twain
Wallace, E.
Waugh, E.
Wells
White, A.
White, W.H.
Williamson, H.
Wodehouse
Woolf, L. and V.
Zangwill
Zola

Overseas Visitors
Abbas
Adams, H.B.
Adams, J.
Ambedkar
Arnold
Barbosa

236

Street index

Berwick Street, W1	*Matthews*
Bethnal Green Station, E1	*Wartime Disaster*
Beverley Lane, Kingston	*Melba*
Bexley High Sreet, Bexley	*Thorpe*
Bidborough Street, WC1	*Nash*
Billet Road, E17	*Monoux*
Birchin Lane, EC3	*Binney*
Birchwood Road, Petts Wood	*Evans (G.)*
Blackfriars Road, SE1	*Hill (R.), Wollstonecraft*
Blandford Street, W1	*Faraday*
Blenheim Road, NW8	*Santley*
Blenheim Road, W4	*Yeats (J.B. and W.B.)*
Bloomsbury Place, WC1	*Sloane*
Bloomsbury Square, WC1	*Chesterfield, D'Israeli, Willan*
Bolden Street, SE8	*Sturdee*
Bolton Gardens, SW5	*Arnold*
Bolton Street, W1	*Burney*
Borough High Street, SE1	*Bible, George inn, Harvard, St Margaret, St Thomas, Stones End, Suffolk, White Hart*
Bourdon Street, W1	*Donovan*
Bouverie Street, EC4	*Hazlitt*
Bow Road, E3	*Lansbury, Match Tax, Sheffield*
Bow Street, WC2	*Bow Street, Gibbons, Radcliffe, Sackville, Wycherley*
Bracknell Gardens, NW3	*Huxley (A.L., J.S. and L.)*
Branch Hill, NW3	*Charles*
Brent Street, NW4	*Parish cage*
Bridge Street, SW1	*Knight (J.P.)*
Broadwick Street, W1	*Bridgeman*
Brockley Hill, Stanmore	*Sulloniacae*
Bromley High Street, Bromley	*Wells*
Brompton Road, SW7	*Lind*
Brompton Square, SW3	*Benson, Mallarmé, Place*
Brook Green, W6	*Short*
Brook Green Road, W6	*Silver Studio*
Brook Street, W1	*Campbell (C.), Handel, Hendrix, Wyatville*
Brooke Street, EC1	*Chatterton*
Broom Road, Teddington	*Cooper, Hancock, Handl, Hill, James (S.), Jewel, Morecambe, Nixon, Winters, Worth*
Broomwood Road, SW11	*Wilberforce*
Bruton Street, W1	*Elizabeth II*
Bryanston Square, W1	*Reschid*
Buckingham Gate, SW1	*Scawen-Blunt*
Buckingham Street, WC2	*Pepys, Stanfield*
Burnley Road, SW9	*Szabo*
Burroughs, The, NW4	*Court Leet*
Butcher Row, E14	*Groser*
Cable Street, E1	*Berg, Billig, Perkin*
Cadogan Place, SW1	*Jordan, Wilberforce*
Cadogan Square, SW1	*Bennett*
Cadogan Terrace, E9	*Murder on train*
Calthorpe Street, WC1	*Lethaby*
Camberwell Grove, SE5	*Chamberlain*
Cambridge Street, SW1	*Ashley, Beardsley*
Camden Park Road, Chislehurst	*Willet*
Camden Passage, N1	*Cruden*
Camden Road, Sutton	*Tate*
Camden Square, NW1	*Krishna Menon, Symons*
Campden Grove, W8	*Joyce*
Campden Hill, W8	*Macaulay*
Campden Hill Gardens, W8	*Rambert*
Campden Hill Road, W8	*Ford, Newbolt*
Campden Hill Square, W8	*Morgan, Sassoon, Stuart (J.M.), Underhill*
Cannon Hill, NW6	*Boult*
Cannon Lane, NW3	*Parish lock-up*
Cannon Place, NW3	*Du Maurier (Gerald), Petrie*
Cannon Street Station, EC4	*St Mary Bothaw*
Canonbury Park South, N1	*MacNeice*
Canonbury Square, N1	*Orwell, Phelps*
Canterbury Crescent, SW9	*Ellis*

Carlisle Place, SW1	*Manning*
Carlisle Street, W1	*Smith (J.C.)*
Carlton Gardens, SW1	*De Gaulle, Kitchener, Palmerston*
Carlton Hill, NW8	*Fleischmann, Voysey*
Carlton House Terrace, SW1	*Curzon, Gladstone*
Carlyle Square, SW3	*Sitwell (O.), Thorndike*
Carnarvon Road, E10	*Plaatje*
Carter Lane, EC4	*Bell inn*
Cartwright Gardens, WC1	*Hill (R.)*
Catford Road, SE6	*New Cross Fire*
Cato Street, W1	*Cato Street Conspiracy*
Cavendish Place, W1	*Clover, Street*
Cavendish Square, W1	*Asquith, Hogg, Hutchinson, Ross (R.)*
Cavendish Street, N1	*Greenaway*
Caxton Street, SW1	*Churchill (W.S.)*
Chagford Street, W1	*Bentley car*
Chalcot Crescent, NW1	*Rizal*
Chalcot Gardens, NW3	*Rackham*
Chancery Lane, WC2	*Old Serjeants' Inn, Thurloe*
Chandos Place, WC2	*Dickens*
Change Alley, EC3	*Marine Society*
Charles Street, W1	*Clarence, Nevill, Rosebery*
Charlotte Street, W1	*Smirke*
Charlton Church Lane, SE7	*Svevo*
Charlton Place, N1	*Chisholm*
Charlton Road, SE7	*Barlow*
Chase Side, Enfield	*Lamb*
Cheapside, EC2	*Becket*
Chelsea Bridge Road, SW1	*Jerome*
Chelsea Embankment, SW3	*Ripon*
Chelsea Park Gardens, SW3	*Munnings*
Chepstow Villas, W11	*Kossuth*
Chesham Place, SW1	*Russell (J.)*
Chester Square, SW1	*Arnold, Shelley (M.W.), Wilhelmina*
Chester Terrace, NW1	*Cockerel*
Chesterfield Street, W1	*Brummell, Maugham*
Chesterfield Walk, SE10	*Chesterfield, Wolseley*
Cheyne Gardens, SW3	*Henry VIII*
Cheyne Row, SW3	*Carlyle, Dawson*
Cheyne Walk, SW3	*Crosby Hall, Eliot (G.), Henry VIII, Rossetti (D.G.), Swinburne, Turner*
Cheyne Walk, SW10	*Belloc, Brunel, Gaskell, Greaves, Pankhurst, Steer, Tweed, Whistler*
Childs Hill, NW2	*Edgware turnpike, Tollgate*
Chiswell Street, EC1	*Caslon, Whitbread*
Chiswick Lane South, W4	*Pope*
Church End, NW4	*Church House*
Church Road, Shortlands	*Keeping, Muirhead*
Church Road, SE19	*Zola*
Church Row, NW3	*Park*
Church Street, Edmonton	*Keats, Lamb*
Church Street, NW8	*Royal Marylebone Theatre*
City Road, EC1	*City Road turnpike, Wesley (J.)*
Clapham Common, SW4	*Clapham Sect , Wilberforce*
Clapham Common North, SW4	*Barry, Burns,Walter*
Claremont Square, N1	*Irving (E.)*
Clarendon Place, W2	*Scott (Giles G.)*
Clarges Street, W1	*Fox*
Clement's Lane, EC4	*Obradovich*
Cleveland Street, W1	*Morse*
Clifton Gardens, W9	*Fleming (J.A.)*
Clifton Hill, NW8	*Frith, Klein*
Clink Street, SE1	*Clink Prison*
Clissold Crescent, N16	*Brooks*
Cloak Lane, EC4	*Cutlers' Hall*
Coborn Street, E3	*Barnardo, Coborn*
Colby Road, SE19	*Besant (A.)*
College Hill, EC4	*Buckingham, Turners' Hall, Whittington*
Collingham Gardens, SW5	*Carter*

Colyton Road, SE22	*Oliver (P.L.)*
Commercial Road, E1	*Anderson*
Commercial Street, E1	*Mallon*
Compayne Gardens, NW6	*Sokolow*
Connaught Place, W2	*Churchill (R.)*
Connaught Square, W2	*Taglioni*
Coombe Road, Croydon	*Horniman*
Cornhill, EC3	*Gray (T.), Guy, Standard in Cornhill*
Cornwall Gardens, SW7	*Compton-Burnett, Nabuco*
County Hall, SE1	*County Hall, GLC, Inner London Education Service*
Coventry Street, W1	*Delfont*
Craigton Road, SE9	*Hope (B.)*
Cranbourn Street, WC2	*Webb (S. and B.)*
Craven Road, W2	*Handley*
Craven Street, WC2	*Franklin, Heine*
Creek Road, SE8	*McMillan*
Crescent Road, Bromley	*Kropotkin*
Crescent Wood Road, SE26	*Baird*
Cresswell Place, SW10	*Christie*
Cromwell Avenue, N6	*Savarkar*
Cromwell Place, SW7	*Bacon, Hoppe, Lavery, Millais*
Cromwell Road, SW7	*Freake*
Crondall Street, N1	*Gunpowder Plot*
Croom's Hill, SE10	*Waugh (B.), Day-Lewis*
Crown Office Row, EC4	*Lamb*
Cudham Lane South, Cudham	*Relph*
Cunningham Place, NW8	*Davies*
Curtain Road, EC2	*Holywell priory, St John the Baptist, Shakespeare,*
Curzon Street, W1	*Disraeli, Isaacs, Mitford*
Dagnall Park, SE25	*Coleridge-Taylor*
Danvers Street, SW3	*Fleming (A.)*
Dartmouth Hill, SE10	*Glaisher*
Dean Street, W1	*Marx, Rogers*
Delancey Street, NW1	*Thomas (D.)*
Deptford High Street, SE8	*London and Greenwich Railway, Peter the Great*
De Vere Gardens, W8	*Browning, James (H.)*
Devonshire Terrace, W2	*Dickens*
Digby Street, E2	*Godley*
Dorset Square, NW1	*Grossmith (senior), Lord, MCC*
Dorset Street, W1	*Babbage*
Doughty Street, WC1	*Brittain, Holtby, Dickens, Smith (Sydney)*
Douro Place, W8	*Palmer*
Draycott Place, SW3	*Jellicoe*
Drayton Gardens, SW10	*Franklin, Peake*
Duke Street, W1	*Bolivār*
Duncan Terrace, N1	*Lamb, Suess*
Dunraven Street, W1	*Wodehouse*
Durley Road, N16	*Howard (E.)*
Ealing Broadway Centre, W5	*Richards*
Eardley Crescent, SW5	*Jacques*
Earls Terrace, W8	*Daniell*
East End Road, N3	*Stephens*
East Heath Road, NW3	*Barrett, Bliss, Mansfield, Murry*
East Street, SE17	*Drysdale*
Eastcheap, EC3	*St Leonard' s Church*
Eastern Road, SE4	*Williamson*
Eaton Place, SW1	*Avebury, Chopin, Ewart, Kelvin*
Eaton Square, SW1	*Baldwin, Boothby, Chamberlain (N.), Halifax, Leigh, Metternich, Peabody*
Ebury Street, SW1	*Evans (E.), Fleming (I.), Moore (G.A.), Mozart, Nicolson, Sackville-West*
Eccleston Square, SW1	*Churchill (W.S.)*
Edgware Road, W2	*Tyburn Tree*
Edith Road, W14	*Goossens family*
Edwardes Square, W8	*Dickinson, Foscolo, Howerd*
Eglington Road, SE18	*Gladstone*
Elder Street, E1	*Gertler*
Elgin Crescent, W11	*Nehru*
Eliot Place, SE23	*Ross (J.C.)*

240

Elm Park Gardens, SW10	*Cripps*
Elm Row, NW3	*Cole*
Elstree Hill, Elstree	*Everett*
Elswick Road, SE13	*Nesbit*
Elsworthy Road, NW3	*Wood (H.J.)*
Enfield Town station	*Keats*
Englefield Road, N1	*Leybourne*
Englewood Road, SW12	*Hobbs*
Essex Street, WC2	*Essex Street, Barbon, Bridgeman, Johnson (S.), Savage, Stuart (C.E.)*
Eton Villas, NW3	*Stevens*
Exmouth Market, EC1	*Grimaldi*
Fairfield Road, E3	*Match girls*
Farringdon Lane, EC1	*Clerks' Well*
Farringdon Road, EC1	*Coppice Row, Zeppelin raid*
Farringdon Street, EC4	*Bridewell, Labour Party*
Fenchurch Street, EC1	*St Gabriel Fenchurch*
Finchley Central station, N3	*Beck*
Finchley Road, NW2	*Fry (C.B.)*
Finchley Road, NW8	*Kokoschka*
Finsbury Square, EC2	*Bruckner*
Fitzjohn's Avenue, NW3	*De Laszlo*
Fitzroy Road, NW1	*Yeats (W.B.)*
Fitzroy Square, W1	*Eastlake, Hofmann, Salisbury (R.A.), Shaw (G.B.), Woolf*
Fitzroy Street, W1	*Flinders*
Fleet Street, EC4	*Automobile Association, Bright, Cobden, Devil tavern, Graham, Johnson, Mitre tavern, Tompion*
Foley Street, W1	*Fuseli*
Footscray Road, SE29	*Jefferies*
Fordwych Road, NW2	*Bomberg*
Fore Street, EC2	*Bomb (first of 2nd WW)*
Forest Hill Road, SE23	*Karloff*
Forest Road, E17	*Lloyd (E.), Morris*
Fortess Road, NW5	*Brown*
Fortune Street, EC1	*Fortune Theatre*
Forty Lane, Wembley	*Lucan*
Foster Lane, EC2	*St Leonard*
Founders' Court, EC2	*Founders' Hall*
Foxley Road, SW9	*Cox*
Frederic's Place, EC2	*Disraeli*
Friern Barnet Road, N11	*Waugh (B.)*
Frith Street, W1	*Baird, Hazlitt, Mozart, Snow*
Frognal, NW3	*De Gaulle, Ferrier, Gillies, Greenaway, Karsavina, Knox, MacDonald, Stewart*
Frognal Gardens, NW3	*Besant (W.), Brain, Gaitskell*
Frognal Way, NW3	*Fields*
Fulham Road, SW6	*Gaudier-Brzeska*
Garbutt Place, W1	*Hill (O.)*
Geldeston Road, E5	*Tandy*
George Lane, SE13	*McMillan*
George Street, W1	*Moore (T.)*
Gerald Road, SW1	*Coward, Gerald Road police station*
Gerrard Street, W1	*Burke, Dryden, Lamerie, Johnson, Reynolds, Turk's Head tavern*
Gillingham Street, SW1	*Conrad*
Gilmore Road, SE13	*Flecker*
Gilston Road, SW10	*Fortune, Du Boulay*
Giltspur Street, EC1	*Giltspur Street Compter*
Gloucester Gate, NW1	*Jacobs (W.W.), Wellcome*
Gloucester Place, W1	*Arnold (B.), Browning, Collins (W.W.), Godley (J. R.), Kelly, Ray-Jones*
Gloucester Road, Kew	*Pissarro (C.)*
Gloucester Square, W2	*Bonham-Carter, Stephenson*
Gloucester Walk, W8	*Sibelius*
Golden Square, W1	*Hunter (J.), Mackenzie, Portuguese embassy, Pompal*
Golders Rise, NW4	*Morden*
Gordon Square, WC1	*Bloomsbury Group, Herford, Keynes, Strachey, Woolf*

Gough Square, EC4	*Johnson (S.)*
Gower Street, WC1	*Anaesthetic, Dance, Darwin, Fawcett, Morrell, Pre-Raphaelite Brotherhood, Robinson (J.), Trevithick*
Gracechurch Street, EC3	*Curtis, St Benet*
Grafton Street, W1	*Brougham, Irving (H.)*
Grafton Way, W1	*Bello, Miranda*
Graham Road, E8	*Lloyd (M.)*
Grange Gardens, NW3	*Lewis (J.)*
Granville Park, SE13	*Smiles*
Granville Road, N12	*Grimaldi*
Gray's Inn Square, WC1	*Romilly*
Great Marlborough Street, W1	*Liszt*
Great Newport Street, WC2	*Colyer, Reynolds*
Great Ormond Streeet, WC1	*Howard (J.)*
Great Portland Street, W1	*Boswell, Hughes (D.E.), Weber*
Great Pulteney Street, W1	*Polidori*
Great Russell Street, WC1	*Caldecott, Dickens, Du Maurier (George), Pugin, Wyatt*
Great Windmill Street, W1	*Hunter (W.)*
Green, The, N14	*Southgate local government, Waugh (B.)*
Green Street, W1	*Sopwith*
Greenwell Street, W1	*Flaxman*
Greenwich Park, SE10	*Wolfe*
Grenville Place, SW7	*Booth (C.)*
Gresham Street, EC2	*St John Zachary*
Grey Close, NW11	*Hancock*
Grosvenor Gardens, SW1	*Pitt-Rivers, Smith (F.E.)*
Grosvenor Place, SW1	*Campbell-Bannerman*
Grosvenor Square, W1	*Adams (J.B.), Eisenhower, Page, Peczenik*
Grosvenor Street, W1	*Oldfield*
Grove, The, N6	*Coleridge, Priestley (J.B.)*
Grove End Road, NW8	*Alma-Tadema, Beecham*
Grove Hill, Harrow	*Motor accident*
Grove Road, E3	*Flying bomb*
Gunnersbury Avenue, W5	*Haynes, James (S.)*
Gunter Grove, SW10	*Ireland*
Gunterstone Road, W14	*Haggard*
Gutter Lane, EC2	*Broderers' Hall*
Gwendolen Avenue, SW15	*Benes*
Hackford Road, SW9	*Van Gogh*
Hadley Green, Barnet	*Livingstone, Trollope (F. and A.)*
Half Moon Street, W1	*Ives*
Hallam Street, W1	*Rossetti (D.G.)*
Halliford Street, N1	*Britten*
Ham Street, Ham, Richmond	*Newman*
Hamilton Terrace, NW8	*Bazalgette, Hertz, MacFarren, Strang*
Hammers Lane, NW7	*Murray*
Hammersmith Bridge, W6	*Wood (C.C.)*
Hammersmith Terrace, W6	*Herbert, Johnston, Walker*
Hampstead Grove, NW3	*Du Maurier (George)*
Hampstead High Street, NW3	*Sitwell (E.), Stanfield*
Hampstead Road, NW1	*Cruikshank*
Hampstead Square, NW3	*Hall (N.)*
Hampton Court Green, Hampton	*Wren*
Hampton Court Road, Hampton	*Faraday, Garrick*
Hanbury Street, E1	*Flanagan*
Handen Road, SE12	*Unwin*
Hanover Square, W1	*Talleyrand*
Hanover Terrace, NW1	*Salvin, Vaughan Williams, Wells*
Hans Place, SW1	*Austen*
Harley Gardens, SW10	*Dobson (F.)*
Harley Road, NW3	*Butt*
Harley Street, W1	*Dick-Read, Gladstone, Lyell, Nightingale, Pinero*
Harrington Gardens, SW7	*Gilbert*
Hatton Garden, EC1	*Maxim, Mazzini*
Haymarket, SW1	*Ho Chi Minh, Wilde*
Heath Street, NW3	*Clock tower*
Heather Walk, Edgware	*Trowbridge*

Hendon Way, NW2	Johnson (A.)
Henrietta Street, WC2	Austen
Hercules Road, SE1	Blake
Hereford Road, W2	Marconi
Hereford Square, SW7	Borrow
Herne Hill, SE24	Rohmer, Ruskin
Hertford Street, W1	Burgoyne, Cayley, Sheridan
High Holborn, EC1	Furnival's Inn
High Holborn, WC1	Dickens, Earnshaw
High Road, E10	Great House, Oliver (T.)
High Road, E11	Hitchcock, Mackenzie
High Road, Loughton	Collins (J.)
High Road, N15	Williams (J.)
High Street, Bushey	Bushey police station, Kemp-Welch
High Street, Cheam	Gilpin
High Street, Hampstead, NW3	Richardson
High Street, Highgate, N6	Marvel
High Street, Kingston	Picton
High Street, Pinner	Turner, Ware
High Street, Southgate, N14	Lawrence (J.L.), Southgate village hall
High Street, Sutton	Rowland
High Street, Whitechapel, E1	Rosenberg
Highbury Grange, N5	Cheesman
Highbury Grove, N5	Cruft, Highbury Barn
Highbury Place, N5	Chamberlain (J.), Sickert
Highway, The, E1	Cook
Highwood Hill, NW7	Raffles
Hinde Street, W1	Macaulay (E.R.)
Hobury Street, SW10	Meredith
Hogarth Lane, W4	Hogarth
Holford Road, NW3	Von Hügel
Holland Park Avenue, W11	McBey
Holland Park Gardens, W14	Barbosa
Holland Park Road, W14	Leighton, May
Holland Street, W8	Crane, Hall (M.R.)
Holloway Road, N7	Meek
Holly Bush Hill, NW3	Romney
Holly Place, NW3	Walton, Watch house
Holybourne Avenue, SW15	Hopkins
Honor Oak Road, SE23	Clarence, Jordan
Hook Road, Chessington	Blyton
Horton Street, W8	Stanford
Howitt Road, NW3	Macdonald (J.R.)
Howley Place, W2	Tilak
Hoxton Market, N1	Burtt
Hoxton Square, N1	Parkinson
Hoxton Street, N1	Pollock's toy shop
Huggins Hill, EC4	Cleary
Hyde Park Gate, SW7	Baden-Powell, Bagnold, Churchill (W.S.), Epstein, Stephen (L.)
Hyde Park Street, W2	Smith (W.H.)
Islington Green, N1	Collins' music hall
Islington High Street, N1	Paine, Peacock inn
Jermyn Street, SW1	Newton
Jerusalem Passage, EC1	Britton
John Adam Street, WC2	Rowlandson, Royal Society of Arts
John Street, WC1	Kirk
Keats Grove, NW3	Keats
Kendal Street, W2	Tauber
Kennington Oval, SE11	Montgomery
Kennington Road, SE11	Chaplin
Kensington Church Street, W8	Clementi
Kensington Court, W8	Crompton (R.E.B.)
Kensington Court Gardens, W8	Eliot (T.S.)
Kensington Gore, SW7	Sargent (M.W.)
Kensington High Street, W8	Low
Kensington Park Gardens, W11	Crookes
Kensington Square, W8	Burne-Jones, Campbell (P.), Mill, Parry, Simon
Kent Terrace, NW1	Shepard

Kew Green, Richmond	*Hughes (A.), Pissarro (C.)*
King Edward Memorial Park, E1	*Willoughby*
King Edward Street, EC1	*Poulters' Hall*
King Henry's Road, NW3	*Ambedkar*
King Street, SW1	*Napoleon III*
King Street, WC2	*Arne, Russell (E.)*
King's Cross station, NW1	*Gresley*
King's Road, Kingston	*VE and VJ Day*
King's Road, SW3	*Astafieva, Grainger, Reed, Terry*
Kingsland Road, N1	*Cavell*
Kingston Hill, Kingston	*Eisenhower*
Knightrider Street, EC4	*Linacre*
Ladbroke Road, W11	*Dukes, Rambert*
Ladywell Road, SE13	*Ladywell mineral spring*
Lambeth Road, SE1	*Bligh, Greet*
Lancaster Avenue, Hadley Wood	*Booth (W.)*
Lancaster Gate, W2	*Harte*
Lancaster Road, W11	*Purkovic*
Lanercost Road, SW2	*Mee*
Langford Place, NW8	*Adams-Acton, Knight (L.)*
Langham Street, W1	*Malone*
Langland Gardens, NW3	*Beaton*
Langley Park Rd, Sutton	*Wells*
Lansdowne Road, W11	*Forbes, Philpot, Pryde, Ricketts, Robinson, Shannon*
Laurence Pountney Hill, EC4	*Laurence Pountney church*
Lauriston Road, Wimbledon	*Graves*
Lavender Gardens, SW11	*Henty*
Lawford Road, NW5	*Orwell*
Lawrence Road, E13	*Thorne*
Lawrence Street, SW3	*Chelsea China, Smollett*
Lawrie Park Road, SE26	*Grace*
Laystall Street, EC1	*Mazzini*
Leicester Square, WC2	*Reynolds*
Leighton Road, NW5	*Cook (D.)*
Lenham Road, Sutton	*Coward*
Leydon Street, E1	*Strype Street*
Lincoln's Inn Fields, WC2	*Marsden, Perceval*
Lingards Road, SE13	*Duncan*
Linthorpe Road, N16	*Calman*
Lisson Grove, NW1	*Haydon, Rossi*
Little Britain, EC1	*Bray, Wesley (C.)*
Liverpool Road, Kingston	*Muybridge*
Liverpool Street, EC2	*Bethlehem Hospital*
Lombard Street, EC3	*De Rokesley, Lloyds coffee house, Pope*
London Road, SE23	*Horniman*
London Road, Stanmore	*Attlee*
London Road, Wallington	*Hughes (A.)*
London Wall, EC2	*Bethlehem Hospital, Howard (E.)*
Long Acre, WC2	*Baird, Johnson (D.)*
Longley Road, SW17	*Lauder, Tate*
Lower Clapton Road, E5	*Howard (J.), Priestley (J.), Watson*
Lower Mall, W6	*Devine*
Lower Road, Loughton	*Jacobs*
Lower Terrace, NW3	*Constable*
Lower Thames Street, EC3	*Old London Bridge*
Ludgate Broadway, EC4	*Blackfriars priory*
Ludgate Circus, EC4	*Daily Courant, Wallace (E.)*
Ludgate Hill, EC4	*Ludgate*
Lyall Street, SW1	*Cubitt*
Mackenzie Road, Beckenham	*De La Mare*
Maida Avenue, W2	*Lowe*
Maida Vale, W9	*Lawrence (P.)*
Maiden Lane, WC2	*Terriss, Turner (J.M.W.), Voltaire*
Main Road, Biggin Hill	*Biggin Hill*
Main Road, Gidea Park	*Repton*
Maitland Park Road, NW3	*Marx*
Mallord Street, SW3	*John, Milne*
Manchester Square, W1	*Bastian, Benedict, Jackson, Milner*
Manchester Street, W1	*Beaufort*

Mandeville Place, W1	*Tosti*
Manor Mount, SE23	*Bonhoeffer*
Manor Place, Chislehurst	*Shepheard*
Mansfield Street, W1	*Lutyens, Pearson (J.L.), Mayer, Stanhope*
Mansion House, EC4	*Stocks market*
Mare Street, E8	*Fry (E.), Wollstonecraft*
Maresfield Gardens, NW3	*Asquith, Freud, Sharp*
Maresfield Road, NW3	*Westfield College*
Market Road, N7	*Copenhagen House*
Marlborough Place, NW8	*Huxley (T.H.)*
Marlborough Road, N19	*Stopes*
Marloes Road, W8	*Lang*
Marshall Street, W1	*Blake*
Martin Lane, EC4	*St Martin Orgar*
Marylebone High Street, W1	*Stokowski*
Marylebone Road, NW1	*Dickens, VJ Day*
Maze Hill, SE10	*Vanbrugh*
McNair Road, Southall	*McNair*
Meadway, NW1	*Donat*
Meard Street, W1	*Hearne*
Meath Gardens, E2	*Cole*
Mecklenburgh Square, WC1	*Doolittle, Khan, Tawney*
Melbury Road, W14	*Fildes, Hunt (W.H.), Stone, Thornycroft*
Methley Street, SE11	*Chaplin*
Middlesex Street, E1	*Board of Guardians*
Mile End Road, E1	*Cook (J.)*
Mile End Road, E3	*Ashbee*
Milk Street, EC2	*City of London School*
Millbank, SW1	*Millbank prison*
Milton Road, Harrow	*Wealdstone rail disaster*
Mitre Square, EC3	*Holy Trinity*
Monkhams Avenue, Woodford	*Attlee*
Montagu Square, W1	*Trollope (A.)*
Montague Road, Richmond	*Chadwick*
Montpelier Row, SE3	*Blackheath FC*
Montpelier Row, Twickenham	*De La Mare, Tennyson*
Moorgate, EC2	*Keats, Moor Gate*
Morden Road, SE23	*Gounod*
Moreton Place, SW1	*Hughes (W.M.)*
Mornington Crescent, NW1	*Sickert*
Morpeth Street, E2	*Lynch*
Mortimer Road, N1	*Gosse*
Mortimer Street, W1	*Nollekens*
Moss Lane, Pinner	*Robinson (W.H.)*
Mottingham Lane, SE9	*Grace*
Mount Park Road, Harrow	*Ballantyne*
Mount Street, W1	*Buchanan*
Mount Vernon, NW3	*Dale, Stevenson*
Muswell Hill Road, N6	*Sellers*
Myddleton Square, EC1	*Brockway*
Neal's Yard, WC2	*Python*
Nelson Square, SE1	*Shelley (P.B.)*
Netherhall Gardens, NW3	*Edwards, Elgar, Webb (S. and B.)*
Netherwood Road, W14	*Collins (M.)*
Nevill Road, N16	*Bomb (first of 1st WW)*
New Bond Street, W1	*Nelson*
New Cavendish Streeet, W1	*Waterhouse, Weisz*
New Change, EC4	*St Paul's School*
New Cross Road, SE14	*Tallis, Wallis, Woolworth's V2*
New Road, E1	*Salvation Army*
Newark Street, E1	*Green*
Newcomen Street, SE1	*Marshall*
Newgate Street, EC1	*Christ's Hospital, Grey Friars monastery, Marconi, Newgate*
Newman Street, W1	*Stothard*
Nightingale Lane, SW12	*Bateman, Spurgeon, Wandsworth*
Noel Road, N1	*Orton*
Norman Grove, E3	*Pankhurst*
North End, NW3	*Blake, Linnell, Unwin, Ventris*

North End Avenue, NW3	*Pitt*
North End Crescent, W14	*Burne-Jones*
North End Road, NW11	*Pavlova, Waugh (E.)*
North End Way, NW3	*Hoare*
North Gower Street, NW1	*Mazzini*
North Road, Highgate, N6	*Dickens, Housman*
Northampton Square, EC1	*Baxter*
Nottingham Place, W1	*Kempe*
Oak Hill Gardens, Woodford	*Hilton*
Oak Hill Park, NW3	*Hopkins*
Oakdale, N14	*Lipton*
Oakley Gardens, SW3	*Gissing*
Oakley Road, Bromley	*Crompton (R.)*
Oakley Street, SW3	*Scott (R.F.)*
Old Broad Street, EC2	*Newman, Gresham*
Old Brompton Road, SW3	*Potter*
Old Church Street, SW3	*De Morgan*
Old Ford Road, E2	*Zangwill*
Old Gloucester Street, WC1	*Challoner*
Old Redding, Harrow Weald	*Shaw (R.N.), Goodall, Gilbert (W.S.)*
Old Road, Lee, SE13	*Baring (F.)*
Old Town, Clapham, SW4	*Bentley*
Onslow Gardens, SW7	*Froude, Law, Lecky*
Onslow Square, SW7	*Fitzroy, Thackeray*
Orme Square, W2	*Hill (R.)*
Orsett Terrace, W2	*Herzen*
Osnaburgh Street, NW1	*Fabian Society, Williams*
Outer Circle, NW1	*Beatty, Cochrane*
Outram Road, Croydon	*Creed*
Paddington Street, W1	*Chateaubriand*
Page Street, NW7	*Nicoll*
Palace Court, W2 '	*Meynell*
Palace Gardens Terrace,W8	*Beerbohm, Lewis (P.W.), Maxwell*
Palace Gate, W8	*Millais*
Palace Green, W8	*Thackeray*
Pall Mall, SW1	*Gainsborough, Gwynne*
Pancras Lane, EC4	*St Benet Sherehog, St Pancras church*
Pandora Road, NW6	*Harmsworth*
Paradise Road, Richmond	*Woolf*
Paradise Row, E2	*Mendoza*
Park Crescent, W1	*Lister, Tempest, Wheatstone*
Park Hill, Carshalton	*White (W.H.)*
Park Lane, W1	*Disraeli, Hall (K.C.), Montefiore, Neagle, Wilcox*
Park Road, NW1	*San Martín*
Park Road, Barnet	*Acres*
Park Street, SE1	*Anchor brewery, Globe, Shakespeare*
Parkhill Road, NW3	*Mondrian*
Parliament Hill, NW3	*Orwell*
Pauntley Street, N19	*Tollgate*
Pavement, The, SW4	*Macaulay (T.B.), Macaulay (Z.)*
Peel Street, W8	*Flint*
Pelham Crescent, SW7	*Playfair*
Pendennis Road, SW16	*Bax*
Percy Circus, WC1	*Lenin*
Percy Street, W1	*Laughton, Patmore*
Perham Road, W14	*White (A.)*
Phillimore Place, W8	*Grahame*
Piccadilly, W1	*Palmerston*
Pilgrim's Lane, NW3	*Cory, Du Pré*
Platts Lane, NW3	*Masaryk*
Poland Street, W1	*Shelley (P.B.)*
Pond Road, SE3	*Hawthorne*
Pond Street, NW3	*Blackwell, Huxley (J.S.), Orwell*
Pont Street, SW1	*Alexander, Langtry*
Poole Street, N1	*Gainsborough Studios*
Porchester Square, W2	*Zygielbojm*
Porchester Terrace, W2	*Loudon*
Portland Place, W1	*Adams (H.B.), Burnett, Gage, Roberts, US Embassy*
Portobello Road, W11	*Garth, Orwell*

Portsea Place, W2	Schreiner
Poultry, EC2	Fry (E.), Hood, St Mary Cole, St Mildred
Powis Road, E3	Gandhi
Praed Street, W2	Fleming (A.)
Prince of Wales Drive, SW11	O'Casey
Princelet Street, E1	Garthwaite, Moses
Princes Gate, SW7	Kennedy
Princes Street, EC2	General Letter Office
Pudding Lane, EC3	Faryner
Putney Bridge Station, SW6	Simms
Putney Hill, SW15	Swinburne, Watts-Dunton
Pyrland Road, N5	Taylor
Quadrant, The, NW4	Cattle Pound
Queen Anne Street, W1	Berlioz, Pearce, Still, Turner
Queen Anne's Gate, SW1	Fisher, Grey, Haldane, Palmerston, Smith (W.), Townley
Queen Caroline Street, W6	Brangwyn
Queen Street, EC4	St Thomas the Apostle
Queen Victoria Street, EC4	Doctors' Commons
Queen's Gate, SW7	Hill (B.)
Queen's Gate Mews, SW7	Thomas (T.)
Queen's Grove, NW8	Frampton
Queens Road, SE15	Moody
Queensborough Terrace, W2	Bennett, Cavafy
Ram Street, SW18	Surrey Iron Railway
Randolph Mews, W9	Hall (H.)
Ranelagh Road, SW1	MacMillan
Rannoch Road, W6	Phillips
Ravenscourt Road, W6	Whall
Ravenscourt Square, W6	Ouida
Ravenshaw Street, NW6	Hagedorn
Reardon Street, E1	Bligh
Red House Lane, Bexleyheath	Red House, Morris (W.)
Red Lion Square, WC1	Burne-Jones, Rossetti (D.G.), Morris (W.) Harrison
Redcliffe Gardens, SW10	Copeman
Redcliffe Street, SW10	Dobson (H.A.)
Regent's Park Road, NW1	Engels
Richmond Terrace, SW1	Stanley (H.M.)
Ridgeway, The, NW7	Collinson, Rosebank, Wilberforce
Ridings, The, W5	Blümlein
Robert Street, WC2	Adam
Rochester Terrace, NW1	Willis
Rodenhurst Road, SW4	Henderson
Rosary Gardens, SW7	Tree
Rose Hill, Hampton	Beard, Ewart
Rossendale Street, E5	Air raid
Rosslyn Hill, NW3	Vane
Routh Road, SW18	Lloyd George
Rudall Crescent, NW3	Gertler
Russell Road, W14	Jinnah
Russell Square, WC1	Denman, Eliot (T.S.), Romilly, Williams (G.)
Russell Street, WC2	Boswell, Johnson (S.), Davies (T.)
Rutland Gate, SW7	Galton, Lugard
Sackville Street, W1	Yearsley
St Albans Grove, W8	Anstell
St Anne's Villas, W11	Chevalier (A.)
St Bartholomew's Hospital, EC1	Wallace (W.)
St George Street, W1	Artists Rifles
St George's Square, SW1	Wingfield
St James's Place, SW1	Chichester, Chopin, Huskisson
St James's Square, SW1	Astor, Derby, Eisenhower, Gladstone, Lovelace, Pitt
St John Street, EC1	St John Street turnpike
St John's Wood High Street, NW8	Britten, Pears
St Leonard's Terrace, SW3	Stoker
St Luke's Road, W11	Hudson
St Martin-le-Grand, EC1	Bull and Mouth, Northumberland House, St Martin
St Martin's Lane, WC2	Chippendale
St Mary's Road, W5	Byron

Syon House, Isleworth	*Reynolds*
Tavistock Square, WC1	*Abbas, Dickens*
Tavistock Street, WC2	*De Quincey*
Taviton Street, WC1	*Hughes (H.P.)*
Tedworth Square, SW3	*Twain*
Telegraph Street, EC2	*Bloomfield*
Tennison Road, SE25	*Doyle*
Terrace, The, SW13	*Holst*
Theobalds Road, WC1	*Disraeli*
Thistlethwaite Road, N5	*Synagogue*
Thornsett Road, SE20	*Crapper*
Threadneedle Street, EC2	*St Anthony's Hospital, St Bartholomew, St Martin Outwich*
Thurleigh Avenue, SW12	*Elen*
Thurloe Square, SW7	*Cole*
Tite Street, SW3	*Haden-Guest, Sargent (J.S.), Warlock, Wilde*
Tooley Street, SE1	*Braidwood*
Torrington Park, N12	*Morecambe*
Torrington Square, WC1	*Rossetti (C.G.)*
Totteridge Lane, N20	*Vardon*
Toynbee Street, E1	*Shinwell*
Trebeck Street, W1	*Mayfair*
Tressillian Crescent, SE4	*Wallace (E.)*
Trinity Road, SW17	*Hardy*
Trinity Square, EC3	*Clayton, Wakefield (C.C.)*
Tufton Street, SW1	*Balcon, Rathbone*
Twickenham Road, Isleworth	*Van Gogh*
Underhill Road, SE22	*Forester*
Upland Road, Sutton	*Sutherland*
Upper Belgrave Street, SW1	*Bagehot, Tennyson*
Upper Berkeley Street, W1	*Anderson*
Upper Brook Street, W1	*Bonn*
Upper Cheyne Row, SW3	*Hunt*
Upper Grosvenor Street, W1	*Peel*
Upper Harley Street, NW1	*Maurice*
Upper Mall, W6	*Clark, Cobden-Sanderson, Macdonald, Ravilious, Ronalds*
Upper Montague Street, W1	*Du Pré*
Upper Richmond Road, SW15	*Oates*
Upper Street, N1	*Greenaway*
Upper Thames Street, EC4	*Joiners and Ceilers*
Upper Wimpole Street, W1	*Doyle, Rees*
Uxbridge Road, Hatch End	*Beeton*
Uxbridge Road, W12	*Pritt*
Vale of Health, NW3	*Hammond, Hunt (J.L.), Lawrence (D.H.), Tagore*
Vallance Road, E2	*Hughes (M.)*
Vanbrugh Hill, SE3	*Dyson*
Vernon Road, E3	*Edwards*
Vestry Road,Walthamstow	*Cage, Church Common*
Vicarage Crescent, SW11	*Wilson*
Vicar's Moor Lane, N21	*Hood*
Victoria Road, W8	*Corbould*
Victoria Square, SW1	*Campbell (T.)*
Victoria Street, SW1	*VE Day*
Villiers Street, WC2	*Kipling*
Vineyard, The, Richmond	*O'Higgins*
Walbrook, EC4	*St Mary Woolchurch Haw*
Waldegrave Road, Teddington	*Coward*
Waldrons, The, Croydon	*Barker*
Walthamstow Marshes, E17	*Roe*
Walworth Road, SE17	*Babbage, Chaplin, Faraday*
Wapping Lane, E1	*Wainright*
Wardour Street, W1	*Clarkson, Sheraton*
Wardrobe Place, EC4	*King's Wardrobe*
Warrington Crescent, W9	*Ben-Gurion, Turing*
Warwick Court, WC1	*Sun Yat Sen*
Warwick Crescent, W2	*Browning*
Warwick Gardens, W14	*Chesterton*
Warwick Lane, EC4	*Royal College of Physicians*

Index by postal district

253